JOSEPH SCHULL

Rebellion

The Rising in French Canada 1837

Macmillan Canada
Toronto

Canadian Cataloguing in Publication Data

Schull, Joseph, 1910-1980
    Rebellion : the rising of French Canada, 1837

Reprint of the 1971 ed. with a few minor revisions.
Includes bibliographical references and index.
ISBN 0-7715-7402-9

1. Canada - History - Rebellion, 1837-1838.
I. Title.

FC450.S38 1996   971.03'8   C96-931160-5
F1032.S38 1996

1 2 3 4 5 FP 00 99 98 97 96

Cover design by Dennis Boyes

Cover illustration: Back view of the church of St-Eustache and dispersion of the
insurgents, 14 December, 1837, by C. Beauclerk (Canadiana Department, Royal
Ontario Museum)

Macmillan Canada wishes to thank the Canada Council, the Ontario Ministry of
Culture and Communications and the Ontario Arts Council for supporting its
publishing program.

Macmillan Canada
A Division of Canada Publishing Corporation
Toronto, Ontario, Canada

Printed in Canada

For

Hélène, Christiane, Joseph, and Michael

Canadians and Québécois

Contents

List of Maps and Illustrations   vi
Preface to the 1996 edition   viii

Preface   xi

ONE   The Uncompleted Conquest   1
TWO   "The Governor sleeps in his chateau"   18
THREE   "Penury is great and misery complete"   31
FOUR   "You must either put him down..."   48
FIVE   "Nos tetes son en jeu maintenant..."   72
SIX   The Grand Brulé   92
SEVEN   "Une sorte de César sans emploi"   127
EIGHT   "To have tranquillity..."   150
NINE   "Dans l'abaissement"   181
TEN   "Let me take this instrument..."   194

Notes   213
Select Bibliography   218
Index   221

Maps and Illustrations

Except where otherwise noted the illustrations are from the Public Archives of Canada. The Public Archives provided all but one of the drawings by Jean-Joseph Girouard. The illustrations by Lord Charles Beauclerk, provided by the Archives, are from his series *Lithographic Views of Military Operations in Canada during the late insurrections,* London, 1840.

Maps

Southern Quebec with insets of Montreal and Quebec City   7
Montreal and the Richelieu River Valley   51
Military Operations at St-Eustache *(Musée du Québec/Luc Chartier)*   116-7

vi

Illustrations

Lord Aylmer by H.W. Pickersgill
Archibald, Earl of Gosford, by T. Phillips
Sir John Colborne by Richmond
The Earl of Durham by T. Phillips
T.S. Brown *(Notman Photographic Archives, McCord Museum)*
Wolfred Nelson by J.-J. Girouard *(collection Jean-Joseph Girouard)*
Captain Jalbert by J.-J. Girouard *(Musée du Québec/Luc Chartier)*
Jean Olivier Chénier by J.-J. Girouard *(collection Jean-Joseph Girouard)*
Jean-Joseph Girouard *(collection Jean-Joseph Girouard)*
W.H. Scott by J.-J. Girouard *(collection Jean-Joseph Girouard)*
Col. Wetherall advancing to the capture of St. Charles,
    25 November, 1837, by C. Beauclerk
The Attack on St. Charles, 25 November, 1837, by C. Beauclerk
Front view of the church of St-Eustache occupied by the
    insurgents. The artillery forcing an entrance, 14 December,
    1837, by C. Beauclerk
St-Eustache after it was burned by the British, 13 December, 1837, `
    by P.J. Bainbrigge
The ruins of St. Benoit, pillaged and burned 15 and 16
    December, 1837, by J.-J. Girouard *(collection Jean-Joseph Girouard)*
The Battle of Odelltown, 9 November, 1838, by Dr. McCallum
Dr. Brien by J.-J. Girouard *(collection Jean-Joseph Girouard)*
Francois-Xavier Prieur by Wiseman
Chevalier de Lorimier by J.-J. Girouard *(collection Jean-Joseph Girouard)*
Louis-Joseph Papineau by Napoléon Bourassa *(Musée du Québec/Luc Chartier)*
Louis Hippolyte LaFontaine by J.-J. Girouard *(collection Jean-Joseph Girouard)*

vii

Preface to the 1996 edition

When a writer who is also a novelist and a journalist delves into history, he cannot set aside his professional background. He must give life to the past. And this is precisely the approach Joseph Schull follows on the 1837 rebellions. His lively style takes the reader through the course of events that shook Lower Canada and his story does not stop with the end of the troubles. He completes his work by showing what happened to each of the main characters.

Rebellion. The Rising in French Canada 1837 was published in 1971, at a time when Québec was fresh from several years marked by violence—violence linked to the idea of independence. In 1970, members of the *Front de libération du Québec* considered themselves to be the heirs and successors to the Patriots of the 1837-1838 rebellion. They demanded a country where only French would be the official language. They did not know, or had forgotten, that Lower Canada's proclamation of independence of February 28, 1838 specified that their republic would have two official languages: French and English.

Back in the 1830s, it was natural for the two Canadas, Upper and Lower—Ontario and Québec—to feel vague impulses towards independence. From the end of the 1810s, Latin Americans had started to overthrow Spanish and Portuguese domination. Europe was facing a series of revolutions. France experienced the three glorious days of the July Revolution of 1830. Unification movements destabilized Italy. Belgium and Greece won their independence in this period known as *The People's Spring*. The idea that the people must rule was shared by leaders such as Louis-Joseph Papineau of the Patriots' Party.

In fact, Lower Canada's push for self-government was comprised of two different movements. In 1837, Papineau and some of his followers declared that independence must be obtained through constitutional means, that they should not resort to arms and violence. During the Six Counties' meeting, they were overtaken by those who were ready for anything. Using the excuse of the anticipated uprising, the leaders of the British army took the initiative. Soldiers marched on the village of St-Charles, but the Patriots stopped them at St-Denis, their only victory. The rebels suffered defeat at St-Charles and St-Eustache. Papineau left the area just before the battle of St-Denis. Joseph Schull does not say whether Papineau took flight or followed the advice of his lieutenants.

The real revolution came in 1838. Robert Nelson, who took over responsibility for the operations, followed the American model. He started with a proclamation of independence, and then tried to form an army to defeat the British forces. He failed and that failure brought about a painful settling of accounts.

Over the past two decades, Québec independence has been the subject of two referendums. The conditions that drove the Patriots to take up arms are no longer found today. However, it is important to return to this era and understand why *Canadiens* were ready to risk their lives for the sake of more freedom. History does not repeat itself, but recalling past events often enables us to understand the present better.

In his lifetime, Louis-Joseph Papineau was considered to be a Messiah, a liberator capable of leading his people to the Promised Land. His sudden departure from St-Denis in November 1837, then his exile to the United States and France, bred a feeling of disappointment. Some francophone Québeckers are ever seeking a new Papineau. A new Messiah appeared in 1887, when Honoré Mercier came to power in Quebec City. He in turn became a disappointment after his involvement in a serious bribery scandal, the Baie des Chaleurs affair.

During the 1970s, Québeckers thought they had found a new Papineau in René Lévesque, after raising some people's hopes, he disappointed them. From the Night of Long Knives to the Beau Risque of 1984, Québec's premier raised a great deal of uneasiness among his followers. Lucien Bouchard's dazzling arrival in Québec's political universe again revived the hopes of the supporters of independence. His mission in turn assumed messianic proportions. The only lesson that Québec's history can teach us is that Québeckers never forgive their Messiahs for deceiving them. Swift though the rise may be, rejection can prove equally sudden.

This is one of the chief reasons why we should revisit the past, revisit Papineau who was the first Messiah. And, to understand Papineau and his era, Joseph Schull's book takes on great importance. What Québec and Canada are currently living through fully justifies both republication in English and translation into French.

As the author himself wrote in his 1971 preface, "The Lower Canada Rebellion was one of the great traumatic experiences of Canadian history." Its consequences are still alive today. The rebellion has a great deal of relevance to the present.

Jacques Lacoursière
Editor and author of *Histoire Populaire du Québec*

Preface

The Lower Canada Rebellion was one of the great traumatic experiences of Canadian history. It was a clash of evolving peoples, of developing philosophies of government, and of conflicting patterns of life. It was a test of men and of leaders, and the leaders failed. The central problems of nationhood that still plague us today are at least in part a result of that failure.

This book is not an analysis of basic causes. It is an attempt, rather, to tell the story of the events and place them in scale. They tend to grow small in the long perspective of history, but they do not diminish in the folk-memory of a people. They are a force yet, to be measured and understood.

My reading and study has been spread out over a good many years, has often been laid aside, and has come together slowly. It was completed at a time when it seemed to take on new relevance, and for that reason, among many others, I hope it has been at least partially successful. I have to thank officials of the Public Archives of Canada, of the Quebec Provincial Archives, and of the British Museum in London for much help. I owe thanks to Norah Story and to Joan St-George Saunders for considerable help in research. Rosanna Seaborn Todd, formerly of Montreal, was one of the first to stimulate my interest in the battle-scarred church of St-Eustache. The Canadian Broadcasting Corporation, several years ago, encouraged me to further studies. John Gray of Macmillan and Hugh Shaw and Frank Lowe of *Weekend* Magazine have done much by their interest in support of the present work. I should like to thank my sister, Helen, for typing and re-typing a great deal of the manuscript; and my wife, Hélène, for enduring with her usual cheerfulness the ordeal of another book.

JOSEPH SCHULL

Rebellion
The Rising in French Canada 1837

ONE

The Uncompleted Conquest

To officials of the British Colonial Office in the early nineteenth century the problem of Canada must have seemed a never-ending bore. It was as old as the conquest made on the Plains of Abraham, it had come home with Wolfe's bones, and it had haunted British politics ever since. Around it and somehow always involved in it there had been a wreckage of noble hopes and careful plans. Yet it had risen from every ruin, a little thornier than before, to perplex imperial governments and entangle reluctant statesmen.

Through Wolfe's victory, confirmed by the Treaty of Paris in 1763, Great Britain had displaced France as the effective possessor of northern North America. She had removed the threat and the rival to her own Thirteen Colonies. For the two million Englishmen who had been hemmed in on the north by the St. Lawrence valley and blocked off from the west by French control of the waterways, the whole interior of the continent was now open. It seemed that the shape of empire had begun to emerge at last. "In another century," wrote Benjamin Franklin, that staid British citizen of Philadelphia, "all the country from the St. Lawrence to the Mississippi will be filled with British people. Britain herself will become vastly more populous by the immense increase of its commerce, the Atlantic sea will be covered with your trading ships; and your naval power, thence continually increasing, will extend your influence round the whole globe and awe the world."[1]

Upon this transcendent vision the problem of the conquered people hardly impinged. New France was gone, and the armies and power of France were gone with it. The high officials of government had all decamped. So had the richer merchants and the greatest of the old seigneurs, who had lived as demi-nobility on the lands granted them for colonizing by a succession of French kings. There remained now only the neediest of each class and the ever-present Church, almost as poor as its children. Of these there were about eight thousand in the smashed ruins of Quebec, and another five thousand in the gloomy greystone huddle of Montreal. Gathered here in impotence and exhausted by the long war was most of the headless remnant of the colony's professions and commerce, its skills and trades and knowledge. For the rest, along the jagged strip of the seigneuries that lined both banks of the St. Lawrence from a little above the Gaspé to its junction with the Ottawa River, there were the church spires and the priests, the stony farms and the woodlots, and some fifty thousand French-speaking Catholic peasants.

They were a race of cheerfully reluctant warriors who had fought, when they were made to, a great deal better than the regular troops of France. They clung to their land with a thrifty Norman passion, but it had not been their first love. As explorers, traders, and adventurers they had followed the continent's waterways north to Hudson Bay, west to the Rocky Mountains and south to the Gulf of Mexico. Their forts and settlements, trading posts and missions, built for the wars, the fur trade, and the faith, projected the civilization of a thousand years to come. There were still ten thousand of their kinfolk scattered among those outposts, but they counted for nothing now. They would be turning British or turning Indian, or they would drift back to the only homes they knew, among the farms along the St. Lawrence. Only the Canadians of the valley had to be thought of. They had known no government but French colonial absolutism, they were left with no leaders but a few priests and sei- gneurs, and they were almost wholly illiterate. Nothing had seemed more certain than that, in the course of a generation or two, they would be absorbed, made British and Protestant, and integrated with the other colonists of the North American empire.

It was to be done gently, and it was all to be left with con- fidence to the power of the British example and the work of enlightening time. Few wars had ended with less rigour and few régimes had begun with more pious hopes than those involved in the taking over of Canada. To the first military gov- ernor it was the invading merchants of Boston and official blockheads newly arrived from England who were the real enemies to be suppressed. The Canadians, to his mind, were "perhaps the bravest and best race upon the Globe",[2] and they were to be protected from greedy conquerors. Their men, though "generally of a litigious disposition",[3] were mostly Nor- mans, hardy, quick, and adaptable, and their handsome women were bearers of many children. They had fought well and they had lost, and from both considerations they were dear to a sol- dier's heart. To the politicians of the Colonial Office they were attractive for other reasons. Docile under a king, fond of the fid- dle and dancing, and indifferent to forms of government, they were immune from the discontents of the Thirteen Colonies. Their seigneurs were a promising nucleus for a body of country squires, to be tied to the Crown by concern for their own "plan- tations". Even their Church was a tool that could be well used for a while. A British government, with all its official abhor- rence for the "Romish Religion", was well aware of the value of an established church. The priests would pave the way for the Church of England, maintaining order and virtue while Popery was undermined. "His Majesty's New Subjects", vigorous, sturdy, and fecund, pleasure-loving, litigious, and devoted to land and Church, were hardly to feel the changing reins of conquest. While old men lived their lives out comfortable and undisturbed, their children would learn from English schools and dominies. They would "by degrees be induced to embrace the Protestant Religion"[4] and to speak the English tongue, and they would be engulfed or carried onward in the tide of impe- rial growth.

Instead, within twenty years of the Treaty of Paris, the American Revolution had supervened, Benjamin Franklin was no longer a British subject, and the southern half of the continent had been sheared away. It was the Canadians along the St. Lawrence, still French and multiplying, who were the one remaining buttress of British power. They could hardly be called loyal but they disliked change, and disliked Americans more. They were sons of a Church that had now become invaluable, since it detested American Protestantism, feared American democracy, and had given its cool support to George III. They had remained quiescently hostile to invading American armies, and it had been enough to turn the scales in favour of the King. In 1783, as the United States began its course through history, Canada remained British, but ninety per cent of its hundred thousand subjects were French-speaking Roman Catholics.

2

The task of the Colonial Office was now to pick up the pieces of empire and chart a new course. With regard to the French the old presumptions remained, and the delayed work of absorption seemed likely to quicken at last. A handful of British officials administered government. British merchants and traders were pre-empting the country's wealth. Thousands of returning loyalists from the lost colonies to the south were as British in all their sympathies as any man could wish. They wanted land, they wanted compensation for their losses, and they wanted self-government after the model of Britons at home. But they did not wish to establish themselves in the parishes along the St. Lawrence. They were overwhelmingly Protestant and they were restless among the French, who returned their dislike with interest. It all led, in 1791, to the sub-division of the province into an Upper and Lower Canada, with the boundary between the sections along the line of the Ottawa River. Most of the new-come loyalists went west beyond the Ottawa, the French remained where they were, and beside and above the French remained a thriving British establishment. Since this comprised about ten thousand out of a total population which was now estimated at some hundred and fifty thousand, it would have to put up for a while with the French ambience, but a change in the form of government gave hope of early relief. There was to be established in each province a colonial adaptation of parliamentary rule. A governor appointed by the King would act in the King's name, an appointed council would advise him, and an assembly elected by the people might tender its advice to both.

There was no thought that the advice of a popular assembly should carry decisive weight. A colony was not the mother country, nor could any body of colonists, particularly French colonists, be entrusted with the actual powers of a House of Commons. The new Canadas, under the firm hands of the governors, would be guided in all essentials by their best people, of whom the best of the best would be members of the Legislative Council. They would be chosen from the judiciary and the bureaucracy and from among the "respectable" merchants, who were naturally all affluent and naturally all British. They would include in Lower Canada a sprinkling of French seigneurs, respectable because of their land holdings and loyal for fear of losing them. While an inner Executive Council, distilled from the Legislative Council, would be the real centre of power, the bodies would function in common as an embryo House of Lords. "It was at that time contemplated," said a later Colonial Minister, "that an hereditary aristocracy might be formed in these provinces by attaching to seats in the Council titles of honour, which were together to pass to descendants of the original grantees."[5]

As usual in the Canadas, however, nothing went as planned. The loyalists of the upper province, though they had departed the Thirteen Colonies, had carried a taste for democracy along with them and were soon clamouring to apply it. As government began and a frontier gentry developed and began to make provision for sons and nephews, a raucous commonalty seethed beneath them, promising future discord. Yet this in its way was familiar English trouble. The problem in Lower Canada was still the French.

Within twenty years of the establishment of the lower province, vast tracts for settlement had been marked off and surveyed. The seigneuries remained for the most part as they were, the closed preserve of the habitant. Outside the seigneuries, however, lay a cordon of new townships bearing comfortably British names. They invited British immigrants, and a trickle was coming in. Flourishing British bureaucrats, after the best manner of home, were providing themselves with the offices, sinecures, and pensions, and the ample grants of land, that would be suitable to their future state as Lords in Canada. The forward-looking merchants who had taken over the fur trade were also building a trade in grain and timber. They were reaching west by the waterways and looking east to London, while they were building capital and connections through a growing export trade. For them and their friends in government, and their opposites in Upper Canada, the future of the St. Lawrence valley was now clear. It was to be a broad commercial highway, blossoming with British cities, bristling with British warehouses, linking the interior of the continent with the routes of the empire's trade. Commercial men and officialdom were alight with impatient hopes. They had come to see geography as the French had once seen it, but they had not been able to absorb the French or fire them with the new vision.

The vast majority of the habitants still lived by the river, with their horizons narrowed down to the seigneurial lands. In their language, their religion, and their primitive methods of farming, they remained impervious to change. They had given a chill welcome to the English schools and dominies, and the priest and the vestry meeting remained their guide and council. They had not been much interested in the gift of a popular assembly, which most of them saw at first as a new device of the English to impose taxes. Yet when the vote came they had learned to use it, and they had begun to develop in the process a new and disturbing class of British subject. Their principal representatives, all French, were an élite chosen from a people of whom one in twelve could read. The Catholic Church, which would not have English teaching and had small means for primary schools of its own, had pinned its hopes for the future on a cluster of small colleges. They could accommodate only the brightest of the young habitants and the promising sons of families in the two cities, but they taught the few well. Out of them, in addition to many priests, came the doctors, lawyers, and notaries who were soon to become anathema to British governors.

The graduates emerged from the colleges as natural leaders,

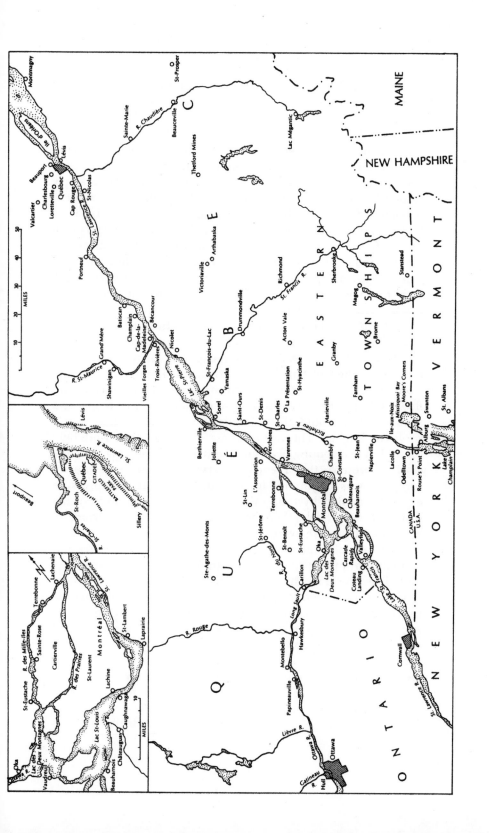

and as the men most keenly irked by conditions around them. They were restricted in their professions because the British controlled commerce and monopolized the posts of government. With a classical education, they had none of the arts of trade, and most of them had no taste for it. They were sometimes brilliant men, and they were all frustrated men. In their own fields, in the way of every ambition they saw a safely settled *bureaucrate* or a younger son from England, come out to make his fortune with the help of established friends. They looked about them in the seigneuries and saw the best land taken up, the farms narrowing as they were divided among many sons, the worried faces of fathers who had no more land to give.

In the townships surrounding the seigneuries the competition for new land meant competition with the English on English terms. The Clergy Reserves and the Crown Reserves lay vacant and closed off. The grants to speculating officials and the grants to disbanded soldiers took up much of the rest, while a haughty British bureaucracy imposed its own priorities in advance of the habitants' claims. It was the immigrants coming from abroad and the Yankees coming from the south who were flowing into the townships and clamouring for roads and schools. They would all be English schools, and roads would serve the English. The vast reserves and land grants were held for an English coming. Everywhere the creeping tentacles were closing around the French. Everywhere the pressure of conquest was beginning to bear down, yet it was pressure explicitly denied by the new Constitution. In the eyes of the British Mother, who had decreed the form of government, French and English were equally British subjects. They were therefore equally entitled to the burdens and fruits of office and to a voice in public affairs. The deputies to the new Assembly, with disastrous French logic, had made the position clear.

They were elected for the first Parliament from a population in which the French outnumbered the English by fifteen to one. A prudent use of the franchise had bettered the proportions in the Assembly, and there were sixteen English members confronting thirty-four French. Among the English, moreover, were a number of substantial businessmen who were expected to redress the balance by their weight and influence. The result proved disappointing. The French moved immediately to impose their choice as Speaker. Over outraged British protests they established the French language on an equal footing with English for all business of the House. They went on to compound these felonies in this and later sessions, and were soon out-studying the English in the subtleties of the Constitution. They were an increasing trial to their rulers and they clogged the wheels of progress. Many were rigid dogmatists with the closed minds of the seminary, and most were of humble origin and despised as country boors. Yet they were, as a class, the most articulate and best-educated in Lower Canada, and there was no gainsaying their right at least to talk.

By the early 1800s talk was becoming theory, and theory was threatening commerce. Disconcerted businessmen began to give up the hopes they had placed in the Assembly. Always dominated by the French, it was attracting English radicals who worked along with the French. From contesting popular elections, the merchant princes turned to seeking appointments, and worked, allied with officialdom, from seats in the Legislative Council. A new struggle shaped itself between the upper and lower Houses. In 1805, with anti-Frenchness sharpening through the long wars with Napoleon, the first explosions came. From Montreal, which was rapidly becoming a British commercial stronghold, there was a proposal to tax land, the first concern of the habitant. There was an immediate counter-proposal to tax trade, the first concern of the merchant. The result was open battle and a foreshadowing of much more, for the very base of bureaucracy was the next to come under attack.

Every officer of the government depended for his position and emolument on three distinct sources. The first was the Civil List, which was the fund appropriated to pay official salaries. The second was the revenue from Crown lands, reserved as the King's Prerogative, while the third was grants or pensions awarded by royal authority and taken from the general fund. All three sources, immune from control by Parliament, had been carefully designed as ramparts against democracy. They were all administered by the Governor and the Governor's friends in Council, and they had preserved the friends in security and independence. By 1810, however, both those blessings were threatened. The men of the lower House, from which most of the English leaders had now departed, were asserting the broader powers of a House of Commons. Demanding control by Parliament of every source of revenue, they were threatening the place and power of every official. They were at war not only with merchants but with the whole sacrosanct fabric of British colonial policy. A "British Party" and a "French Party" had taken shape in the province, there were new and venomous newspapers disputing on the same lines, and Craig, the tenth governor, had imprisoned members of the Assembly. They had not been long in durance but Craig had become a legend, and the sleeping rancours of conquest were at last fully awake.

These were directed at first not at the British Mother but at British colonial Tories who distorted the Constitution. Through the War of 1812, and for fifteen years thereafter, French loyalty to the Crown was quite as dependable an asset as British loyalty. But the French-Canadian habitant would not be made English. The French-Canadian Catholic would not be made Protestant. And the French-Canadian legislators, always a little more skilful in debate and agitation, would no longer vote the subsidies that supported a colonial oligarchy. They had discovered the power of the purse and meant to use it, for the rooting out of *bureaucrates,* for the control of the Legislative Council, and even for the better guidance of irate colonial governors. By 1831, as a result of savage controversy, much of this had been gained. The mother country, which had sided with her merchants and officials and then wearied of them as their ways became better known, had abandoned the hope of a colonial aristocracy. She had accepted the ruder ways of North America, with all the distasteful levelling these entailed. She had almost accepted representative government, with the dreaded implication of majority rule. Except for the Civil List and the fund from the Crown lands, the Assembly of Lower Canada would control the revenue.

Even the Civil List, the central bone of contention, had been sharply and sadly pruned. It was to provide now only for the salaries of the governor and the senior officials round him, most of them aging patriarchs nesting high in the bureaucracy. From their eyries in the two Councils they had fought the long battle against Frenchness and popular government, and the battle was turning against them. Their numbers had been reduced, their privileges had been curtailed, and they were sharing their seats in council with increasing numbers of French. It meant little in fact, for the newly appointed French were still outnumbered and a British majority held its grip on the Councils. Yet more and more, as power passed to the Assembly, the ominous signs grew clear. There were no more princely land grants at the stroke of a governor's pen. Sinecures were growing fewer and even pensions were threatened, though they were pledged on the faith of the King. They depended now solely on the King's Prerogative, the fund from the Crown Reserves, still withheld from the grasping hands of legislators. Yet even this was vulnerable and under increasing attack. The King's servants, the distilled essence of Englishness and the aristocratic dream, looked out unbelievingly on ever-advancing Frenchness. While their salaries remained assured to them they were beyond removal or control, but they were locked into a citadel that was crumbling under their feet.

If the auguries dismayed the *bureaucrates*, they were even worse for the merchants. Their quarrel was not with Frenchness but with stagnation, yet all stagnation seemed to come from the French. Year by year, as the endless, maddening ritual of sessions and debate went on, the province had been frittering away its golden hopes. Upper Canada was building canals and waterways, widening and deepening the channels that fed trade to the St. Lawrence. The Assembly of Lower Canada would vote no funds for the work. It still saw such progress as a solely English concern. It watched with surly apathy as the younger province grew, and the grain trade and the timber trade began to fill the river. The apathy became hostility as the ships that went to England laden with timber returned with British immigrants to compete for the province's land. Commercial hopes lay dormant and commercial men grew desperate as the Erie Canal was built, and then the Champlain Canal, completing American waterways that drained trade from the St. Lawrence.

In 1822, pointing to the growing strength of the upper province, the canals and roads unbuilt, the chances slipping away, the merchants of Lower Canada had taken their case to England. They had moved in the name of progress for a reunion of the two Canadas that would at last root out Frenchness by a combined British majority. They had only blown up a storm that blew them down. As the Union Bill was framed and the French united to oppose it they had been joined by English reformers who were at war with Tory government. French and English leaders had crossed the Atlantic, bearing a huge petition against the Bill. Of its sixty thousand names thousands were signed with crosses, and the "Knights of the Cross" excited much derision. Yet they had proved effective pleaders, and they had found friends in London. They had won the support of powerful men in Parliament and the measure had been defeated.

The first bitter blow to colonial Tories had been followed by many others. Proposals to cede Montreal to Upper Canada, to create a separate province from the English townships, to unite the English somehow for the overcoming of the French, had all failed. It seemed to the British leaders, firm in their old ideas, that the obvious destiny of the country was being mocked. Education was lagging along with commerce, for the French would not be taught in Protestant schools. Lesser irritations were becoming rasping sores. French civil law, tolerated still by a too-indulgent England, perplexed the many transactions of British business. French seigneurial tenure hovered in feudal complexity over transfers of British land. And worst of all were the French-Canadian legislators, brushing aside the interests of the country. Amid their endless sterile quarrels with governors and the upper House, bills died, acts expired, revenues were uncollected, and improvements were left unmade. The province was standing still, the province was still French, and every hope of the conquest seemed farther off than ever.

3

There were other considerations, and they centred on one man. In 1831 Louis-Joseph Papineau, a lawyer and the son of a notary, was forty-five years old. He was the owner of one of the newer, rawer seigneuries, west of Montreal on the Ottawa River. It bore the resounding name of La Petite Nation, but it was land purchased by his father; Louis-Joseph was a parvenu seigneur. He had been a member of the Assembly for over twenty years, and its Speaker for fourteen. He was not enjoined to silence; the Speaker of those days spoke as the party leader, and the flood of Papineau's eloquence had washed him high. As first officer of the House he enjoyed a salary of £1,000 a year, which compared reasonably well with the salaries of senior *bureaucrates*. It had been bequeathed to him in palmier days when governors still had hopes of him, but the hopes had long since vanished. The new-made aristocrat had a keen respect for money, and was prouder of his rank and title than most of the old seigneurs, but he was not malleable. A ceaseless war with bureaucracy, and with the governors who paid *bureaucrates*, had coloured his whole career and shaped the man.

He was not quite yet the undisputed leader, either of the French fighting for survival or of the reforming Scots and Englishmen who adhered to the French Party. There had been men before him setting the shape of battle, and there were stronger, steadier men around him now. But he had the leader's presence and the touch of magic. "I have never seen anyone," wrote one British observer, "who appeared more versed than this Canadian orator in the tricks and the mastery of means by which one man dominates the minds of a great number."[6] He was no rough countryman; he had been born and made his home in Montreal, Quebec was his theatre of action, and there were few of the "Château Clique" around the Governor who rivalled Papineau's grace or ease of manner. But it had become the guarded grace of a declared enemy. He moved among them, a Canadian, the equal of any one and the superior of most, seeing them all as "birds of prey and passage",[7] the wreckers of New France, the rootless, ruthless exploiters to whom only Britain was home. He had drawn into himself, through twenty years of parliaments, the gloomy, angry pride of a trapped people, and a brooding sense of destiny as some of the bars went down. Reform was half-won, Parliament was half-free, and it was not his work alone. Others had helped to trim the power of governors and prune the fat bureaucracy, yet always more and more it was work done in his name. And always a little less, whatever the work accomplished, was it able to content Papineau.

He was growing and hardening in his purposes as he rose taller in the country. The grant of a share in government was now no longer enough. It had no meaning for Papineau while a Civil List remained, buttressing his old enemies and confirming English rule. So long as appointed autocrats were paid in the King's name there would be no budging them, no changing them; they would somehow have their way. They must be torn loose from those salaries and pitched out in the American fashion to the tender mercies of the people. Every office of government must be made elective, and there could be no doubt of the result. The population of the province, by the beginning of the 1830s, was still about four-fifths French.

Even that fraction did not tell all the story. The Irish were coming now, disgorged from the timber ships, and hatred of England was part of the air they breathed. Americans from New York and Vermont were clustered in the Eastern Townships along the border, with their own grievances against law officers and land officers who grabbed the best for themselves, built no roads or schools, and reeked always of the autocratic Englishness that had been driven from the Thirteen Colonies. There were new men from an England where reform was changing Parliament, and others from a seething Europe that was beginning to tumble its kings. They were all ripe for Papineau, and Papineau was ripe for them. Restlessness and revolution were in the air, vying with Frenchness and assisting Frenchness. The little prophets were gravitating round the greater,. and they were lifting and thrusting him on. The very idea of monarchy was under attack, and even the authority of the Church. The French Party was becoming the Papineau Party, and it was possible to look beyond it. One could see the last of Britishness expelled from elective councils. One could even see Papineau as president of a French republic.

It was not to be thought of seriously, but it was being thought of. It was obviously in the minds of orators who declaimed on the many virtues of government in the United States. It was being scribbled about by journalists, who were Irish where they were not French. Rejected by moderate men of all persuasions, it was still a noxious breath in thickening air. For the Honourable George Moffatt, merchant of Montreal and member of the Legislative Council, the air required a clearing.

He had not been long with the Council, having just taken his seat in November of 1831. As a comparative freshman in politics, he regarded the honour seriously, and he had a high opinion of himself, for good reasons. A penniless boy from England, he had gone west with the fur trade just at the turn of the century. He had come back ten years later with the base of a fortune laid, and had branched out from furs into timber and grain and staples. He was a banker now as well, a member of the Board of Magistrates that governed Montreal, and one of the most powerful men in Lower Canada. Forty-five years old, in full and vigorous prime, he had a somewhat simplistic view of public affairs. This was a British colony, conquered by British arms, developed by British enterprise, ruled by a British king. French intransigence must end and British progress resume, and the time had come to act. The authority of British government, entrenched in His Majesty's Council, must be restored without delay. It must be restored once and for all, in a way that was clear to all.

4

The opportunity presented itself in January of 1832. Of the journalists supporting Papineau in Montreal, two of the most obnoxious were Ludger Duvernay of *La Minerve* and Daniel Tracey of *The Vindicator*, and both had chosen to salute the Council in their New Year editorials. They had often done so before and would again, and their words at the festive season were comparatively mild. They considered the Council an "incubus" and found that the latest batch of appointments, of which George Moffatt's was one, added "eight or ten men with scarcely common talent". The body governed by "caprice" and defeated the wishes of the people. They demanded its abolition.[8]

There was talk much worse than that circulating every day among the snowdrifts and horse droppings and grey-stone shops and warehouses of wintertime Montreal. At Quebec, where Parliament was sitting, the seasoned members of the Council plumped for lofty contempt and silence. To George Moffatt, however, another course was called for, and he commanded formidable influence. He brought it to bear on several reluctant colleagues, and a brief debate resulted in drastic action. On January 17 the Serjeant-at-Arms appeared at the bar of the House. He announced that he had in custody, by virtue of the Council's order, the persons of Ludger Duvernay and Daniel Tracey. Each in turn they were summoned to appear at the bar, marched out while their sentence was being considered, and marched back to hear it. They had been found guilty "of a high breach of the privileges of this House,"[9] and for the remainder of the session of Parliament they were to be lodged in the Quebec jail.

There was nothing else that the Council could devise as punishment, and it lived for the next few weeks through a storm of abuse and ridicule. On February 25 the session closed, and a day later the culprits were the idols of French and Irish Montreal. They returned unrepentant, and their unrepentant newspapers were immediately in full cry. Spring came on and the shipping season approached. The narrow streets and dank alleys opening up from the waterfront became uglier and noisier with the bustle of preparations. Stevedores not yet employed and swarming dockside "sunfish" who were not seeking employment came out of their winter hiding. Alert, expectant, idle and ripe for trouble, the town still talked of its heroes. Officialdom let them be, nursing its burnt fingers but ready and eager to try a new approach. It was no time for an election, but a by-election came.

The vacant seat was a Montreal constituency, and Tracey, the people's martyr, was at once the people's candidate. George Moffatt had made him, and Papineau's French and Irish lost no time in enlarging him. He was opposed by a George Bagg who discovered his own friends, and numerous friends on both sides were soon equipped with clubs. "While there was a man in the city who could be bought," said Tracey's newspaper, "no pains were spared to buy him," and according to the same authority the campaign was "spun out to the great annoyance of the public and the suspension of almost all the business of this city."[10]

From April 24 to May 21 the endless ritual of open polling went on. The doors of the returning office opened on Place d'Armes, and gangs of rival "whackers" milled in the square. As each voter arrived he was forced to run a gauntlet of both persuasions, and often as he finished voting he remained to support one. It was a neck-and-neck race, with the tally announced in the newspapers day by day, and a daily quarrel ensuing as to the methods of each party. On May 21, as the voting rose to its climax, Place d'Armes was black with people and there was promise of a full-fledged riot. At five in the afternoon, as Tracey was declared the winner and his forces gathered to form a victory procession, the riot duly came. The hired bullies pitched into each other with their clubs, the unpaid outriders contributed a shower of stones, and jubilant battle swayed across the square.

It began to approach the church of Notre Dame, with a light rain falling and the May dusk closing in. Few appeared to have noticed that there was an ominous patch of red, just on the edge of the tumult. Custom forbade the presence of troops at elections, but the Montreal magistrates, of whom George Moffatt was one, had decided to set a precedent. They had sent a call to the garrison on St. Helen's Island, and a company dispatched from there was stationed in the shadow of the church. The soldiers were standing at ease, curious and amused, enjoying with official blessing the first such spectacle they had seen. As the fight surged toward them with a sudden, meaningless rush, the relaxed ranks stiffened. George Moffatt, present in his capacity as Magistrate, was waving his arms at their officer, and as stones showered the troops the officer called for an advance. The men went into the mob with their rifles high, trying to clear a front. Then, as the fighting thickened, some of the barrels came down. There was the sharp bark of an order, and the levelled muzzles were suddenly spitting fire. The waves of the crowd lapped back around a little patch on the cobblestones where three men lay dead. Pierre Billet, François Languedoc, and Casimir Chauvin, two labourers and a printer, had established their own precedent. For the first time since the Conquest the bullets of British infantry had spilled Canadian blood.

TWO

"The Governor sleeps in his château"

For an hour or so after dusk, in the light of lanterns and torches under a steady drumming of rain, the bodies lay in the square. A bewildered coroner stood over them, a cordon of troops surrounded them, and beyond the troops was the mob, stunned, murmurous, and deadly. It parted to admit Papineau followed by a dozen friends, and politics entered at once on a new dimension.

Would the officer in command of the troops say who had given the order to fire? He would not; he would answer only to superior military authority. Would the coroner proceed with the inquest on grounds laid out by Papineau? He would not; he would adjourn to the following day. The bodies were carried off, the littered square emptied, and the morning's first wet news sheets brought the start of the public outcry.

It was assisted at every turn by Matthew, Baron Aylmer, the latest of Wellington's generals to govern Canada. Amiable, dithering, and inane, he held aloof at Quebec, concerned for his friends in Council and the reputation of his soldiers, attempting to divert inquiry into the labyrinth of the courts. It would not be so diverted while Papineau had a voice. "The Governor sleeps in his château, and they leave us with these murderers!"[1] For three weeks the storm rose. Then it became a background, unforgotten. Whipped up by orators, newspapers, committees of investigation, and the confused and competing testimony of hundreds of witnesses, it was to return with a new venom at the autumn session of the legislature. But the summer came first, and there were grislier times at hand.

There had been warnings from London late in the previous year that Asiatic cholera, rising in the delta of the Ganges and sweeping across Europe, might make an appearance in Canada. It seemed to be a disease that followed migrant men, and they were flowing in from the Motherland in yearly increasing numbers. In the single season of 1831, fifty thousand men, women, and children had been poured out onto the waterfronts at Quebec or Montreal. Some were the well-provided who stepped ashore from comfortable first-class cabins, picked their way through the mud and stench of the docksides, and departed with funds and baggage for the purer air beyond. Others were of the stout British yeoman class, much celebrated in the oratory and advertising of the times, who at least brought skills and ambition and usually a pouch of coins. As they flowed out to the townships or on to Upper Canada, the wealth and Britishness of the country grew around them. It was the lifeblood of the future and one of the bases of trade, this tide of immigration.

Yet it also brought with it, in large and increasing proportions, another class of humanity. There were thousands of Irish, famine-ridden and destitute, who had been dispossessed by landlords in their own country and left to the charge of parishes that had no means to support them. There were other thousands as miserable from the slums of English cities. Both classes, to concerned authority in England, were highly favoured cargo either as sweepings to be got rid of or as ballast for the timber ships, and they were usually helped on their way with a little money. They were also frequently deluded as to the length and conditions of the voyage and their welcome in the new world.

They were herded with their wives and children and their scraps of baggage and provisions onto the docks of British

19

ports. The "fast, commodious vessel" to which they had been led by glowing advertisements proved, more often than not, to be a racked and leaky timber drogher or an old, third-rate tramp with its holds unwashed and stinking from a dozen previous passages. The promised day of sailing was usually put off for weeks, while they ate the last of their provisions and spent most of their money. Then, with nothing to live on except what they could purchase from ship's stores, they would be battened down in the noisome well of the steerage and the Atlantic voyage would begin. It sometimes went on for seventy or eighty days, frequently under captains who might well have graced the slave trade. The medical stores of one ship consisted of three pints of castor oil and three pounds of Epsom salts. The ship's "doctor" in another was vague as to whether the tibia and the fibula were bones of the arm or the leg. There were numerous dead flung overboard in the wake of all these ships, and sometimes as they came into the St. Lawrence their dying were simply abandoned along a stretch of desolate shore. Yet there were still thousands of survivors when the vessels arrived at Quebec, some to be emptied there and some to be towed upriver by the tugs and paddlewheel steamers that plied to Montreal.

At neither port was any provision made for the new arrivals. Dazed, friendless, and exhausted after weeks of foul air, foul water, and wretched food, they were herded along through great barnlike immigrant sheds and tumbled out onto the dockside to make their way as they could. At Quebec, below the heights was a sprawl of wharves and warehouses and the jumble of the lower town, filthy, bustling, and crowded, with its timber rafts upriver, its hooting tugs and steamers, and its constant clutter of sail. The upper town loomed over, feeding its streams of sewage down the bare face of the rock, and climbing up from the waterside were the narrow ribbon of Mountain Street and the gap of Break-Neck Stairs. But the immigrant seldom climbed, for he was not welcome above. His way was along Champlain Street, twisting between the warehouses and the dank wall of the cliff, with the ruinous stone hovels of its grog shops and boarding houses, its sailors and sailors' women, and its hard-eyed crimps and foremen on watch for the strongest backs. For some of these there was work to be had at The Coves, where the shipyards and lumberyards lined both banks of the river. A few men went to the timber rafts, a few to the pick-and-shovel gangs, and others shipped back home in the outbound droghers. But most stayed, with their wives and children round them, and most were idle and starving.

Some took off in tattered tribes of families to walk to Montreal, where the muddy flats of the waterside were being cleared for new docks and there was much digging and building. But the vessels towed upriver had arrived well ahead of them and the jobs were usually gone. There was only the same wretchedness they had left behind in Quebec. Some moved on again for the woods beyond the Ottawa, but many more did not. They sickened and died in alleys, infested the waterfront hovels, and traipsed about through the summer in listless, rag-hung droves. Where they went when the snow came no man knew for sure, but the used ballast of the timber trade was not easily disposed of.

By 1831, as private charity gave out and typhus and dysentery grew to be chronic threats, the nuisance had become intolerable. Urged on by church societies and philanthropists who had no more means to provide food or care, the leading merchants in Quebec and Montreal had been persuaded with some difficulty to contribute to an Emigrant Fund. It provided about five shillings per head, not for the wretched lingerers in the two cities, but as an inducement to some of the derelicts to continue their journey west. Some four thousand had thus been emptied out. Yet there would be new thousands arriving in 1832, and with the timber trade booming and the cholera warning in mind, there had been strong hints from London that other measures were called for. A quarantine station was to be established at Grosse Ile, a pretty island in the St. Lawrence about thirty miles down from Quebec. There were to be Boards of Health appointed in both Quebec and Montreal. Beyond that, to establish a public fund for the sick and indigent, there was to be a tax of five shillings, paid by the captain of the ship, on each immigrant landed.

To this last, though the bill was proposed in the Assembly with the approval of the Governor, the merchant princes of the Council had raised violent objection. The other public provisions, involving an assault on the treasury, were quite painful enough. But a head tax on immigrants was a tax on British trade. It was a measure supported by the French, to whom immigration was anathema. It restricted the right of freeborn British subjects to move wherever they pleased, and it would infallibly divert thousands of them to ports in the United States. George Moffatt, once more wielding his influence in the Council, had led the fight to block the bill during February of 1832, and the combatants had not been sweetened by the thought of Tracey and Duvernay reposing in Quebec jail. Yet on February 25, the last day of the session, a few hours before the cell doors creaked open to release the journalists, the measure had gone through.

By late April, as the ice moved out of the river, the quarantine station was ready on Grosse Ile. It was staffed with doctors and officials of the new Boards of Health, and large sheds of fresh-smelling pine and spruce stood near the waterside for the temporary accommodation of sick passengers. The flag climbed on a tall staff, giving authority to the new institution, two landing places had been marked out on the rocky shore, and there were cannon set up to command both sides of the channel. One of the green meadows near the water was whitened with the tents of soldiers who were stationed as permanent garrison. It was all a refreshing sight to weary passengers as the ships came upriver after the fogs and battering of the Gulf.

2

It had no such effect on the captains, who were faced with new delays, new expense, and official interference with the established ways of trade. On April 28 *Constantin* of Limerick was signalled to anchor, and the first surly master greeted the doctors' boat. Of his hundred and seventy passengers twenty-nine had died, but it was not an abnormal figure. He reported none sick now, the inspecting doctors concurred, and the ship was allowed to proceed. *Robert, Elizabeth,* and *Carrick* came in during the following week to report in all seventy-five deaths during their voyages and twenty or thirty cases of typhus and "ship fever". The sick were taken off, the vessels allowed to go on, and the stream of the summer's shipping began to grow.

On June 7 *Voyager* limped in. She was obviously a wretched old hulk with a seething mass of trouble and misery in her steerage, but there were other ships pressing behind her and doctors were overworked. The sheds on shore were already becoming crowded and were no longer smelling sweetly. Captains in haste were ignoring the proper landing places and dumping their sick where they could. Immigrants were wandering the island, confusion was growing everywhere, and inspection was becoming as hasty as the captains themselves. *Voyager* went up the river the same evening, bound for Montreal. She stopped for her tug at Quebec, and went on. By dawn she was forced to turn back. The ship was leaking in the choppy swells of the river, the steerage was filling with water, and its drenched and frenzied occupants were swarming up to the deck. They were dragging their sick after them, heaving overboard the wet masses of rags and straw on which some had already died, and screaming to be put ashore. By the night of June 8 *Voyager* was back in Quebec. The captain landed some two hundred of his worst "trouble-makers" and started upriver again.

About fifty of those disembarked found shelter in the dank stalls of a boarding house on Champlain Street. One of them died in the night. Another died in the morning and by the evening of June 9, from this house and from others along the street, sixteen patients had been admitted to a Quebec hospital. Their symptoms indicated cholera and by nightfall eight were dead.

Rumours could not be allowed to sweep the city. They were bad for immigration and bad for trade. By this time some 28,000 of the summer's immigrants had landed and the flow could not be stopped. Timber was waiting to be loaded, goods ordered from abroad were urgently required by the merchants; business must go its way. As talk simmered in the streets, newspapers damped it down with angry denials. The Board of Health, only recently appointed and official in all its ways, prudently avoided expenditures for supplies or hospital space until the need should become manifest.

On June 13, however, came the first public announcement. There had been ninety-four cases of cholera in the past twenty-four hours, and twenty-three deaths. On June 15 the thunderbolt struck the city with full force. There were now 1,204 officially reported cases of whom 230 had died, and there was

23

no certainty that all cases had been reported. In the next two days 475 were added to the sick list and there were 102 "ascertained deaths".

Trade flowed on. The barques and brigs came up the stream from Grosse Ile, lightened of their sick and dead but still crowded. The timber droghers pushed in, hastily inspected, half-inspected, with some among them who had evaded all inspection. There was no time and there was little inclination for doctors to linger long in any of the holds. The men on the island were coping with thousands now, the new sheds were pesthouses from which all who could escaped, and troops were digging burial pits while the infected roamed at large. The people freed from Grosse Ile poured out onto the wharves of Quebec, wailing for the dead and dying left behind them, gaunt, destitute, and bewildered, much as in other years. But this year, in the filthy, hostile city, even the low doors open to them had almost all been closed.

By the end of June every hospital was filled and there were hundreds of sick in tents on the Plains of Abraham. Of the city's people those who could leave were gone, but many were dying at home. Of the newcomers, many were dying in holes and corners of the streets, passing forever beyond the grasp of records. That was as well; the records were bad enough. The Board of Health had moved at last and the immigrant shed was now L'Hôpital des Emigrés, where no one came who could walk. Those still on their feet waited outside, with their wives and children round them, sickening while they waited. They streamed out along the river banks, to lie on the rocks in the heat, or shiver in the night damp till they became eligible for care. Inside the hospital the sick lay in their rags, two or three to a mattress, some of them already dead. All mattresses were soon wet and reeking. There was a shortage of all medicines, there were no instruments for the hastily recruited doctors, and there were no chamberpots. Going from pallet to pallet, attendants waded in galoshes through the ankle-deep filth on the floor.

The few exhausted women who attempted to care for the sick were presided over by one of those savage harpies who seem to appear with plague. The matron, as an appointee of the Board of Health, was above the control of doctors. Such medicines as the doctors prescribed were not administered, even if they were there to be had. Food supplies and liquor rations were stolen, and attendants who dared to protest were ordered out. The matron's favourites held sway, while some of her chosen enemies were retained to be worked to death. Doctors who had scoured the city to find help were unable to keep their nurses or protect them. One devoted girl, driven for thirty-six hours without a break, was refused a mattress to sleep on and died on the floor by the pallets. A league of drunken assistants, presided over by the matron, did a profitable business in selling the effects of the dead. The ships came in, the black figures in the newspapers climbed and the terror in the city rose, while the officials of the Board of Health kept their usual office hours of nine to five. Doctors, ordered to report each new case within twelve hours, found the Board's office closed for sixteen hours a day. Often officials refused to receive reports, and all, "with a prudence personal rather than official, religiously avoided the scenes of the plague."[2]

The ignorance about the disease was complete, and most of the remedies prescribed came out of the memories of the middle ages. Quebec newspapers warned their readers against putting bare feet on a cold floor, or sleeping with windows open, or drinking on an empty stomach. They suggested camphor fumigations, tinctures of lavender, opium, or rhubarb, and recommended liberal use of warm, spiced drinks, or brandy and water, or maple syrup and ginger. It was debated whether more Catholics than Protestants caught the disease. Tuesdays and Wednesdays were considered the most dangerous days because of the weekend excesses that preceded them. It was suggested that cannon be fired to clear the air, and among groups who huddled in the refuse-laden streets or passed by the open sewers there were endless discussions of vomitifs, revulsifs, borborogymes, diarrhoea, washings, and vomitings. People should remain cheerful, that was considered imperative; yet everyone watched himself and those near him for the failing appetite, the white, furred tongue, the nausea and sinking of the stomach or rumbling of wind in the bowels that might be the first warning, to be followed by the spasms and cramps, the numbness and apathy, the cold, bluish pallor, and the shrinking and wasting of the face.

The summer weather alternated for the most part between

25

days of humid, stifling heat and days of wild rainstorms that ripped down the tents on the Plains of Abraham and drenched the many hundreds who were sheltering along the river. From there and from the lower town the nightly processions to the "Cholera Cemetery" wound up the steep defile of Mountain Street, passed through the upper town to the monastery of the Franciscans, and ended in a vacant field not far away. Every house in the upper town was barred to pest-carrying strangers, but in the lower town they could not be driven away and what money they had remained in demand still. Here, after ten weeks of the epidemic, the Board of Health had taken no measures to fumigate. When it did move, its methods were peculiarly its own. Whitewash gangs would appear before a house early in the morning, usually a rainy morning in this summer. All the occupants of the house, sick and well, would be ordered into the street, and their furniture, clothes, and provisions would be dumped out beside them. There they would remain for the day while their floors and walls were whitewashed, after which they would be bundled back, soaked, chilled, and feverish, with their wet belongings about them, into the wet rooms.

In many of the houses six or ten families lived crowded into space that was barely enough for one. Fifty people were found in one two-room house, twenty-seven with cholera. Priests and other clergymen waded through garbage and excrement to visit the sick, screamed at from ruinous doorways, followed by wailing women, and often having to close their ears to some. There were more priests than there were ministers, for there were more Catholics than Protestants, but one towering figure was soon familiar. George Jehoshaphat Mountain was Rector of Quebec and Archdeacon of Lower Canada. He was the son of Jacob Mountain, first Bishop of the Church of England in Canada and one of the great upholders of the British establishment, but he was a man of the cloth first. Often, said a visitor to the lower town who had called at some of the hovels where the poor lay stalled bunk fashion in slots cut in the walls, he had seen "a large black mass of clothes"[3] thrust deep into one of the recesses. It was the Archdeacon, leaning in through the darkness over some dying face.

3

The disease was in Montreal within a day of the outbreak in Quebec, and here too a first concern of the merchants was to deny the presence of cholera. Yielding on that, they turned to refute the charge that it was brought by immigrants. They were firm in any case against an interruption of trade. The ships came in relentlessly, towed by the tugs and steamers, sometimes with several vessels on a single line. Between June 7 and June 12 alone, 7,097 steerage passengers were dumped out along the line of wharves and mudbank and among the litter of excavation that constituted the waterfront. Between the river and St. Paul Street, the principal street of commerce, lay a lower town that much resembled Quebec's, and here too among the slimy, cobbled lanes and the boarding houses and brothels, stench, confusion, and panic were growing with each arrival.

The newspapers considered exhaustion to be a common prelude to cholera, and advised against overtiredness if a man felt ill. Yet a man had to live too, and find food for his family. In addition to work on the docks there was a good deal of construction around the city, and the demand for cheap labour was rather better than usual. For the most part it was met; in a macabre, spasmodic way work went on. The masons, sawyers, and labourers sweated in the rare, hot sunshine and the sultry, clammy rain, dropping as the sickness struck: "Men fell down with their hods on their shoulders."[4]

By June 26 the Montreal Board of Health had reported 3,384 cases of cholera and 947 deaths. Here as at Quebec the immigrant shed was now serving as a hospital, and was in much the same condition as the one below. The surplus of the uncared-for flowed out along the riverbank or welled up through the lower town into the city's streets and squares. The strangers were unwelcome and were greeted with black looks, but they were only a rising ripple among the fears and the old angers. Tracey the journalist was already dead of cholera, but the three who had died in May on Place d'Armes were still too well remembered. "The Montreal garrison must be reinforced," said one English newspaper, "to suppress any revolutionary movement to which Papineau may push his rabble."[5] It was one warning to which authority responded promptly. A detachment of four hundred troops was brought over from St. Helen's Island and drilled daily on Champ de Mars under the glowering eyes of the rabble. It was only returned to the purer air of the island after forty-six men had died.

By then there were fewer news sheets, for printers like other craftsmen had begun to desert their work. The knell was sounding from church towers every hour of the day. In the little rectangle of the city, about a mile long and extending back less than half a mile from the river, there was no regular police force and no sanitary system, and the few regulations made by the Board of Health were almost wholly ignored. The garbage flowed in the ditches and the rats ran beside them. In St. Paul Street, with its grey stone or rickety wooden warehouses, most of the merchants still lived over their premises, boarding their clerks. At night, when the narrow windows were closed by iron shutters, drunken old watchmen had swayed along broken pavements, lighting the few oil lamps. As plague came there was darkness. Notre Dame was above St. Paul, an avenue of the élite, but it was now largely deserted. Down Craig Street, the northern boundary of the city, coursed an ancient little rivulet spanned by ten rickety bridges from which housewives tossed their refuse into the stream. It was a girdle of filth encircling the mass of wretchedness that centred in the lower town. Wherever a fine house stood it was usually empty, for the well-to-do had taken refuge in the country. There was no flight for the poor, native or immigrant. Night and day there was no silence and there was no rest. The gin mills and the rum mills somehow plied their business and the women shrilled around them, selling their one ware. The coffin shops had multiplied, and the clatter of hammers and the scream of bandsaws rose above the other noises and gave them meaning.

The disease was raging here with a fury unknown in Europe, and it had struck too suddenly to be dealt with, even if there had been knowledge or care. The unknown dying became the unburied dead, waiting for searchers who were too busy to come. Husbands who had ventured out to work in the morning came home to find their wives dead. Parents, watching their children die, rushed out into the streets shouting for help that was nowhere to be found. All bodies were ordered to be buried within twelve hours; and there was sometimes a sullen reluctance to part with the dead, sometimes a wild haste to be rid of the infected corpse. Bodies were hidden while rosaries were muttered over them, while other bodies were left in fields or streets. At first the evening dark was the time of burial. Then there could no longer be any waiting for the dark. At every hour of the day the open carts rattled to the cemetery beside the cathedral, and at night the long file of hurrying charettes became a torchlit race "like the dances of death one finds on the sculptures of the middle ages". At the buryings themselves roughly knocked-together boxes were trampled down into hastily half-dug holes, sometimes with arms or fingers still projecting, and were beaten in with spades when the earth was too shallow to cover them. Sometimes a frantic woman followed a coffin screaming out to the cartmen that the body they had carried off was still breathing.

4

By the end of August, of the 52,000 passengers who had been recorded at Grosse Ile, 24,000 had been landed as sick. Thousands of these had been sent on later, but many had remained behind. The "ascertained deaths" in Quebec were about 3,800 and in Montreal about 4,000. The dead filled the cemeteries, the hospitals were still crowded, nobody knew how many had gone into the pits at Grosse Ile, and infection was pacing the immigrants up the whole length of the St. Lawrence.

Three Rivers, midway between Quebec and Montreal, had barred immigrant ships and was comparatively free of the disease. But Lévis, Beauport, and Little River, in the Quebec district, had reported cholera by June 12. Near Montreal the Indians of Caughnawaga began to sicken, seventy of them dying out of 150 cases. Lachine and St. Johns were struck on June 12, Chambly on June 29, and by that time reports were coming in from Brockville, Kingston, and Prescott in Upper Canada. In one village there were thirty deaths within thirty hours. "You could see men digging graves and burying their dead by torches, and every few minutes hear the clattering of horses' feet—a messenger despatched for a physician."[6] The disease reached York to kill 2,500, and almost depopulated Galt. It attacked the American cities on the Great Lakes. Then it passed on, following the course of the waters, to spend itself among the Métis of the Red River and the Indian tribes beyond.

By the middle of September the epidemic seemed to have died out in Quebec and Montreal. But it was to return two years later, and its memories were already at work. "In Canada," reported a committee of investigating doctors who came up a few months later from Philadelphia, "party strife had proceeded this spring to great lengths, the passions had been roused, antipathies and hatreds and personal animosities were in the height of bitterness . . . they exercised an unhappy influence by paralysing public measures. The most beneficial and liberal offers coming from one party were regarded with a jealous eye as originating in a sinister intention, and rejected by the other. Instead of unanimity for the public welfare there reigned division, distraction and distrust."[7]

More than a tenth of the population of the two cities had died, and the living were no longer the same. It was a bureaucracy dominated by the English that had bungled every measure for public health. It was an English governor, thinking of English merchants, who had refused to shut the St. Lawrence to the ships that brought the plague. "They must rid themselves of their beggars and cast them by thousands on our shores . . . they must send us pestilence and death."[8] Spurred along by the demagogues, the murmur ran through the valley, "They are preparing the fate of the Acadians for us."[9]

And that year the crops began to fail.

THREE

"Penury is great and misery complete"

For the next five years, with cholera returning in 1834, the wheat fly, the caterpillar, and the grasshopper ravaged the farms of the valley. There were few regions spared in the patchwork pattern of settlement, but it was the habitant of the seigneuries who suffered most. Here, with his diminished strip of river frontage and his crude, homemade implements, he was already contending vainly with the growing exhaustion of his land. With feed poor and scarce and selective breeding unknown, his horses were small, his cattle and pigs lean, and his sheep gave little wool. He was not much at cheese-making or butter-making, even when there was milk to spare. He did not rotate his crops because he had not been taught to, and there would be nothing at all to live on if land lay fallow for a year. All too often, according to his English critics, he carted manure across his starving fields to dump it in the nearest river. Year by year, disliking the English and English innovation, watching the immigrants come and the farms of the English townships grow around him, he had seen his own crops dwindle. He was eating black bread now instead of white, and meat was rare on his table. He was already becoming proverbial for his thin pea soup, thickened with a few potatoes or scraps of fat.

As the pests swarmed, following in the wake of the plague, even this food grew scarce. The weather worked with the insects through a yearly recurring cycle of floods and drought. Seasons of blazing heat alternated with stifling damp, killing the grain or spoiling it. Along the banks of the St. Lawrence, pocked with their thousands of graves, the new spectre of famine began to walk. In 1833, in the region below Quebec, the harvest was a complete failure. The curés of many parishes, brooding over their flocks, divided them into sombre categories; some had enough to live till the next harvest, some would be starving by spring, and some were already starving. There was almost no relief in the next two years, cholera came back in some regions as bad as or worse than before, and the harvest of 1836 was the worst on record.

By the spring of 1837 hunger or the threat of hunger had crept down from Quebec along the whole line of the estuary. Rimouski County was almost bare of food, smallpox and scarlet fever raged in the Beauce, and families who had long since eaten their own livestock were living on the bodies of animals they had found dead in the fields. In many places farms lay unworked or abandoned and only the rising floods of the Chaudière, which closed most of the roads, held back the wagons of the desperate who were preparing to move out. Above Quebec the farms of the Richelieu valley were also stricken, and the district of Montreal, though it suffered less, was speckled with dreary regions of cropless fields. As the effects reached the cities hundreds of uprooted farm people, as well as the jobless poor, came in to fill the workhouses or beg beside the immigrants. "I confess," wrote Louis-Hippolyte LaFontaine, the young lawyer and rising lieutenant of Papineau, "that penury is great and misery complete in Canada."[1]

2

Papineau's own brother had written to the same effect from the stony soil and half-cleared woodlots of the seigneury along the Ottawa. "There is neither straw nor hay nor grain nor meat in the place. People and animals are destitute."[2] Neither these words, however, nor thousands of others like them, nor the evidence of his own eyes, had been enough to deflect the leader from his chosen course. He had grudged and opposed the grants of government assistance that had been made in some of the districts. He had been loud as the Tory merchants in his scorn of official "charity", which would weaken the habitant's fibre and destroy his independence. For Papineau the habitant's duty lay to the seigneur, and the seigneur cared for his own. That the seigneur could no longer do so, and that an English government must, was only a new frustration and an irritant to old rancours. They had grown with the bloody evening on Place d'Armes, and through all the years of misery and famine since. The plague, the pests, and poverty had become a part of his politics, and his cause was not to be weakened by dribbles of public aid. He embodied the woes of Canada in the blight of English rule, and there was to be no cure for any of them until that blight was removed.

The lord of La Petite Nation had come to his fullness now, ripened in the black times. His father was living still, taciturn and old but feeding on long memories. Joseph Papineau had been a boy in a haymow crying out his eyes as the files of the redcoats entered Montreal. He had grown up in the seventeen years of peace, as the French of the west came back to the farms of the seigneuries and the dream of New France died out. He had seen the first of the traders up from New England, and the camp-followers and the sutlers and the flint-eyed Boston merchants, thrusting everywhere, grabbing everywhere, stamping the conquest in. He had been a man in his mid-twenties during the American Revolution and he had made his choice for the King, the devil he knew. After the Revolution he had done well. He had been one of the bourgeoisie, the new and growing class, feeding on law where there was little else to feed on. A prosperous notary in his mid-forties, he had become a power at once in the new Assembly. He liked to talk of those days when

33

the French had taught the English the ways of Parliament, out-studied and outmanoeuvred them and beaten them at their own game. But he had bent to the will of a governor who was set above Parliament. He had been humbled by James Craig, the hater of all things French, the man who had jailed the legislators, and he chafed at the memory still in old age. There had been no more governors like Craig, perhaps there never would be; but there were always the English *bureaucrates* with the bayonet-glint beyond them.

Louis-Joseph had entered the fifth Parliament in 1809, as his father's career was crumbling. He had been twenty-three years old, a boy with a name to live up to, a hot-eyed, brooding student, too impatient for politics to finish his course at the bar. When his degree came he was already a member of the Assembly, and already a marked man. He had been brilliant and difficult in the seminary and he could not be at ease in Parliament, for it had been a place of bitter defeat for his own father. He loved and was dominated and troubled by a puritanical mother, authoritative and possessive. He could not be held to her stern, unbending faith, yet ît was not to be laid aside without loss and pain. A sense of history possessed the boy and centred on his own people; he would be tied and torn forever by the tragedy of New France. He fed on the old glories, enriched them with his own imaginings, and could make no peace with the present. Under every hope for the future lay the rankling wounds of the past.

He had been fifteen when his father acquired the seigneury along the Ottawa, and the new dignity had only deepened conflict. He had become the heir of a seigneur, a part of the pride and legendry that filled his mind from the past, and he was doomed from birth to walk among his conquerors. Yet he was a man who would walk tall, whatever the men around him, and he came at a time when the conquerors seemed to be mellowing. The men who had been joined with his father in the early parliaments had not worked quite in vain, and there was a new awareness in England of the squalors of local tyranny. Among French-Canadian legislators there was a recurring faith in the Constitution and the Crown, and it stirred and steadied Papineau as he rose beside his elders. He had seen the going of Craig and the coming of better men. Allied with the French in the Assembly he had found a leavening of British who were neither oligarchs nor *bureaucrates* and were bent on reforming government. Papineau was drawn to them and they to him. He was drawn by every instinct into the road that led to power. In the War of 1812 he had put on the King's uniform, and he had come out of the war half-reconciled to a life shared with the English.

But the sharing was never real, and never could be. There was no sharing that could satisfy such a man, growing from such roots. The pious, benevolent platitudes blew from across the Atlantic. The mellowing governors came, and most of them were well-meaning. They were prepared to coddle and flatter this born leader. But they were all British and they were all generals, and the martial hackles bristled when colonials forgot their place. They came with the old purposes and the old hopes for the French; they wished to make British subjects wholly British. The immovable bureaucracy surrounded them, steering and shaping governors, always feeding itself, always renewing itself. The grasp of the merchants tightened and Upper Canada grew, promise of the British future, the cloud looming in the west. For a while in spite of it all Papineau, the young reformer, had made his way, trusting in the Constitution and in the wisdom beyond bureaucracy that reposed in the Parliament of England. But it was a trust dwindling as he grew.

On April 29, 1818, he had married Julie Bruneau, a daughter of one of the prominent families of Quebec. Five days before, he had pledged his faith and homage to George III, as seigneur of La Petite Nation, the wedding gift of his father. He had become the lord of two hundred tenants and he had acquired a lady who would never let him forget, even if he ever wished to, the dignity of a seigneur, the pride of a *patriote* leader, and the haunting pain of severance from his dream of the lost New France. He had passed from the influence of his mother to that of a stronger, more insistently dominating, more passionately French and passionately religious woman. In religion she could not control him, but in everything else she would force him into her mould. A new presence began to grow in the Assembly, sombre in discontent, fixed on the tragic past, haughtily and bitterly obstructive to the bleak designs of the present.

He had reached his first crossroads when the merchants attempted to reunite the Canadas, with their loud slogans of progress and their smugly open intention of swamping the

French. He had gone to England to oppose the bill with John Neilson the Scot, a friend and fellow reformer and a man as high as Papineau among the leaders of the French Party. He had found a few like Neilson among British parliamentarians, and they had torn the bill to shreds in a brief debate. Papineau had admired the men and he had seen the value of friends in the British Parliament; he would remember that lesson well. But he had not been reassured by his glimpse of the empire's rulers, nor by a yawning House of Commons that was more than two-thirds empty as the bill went down to defeat. He had sensed for the first time the power and indifference and remoteness of this alien mother country that was mother only to the Briton. He came back to his own people, the friend of Neilson still, but he was changed in something else. He had won reprieve from the English, but he had lost his faith in England.

Year by year, as the new spirit grew in him, he had turned away from the aims of moderate men. He had found himself restless in a Church that supported the ways of authority so long as religion was left undisturbed. He had been restless among the Reformers, though many reforms came. By 1831, as the arrogant old bureaucracy was pushed back to the wall, John Neilson saw a "revolution effected quietly and peaceably"[3] after forty years of struggle. To Papineau the view was otherwise, and he was parting with his old friend. He was parting with other leaders, French as well as English, and he was coming to a parting with the Church. Around him now, with the fiery young of his own people who would make no terms with *bureaucrates,* were the birds of another feather who would make no terms with a king. To them the way for Canada was the way of the Thirteen Colonies. The oligarchy, the seigneurs, the royal government, and the Church, must all be swept away in a new republic.

He listened to them all and disagreed with many. Few of the men or views were quite to his taste. He had lost faith in religion, but he knew the power of priests. He was still and always would be the seigneur and man of property, the lover of due process, the man who swayed by words. He moved parliaments and aroused people; he was not a maker of war. Yet he was more than ever French and more than ever the alien where the Union Jack flew. Better the Stars and Stripes than that rag, or better still the threat of the Stars and Stripes. There was hatred enough of England in the United States, and power enough to sweep the British from Canada. He dared not wish for a Canada made American; it would mean more surely than ever the death of all things French. Yet the thought of that mighty help was always there, hovering in cautious words. "The day is not far distant when America will give presidents and republics to Europe."[4] The threat, the aroused people, the power of words; they were all tools to work with and they were all dangerous. There were dangerous men about him but he moved with them, shaping his course to theirs.

As the spring of 1837 broke rainy and wet, "a season of bad omens", he had come to his second crossroads. In the five years since that May evening on Place d'Armes there had been five sessions of the legislature. With each one Papineau's power had risen and constitutional government had been brought nearer to collapse. Before His Majesty in London, the sailor William IV, the man with a head like a pineapple who would hear no talk of reform, lay a bulky mass of parchment that was now three years old. It was the Ninety-Two Resolutions of the Assembly of Lower Canada, a mighty compendium of all the woes of the past. Much of it was Papineau's work, and the whole breathed of Papineau. "Such is the copiousness and warmth of expression," wrote one baffled minister, "that in many cases it is difficult to discern what is the subject matter to which the writers refer."[5] The ultimate drift, however, was starkly clear. The King's Prerogative was denied, the Civil List was refused. The last powers of the oligarchy and officialdom must pass with control of the revenue to a wholly elective legislature.

To this ground Papineau had held his party, ignoring the fears of moderate men and beating the waverers down. He had lost Neilson's friendship and the support of others like him, but he had hardened his core of power and made himself dominant in the Assembly. He had gone on, always by the due process of a parliamentary majority, to invoke the hallowed privilege of refusing supply. His Majesty's loyal Assembly, while its grievances lay unredressed, had declined to make provision for the expenses of government. Public expenditure had ceased and officials had gone unpaid. Salaries, pensions and emoluments, including the salary of Mr. Speaker, had remained locked in the

37

treasury. Meanwhile, having sealed the pockets of Parliament and almost closed its doors, the leader had turned to the country.

By 1836 the furious British merchants, to whom the Ninety-Two Resolutions had been "the most insolent, disloyal, insane and ridiculous productions that were ever submitted to the consideration of a deliberative body",[6] had banded themselves together as Constitutionalists. They were talking again of union with Upper Canada, and there was still more threatening talk of procuring arms. "Attack them in their dearest parts, their pockets,"[7] Papineau had urged in reply; and with trade already faltering in the gaunt cities the merchants were faced with a series of runs on the banks and with boycotts of British goods. They were hearing the ominous buzz of secret societies, and they were walking by night in darkness. The Parliament that would not grant money had also refused to make laws, and the Acts governing the cities had simply been allowed to expire. Except for the Board of Magistrates who served on unpaid, there was no civic authority in Quebec or Montreal. There were no police and there was no provision for lighting, nor even for the sanitation that had been sketchy enough before. Neglected refuse stank on the broken pavements, and through it gangs of the idle scuffed their way. As the thugs and brawls multiplied, French factions and English factions, recruited in the name of order, became formed into bands that prowled the town by night. The citizen moved with his lantern among the drifting scum of the streets, while the organized vigilantes were even more to be feared.

Amid the confusion and adding to it were the shouts of the loudest newspapers, drowning the few more moderate who were warning in both tongues. The paid press of the oligarchy, savage in abuse of Papineau, was equally savage with governors who proposed any concession. It was answered with new venom by Duvernay's *La Minerve*, and by the scrawny Irish Juvenal who had taken up Tracey's cudgels. Edmund Bailey O'Callaghan, born in Ireland and educated in Paris, had come to Canada as a doctor but was said to have haunted government in search of a political appointment. Whatever the truth, he had found no friends in officialdom and was now its savage enemy. As politician, journalist, and revolutionary republican, he had given the English *Vindicator* a shriller voice than before.

The war of print in Canada was a war of delegations across the Atlantic. Merchants set off for London to bring government to its senses. Agents were there from Papineau, besieging vocal friends in the British Parliament. Nearer at home, and deepening the murk of controversy, there were other forces shaping. The St-Jean-Baptiste Society, inspired by Ludger Duvernay, was directing the work of *patriotes* toward the ending of British rule. At the home of the mild bookseller, the well-loved Edouard Fabre, a Permanent Central Committee of *patriote* leaders was now in constant session. It framed the resolutions and transmitted the propaganda that inspired tumultuous meetings, and it was served by a stream of emissaries who threaded out through the province and were "able in a few days to create a climate of opinion". Even more ominous was the appearance of La Banque du Peuple, organized by Papineau's cousin, Louis-Michel Viger, and fought from its hour of inception by a hostile British establishment. Its innocent open purpose was to attract the habitants' savings, but it was regarded now by both sides as a potential treasury of rebellion.

Over it all was Papineau, and at the heart of it all were the Ninety-Two Resolutions, still unanswered by England. The whole goal of his striving was to force that answer on. To the oligarchy the "ridiculous and insane productions" meant the end of the Constitution and the end of British rule. To Papineau they had become a battleground from which there was no retreat. He could not retreat, for the leader had made the battle and the battle had made him. While the cities seethed, the wagons and walkers streamed across the countryside, gathering at his great meetings. At each town where he came, heralded for weeks before by busy agents, the triumphal arches rose, the homemade banners waved, and the cry went out to his listeners, "We are at war with the old enemies."[9] There had been rich ground for his seed in the stricken valley, and for five years the dragons' teeth had grown well. They had been the years of the final shaping and the years of the lasting imprint that this man would leave on his people. Passionate, eloquent, and electric, alight with his dreams and angers, he had stirred the depths of the parishes and unloosed a rising wind. He had transformed squalor and misery into the living anguish of conquest, and he had wakened a sense of destiny that would never be stilled again.

39

Yet he had been carried to the heights of a prophet while he remained a politician. He thundered against the oligarchy, but he did not expect to change them. His one hope was to rouse opinion in England by the spectre of an aroused colony. The cheers of his country meetings were to be heard across the Atlantic, over the heads of his enemies and impressing his distant friends. He spoke of war to arouse those cheers, but he did not think of war; he was still the man of parliaments who was thinking of minds and votes. The habitants were less subtle. They saw a war with weapons in the way of the Thirteen Colonies. They saw a free people, a nation under Papineau, *la nation canadienne* at last in being. Papineau saw it too, glimmering along the horizon, but he still looked down on huddles of helpless men. He had no arms for them, no plan for them, and even the ultimate goal was still obscure. He was shrewd enough to be aware of it and wise enough to fear it, but there could be no stopping now. He had paralysed colonial government to sway a British Parliament, and it remained his only hope. He must go on or go down.

3

For His Excellency Archibald Acheson, second Earl of Gosford, the other horn of the dilemma was much the same. He had arrived from England in August of 1835 to fulfil a dual role. He was to replace Aylmer as governor, and he was also to head a commission of investigation. The ministers in the Colonial Office, constantly changing as governments rose and fell, had despaired of threading their way through the Ninety-Two Resolutions. Yet the friends of colonial liberties, well-armed by Papineau, were making trouble in Parliament. They were reminiscing ominously of the American Revolution. In a time of precarious majorities and demands for reform at home, all such talk was dangerous. There would have to be peace in Canada, and perhaps Gosford could make it. He might concede much and hint of more, while groping for solid ground. In the meantime his commission was to observe, measure, and report.

As his ship came up the river he had found the condition of

government well symbolized by the state of the Castle of St. Louis, rising on the heights of Quebec under the massive bulk of Cape Diamond. It had housed the rulers of Canada since the days of the French régime. Gaunt, ugly, and changed by many additions, it had been badly damaged by fire in January of 1834, and it glowered down from the rock amid heaps of broken masonry and charred balks of timber. Beneath the rubble, moreover, lay the locked-up coffers of government and the unpaid salaries of bureaucrats. "There the monies lie," the secretary of the Gosford commission was to write pathetically later, "buried in the vaults below the château yard . . . trodden over by men whose rightful earnings they constituted, but who were left for want of them to become the victims of creditors and bailiffs, and some of them to be stripped of the fruits of whole lives of prudence through this merciless infliction in a quarrel not their own."[10]

Nevertheless, there were stately rooms of the Castle still intact and Gosford had settled into them. He had had two months to assess the state of the conflict before convoking Parliament, and he had used the time well. "You will ever bear in mind," ran one line of his instructions, "that you are sent on a mission of peace and conciliation."[11] The mild, liberal Irishman who had fought Orangemen in his homeland and spoke excellent French, had come equipped for the work. In addition to "ten tons of claret and proportionate quantities of champagne and sherry,"[12] he had considerable information and a solid list of concessions. He was soon aware that the colony had been ruled by "a little group of old men who occupy the highest posts . . . avid of privilege, jealous of their authority, and ready to take offense at any examination of the complaints of the people."[13] He disliked them heartily, shunned the strangling embrace that they usually imposed on governors, and turned to the French to lay his cards on the table, or at least most of his cards.

He would listen to all suggestions for reform of the Legislative Council, and a majority of his new appointments would go to the French. His Majesty William IV, "anxious to render his reign a blessing to his Canadian subjects",[14] was prepared to relinquish much of the King's Prerogative, or perhaps even all. The Civil List was not demanded but requested. It was sanctioned by all the highest principles of government. There could be "no real, or at least no irreconcilable, differences of opinion"[15] on the matter of maintaining judges and high officials in independent authority. The amount in question was hardly worth debate. It was unthinkable that there should be conflict, Gosford could quote from his instructions, "for the sake of a sum of money so insignificant as to be scarcely perceptible in the financial operations of Great Britain, and of no considerable moment even in those of Lower Canada."[16] It was linked, of course, with the question of elective government, but even on that thorny subject "His Majesty will not absolutely close the avenue to inquiry."[17]

While the fireside chats went on with the French leaders, a steady trickle of appointments displaced the lesser English. New sheriffs, clerks, and secretaries began to be named, and most of the names were French. The good wine flowed at the Castle, and it was soon brackish to *bureaucrates*. There were more French appearing at the balls and receptions, and it was they who were sought by the Governor and conferred with in private rooms. Their wives and children went home from gay little parties, burdened with Gosford favours, speaking of the kind milord. As usual most of the seigneurs and the French of property and substance were prepared to be won over. The Church breathed easier and many of the legislators softened. There even seemed to be a wintry relenting in Papineau, who sometimes dined with His Excellency. The genial, fatherly civilian was a relief from soldier-governors, and the qualities of the French Canadian were to charm and mystify Gosford to the last day of his life. Yet after the parties came Parliament, and the hard rock of the facts.

One by one, the cards unturned in the discussions had to be brought face up. The relinquishment of the King's Prerogative meant the yielding up of revenue from the land reserves of the Crown. It did not mean the control of land for settlement, nor the control of immigration. Still less did it mean the abandonment of the King's pensioners, those long-enduring thorns in the public body. They would somehow have to be provided for by a grant of public funds. The Civil List, however it might be pruned, remained a non-negotiable principle; there would always be Crown officers who were independent of the Assembly. And above and beyond the bristle of lesser quarrels remained the matter of the Legislative Council. It had been discussed and would be reformed; there would be new French members appointed to replace some of the English. The Council's strength would be balanced, or at least appear to be balanced, as a body answering equally to the claims of the two peoples. It would not, however, become an elective body. There would be no Republic of Canada while the flag waved from the rock.

By the end of 1836 Gosford had faced his second session of Parliament, and had closed it in twelve days. There had been no vote of supply at either session, and there was no hint of peace. The treasury remained locked, the unpaid salaries mounted, and the conciliating Governor was battered from both sides now. He was railed at incessantly by the press of a savage oligarchy that was talking outright war. He had disbanded a rifle regiment that had been organized by Young Tories, and was now the dearest enemy of its frustrated volunteers. Yet the scribes and orators of the *patriotes* had only salt for his wounds. One could not conciliate the French without further envenoming the English. One could not win over Papineau without total surrender. And surrender was not contemplated; the mild man in the Castle was clear enough on that. He had retreated step by step toward the last limit allowed to him, and the next step lay with London.

In January of 1837 Gosford's commissioners left for England with their findings. He himself remained, anathema to both sides now. On March 6, with the commission's report digested, Lord John Russell rose in the House of Commons, the home of Papineau's hope. He presented Ten Resolutions, as the answer of the British government to the Ninety-Two from Canada. They were a flat and formal rejection of every essential claimed. The Legislative Council would not be made elective. The inner, Executive, Council remained as before, responsible only to the Governor. The British American Land Company, with a grant of 800,000 acres in the Eastern Townships, would continue to encourage British immigration. A Civil List was an indispensable condition to the cession of Crown revenues. Moreover, in view of the fact that since October 31, 1832, there had been no provision by the legislature to defray the expenses of government, the Crown revenues should be applied as far as they would go and the Governor be then empowered to take from the treasury "such further sums as shall be necessary to effect the payment of the before-mentioned sum of £142,160. 14s 6d."[18]

4

By April 10 the text of the Ten Resolutions was known in Canada. In late July came word that they had been suspended. William IV had died on June 20, and with the young Queen Victoria now on the throne there had been a gesture to appease controversy. It did not appease the storm that was breaking over the rock. In Montreal and Quebec bands of youthful *patriotes* were tramping the streets, led along by the tricolour and singing the Marseillaise. There were counter-marching English led by the Union Jack, and there were stones flying and clubs waving from under each of the flags. The newspapers flooded in on the man in the Castle, where the French no longer came. They blared of the great meetings that were sweeping across the province, Papineau meetings and Constitutionalist meetings. Each was reported larger than the last, each a little more savage; and with the mounting war of politics came the new sorrows of trade.

In the spring of 1837 the first great British railway boom had reached and passed its climax. In the United States a financial panic almost brought collapse. A crisis that was to continue for four years and bring 33,000 commercial failures had made even New York a dead city, with docks idle and all building at a standstill while thousands filled the workhouses and more begged in the streets. American banks had suspended payments in specie, and Canadian banks had followed. The whole fabric of the economy had collapsed, along with the American, in a sickening downward slide. The grain trade was gone with the failed crops; Canada was importing flour at ruinous prices. Canadian credits were being cut off in England, all imports faltered, and as the few ships of the timber trade ran out their last contracts there seemed to be nothing left. The streets of Montreal, gloomy, filthy, and speckled with stopped construction, took on a Sunday quiet. The river's shipping dwindled to a sparse trickle; the banks would not give credit and could make no payments in coin. "In my day," wrote Peter McGill, president of the Bank of Montreal and merchant of many interests, "such times have never been experienced."[19]

Over all this the voice of Papineau rose, while his old enemies responded with an ever-enriched venom. There was a new pathos now to the thought of those thousands of pounds of idle coin, locked up in the treasury. There was a new spokesman in the person of Adam Thom, Master of Arts and journalist, recently arrived from Scotland to instruct the colonies. Destined to be a trouble-maker for the next seventeen years, he had inspired the rifle regiment that had been laid to rest by Gosford, and he had a short and simple answer to the problem of a French majority. "Crowded as they are," he wrote, "on the level banks of the St. Lawrence and other navigable rivers, they could be reached in almost all their settlements by the long 48-pounder of a gunboat, wheeling on a pivot and describing successive circles of fire and blood from one end of the seignories to the other."[20]

There was another man in the colony now who deplored such talk of weapons. Sir John Colborne had fought with Wellington throughout the Peninsular War, and had commanded a brigade of infantry at Waterloo. He was credited by some with as large a share as the Duke's in winning the battle. He looked a little like Wellington and stood a shade taller, and he had been Governor of Upper Canada for six years. In January of 1836 he had been on his way home, disgruntled like most governors, when new orders from England had sent him posting to Quebec as commander of the military forces. He was soon at odds with Gosford, but he was also quickly at work.

"The less military display is made, the better."[21] It was the maxim of a good soldier, and he had kept it steadily in mind. Quebec was long familiar with departing and arriving troops, and it was hardly noticed now that they came more often than they left. It was hardly to be resented, for the arrivals were rather gay, and soldiers were free-spenders. In the winter months, when ice was thick in the river, detachments had often been landed at Point Lévis and had crossed over in long strings of carrioles, each flying the flag and with a band playing ahead of them. The young faces of the redcoats, after the rigours of an ocean passage, had been tired but quite unmenacing. There had been good humour and good manners and quiet military precision as they fell into their ranks, answered their names to the roll-call, and were marched off to their barracks.

Both Quebec and Montreal were lively stations for their officers. The plays, the *tableaux vivants,* and the brilliant military balls enlivened social life, and the girls of the two cities, the "muffins" of soldier parlance, were bright, witty, and delightful. There was magnificent fishing and hunting, and the winter picnics on the ice or in some rented home upriver were best of all. One took along a band and much champagne, and danced till the small hours. Then there was the drive home, always memorable, over the crisp snow, under the bright stars, swaddled in furs with the muffin warm beside one. Officers in Montreal, in the spring of 1837, organized a pack of foxhounds and rode to them on the south shore. Occasionally, when bands of abusive *patriotes* became a nuisance, they turned to charge with horsewhips. Champ de Mars, the parade ground, was sometimes shared informally with awkward squads of the French, busy at their own drill. They were angry and sometimes offensive when they were laughed at by the professionals, but it was only toward midsummer, when the garrison began to swell and the town's mood grew uglier, that they had to be ordered off.

On July 8, much against his judgment and in response to orders from London, Gosford had summoned Parliament. It was to meet in Quebec on August 18, and it was to vote supply. If not, though the Russell resolutions remained suspended, supply would still be made. A vote of the House of Commons would release the £142,160 14s. 6d. On August 16, a group of Papineau's leaders coming to attend the session arrived from Montreal. They stepped ashore from the steamer in jackets and trousers of crude homespun and "beef shoes" and straw hats that aroused much hostile laughter. They had declined to make use of textiles that paid revenue to the Crown. They had proclaimed smuggling to be a *patriote* duty. They had urged shopkeepers to sell no British goods, and enjoined the habitant to refrain from the tea, sugar, and wine, the leather goods and the linen that earned duties for the King. The injunction was hardly necessary in view of the present resources of the habitant, but it recalled the preliminary acts of the Thirteen Colonies and it had been made at Papineau's bidding. The leader was not among the group but he arrived the following day, his usual

46

immaculate self. One would not have expected Papineau in homespun trousers.

On the 18th the session duly opened. The Speech from the Throne was read, conciliatory as always, and for several days debate wavered in reply. A group of moderates edged away from Papineau, sensing the last impasse. By the 26th, however, enough of these had come back, and the vote was taken. At three o'clock on that Saturday afternoon the members of the Assembly trooped into the Castle for an appointed audience with the Governor. Mr. Speaker Papineau walked at their head. He was growing a little portly now, and the mane of black hair was becoming flecked with grey. But the face that might have been carved on a Roman coin was as impressive as ever. The voice was as beautiful and the message as long, with a shapely, acid eloquence that must have been much edited. The trend was unmistakable from the first paragraphs and there was no surprise in the conclusion. Every familiar phrase came out unchanged. "The application of the elective principle to the Legislative Council" and "the establishment of a popular and responsible government" remained "the only means by which the political connexion with Great Britain can be rendered beneficial to the people of Canada."[22] Until such time, and failing such concessions, Her Majesty's loyal Assembly must suspend its deliberations. There would be no vote of supply.

Gosford rose at the end, courteous as ever. He thanked the honourable members in his graceful French, and regretted the tenor of the reply. "It remains to me only to assure you that I shall exercise to the best of my judgment the powers with which I am invested as the representative of our Sovereign."[23]

By the time the honourable members had returned to the legislative chamber a page had been there ahead of them. A bulky white envelope was lying on the Speaker's chair. Papineau opened it while the members clustered round him. The Clerk of the Crown in Chancery begged to transmit to the Honourable Mr. Speaker a proclamation signed this day by His Excellency the Governor General. The fourth session of the fifteenth Parliament—the last in Lower Canada—stood prorogued. Due process was ended. Outside the windows, on the rock that Wolfe had taken, the guns grinned from the casemates. The sentries paced by the pyramids of roundshot and the flag gloomed in the sky.

FOUR

"You must either put him down . . ."

As the doors of the Assembly closed, Gosford proceeded to unlock the doors of the Treasury. He had been given the key by England, and the arrears of government salaries were now to be paid. Moreover, in this colony starved for credit and almost devoid of money, they were to be paid in hard coin. By the first week of September he had mobilized all the specie to be found in Canada, and had sent an agent to New York equipped with drafts on London to buy what more was required. By early October the chests were coming in, and on the 12th of the month the paymaster's wicket opened at the Commissariat Office in Quebec. Clerks, charwomen and criers, tipstaffs, bailiffs and turnkeys, doormen, coachmen, and masons received their fistfuls of gold and silver. The agents of higher officials appeared with their warrants, the pensioners were paid up, and the sovereign's chosen received their due at last. To ailing old Judge Sewell and the plentiful family he had spawned under every governor for the past forty-four years went a total of £8,949 12s. 9d., while the equally hated and long-enduring Rylands were accommodated with £3,397 14s. 11d. Rapidly and jubilantly, while *patriotes* and *patriote* legislators glowered from afar, most of the £142,160 14s. 6d. was gobbled up. It flowed out from the loyal hands of the *bureaucrates* to the loyal hands of the merchants, a single glitter of comfort in the black confusion of the times.

Mr. Speaker Papineau, who had drawn no salary since 1832, did not appear at the wicket. Gosford had not expected him. He was heard of in Montreal, and in the Richelieu valley and the north. Everywhere he moved, the flags and meetings multiplied, the cloud of rumours flew, and government and law collapsed. The bells and tocsins of assembly had followed the close of Parliament, and to Gosford at least the next step was clear. "We can now make no terms with Mr. Papineau," he had written to the Colonial Minister on September 8. "You must either put him down or submit to let him put you down."[1]

The mild man in the Castle was beginning to harden now, but he was hungering for his own recall. He had issued a proclamation against sedition and had ordered it to be read in all the towns and villages by officers of the provincial militia. They had refused in droves and resigned in droves, and many who had not resigned had been dismissed. They were hardly soldiers but they were the principal keepers of order in every parish, and order had gone with them. Among the appointed French there were few sheriffs and few justices of the peace whose loyalty could be relied on. The Tory press was shrieking for blood and law, the *patriote* press replied with shrill defiance, and the war of words was threatening war in the streets. One could see ahead the wringing of many necks, and Gosford had little taste for it.

He was still supported, at least in his demands for order, by the bishops and most of the clergy and by the French of property and substance who came to him abjuring Papineau. But it was cold comfort in the treacherous murk about him. Now, since the close of Parliament, the letter had come from London confirming the men he had suggested for appointment to the Legislative Council. Seven of the ten were French, and six of the seven had accepted, but without much enthusiasm. They had proved elusive and difficult and it was hard to trust them wholly. It was hard to trust anyone. It was equally hard to establish anyone's guilt. One could not hang a man for words

49

reported in a newspaper, when all newspapers lied. One could not have ears everywhere, and the sleazy work of the informer was becoming a dangerous trade. The sworn statement of one day became the scared denial of the next, and a civilian governor could move only through the courts. His Attorney General and Solicitor General, helped by a corps of agents, were busy across the province and particularly in Montreal. He had sent them to find the evidence that would convict the principal disturbers, and when he had that he would act. He would have to act, but it would be better work for Colborne.

The General waited beside him, steady and disapproving. He deplored weakness and distrusted mildness, and quarrels with his civilian overlord were a matter of old habit. The two were at odds now about the disposition of troops, but Colborne took that lightly. He would get the troops when he needed them and move them as he saw fit. For the moment at least he was not seriously alarmed. His military maps were few, bad and untrustworthy, and so were most of his reports, but what they told was significant. For all the mood of the province, black though that might be, the disturbances were still local. Quebec City, under the guns of the Citadel, flared with the occasional meeting but always relapsed again into sullen quiet. There was little sign of trouble below Quebec. The risings, if there were to be risings, would come in the valley of the Richelieu or to the north of Montreal, where beyond the Rivière des Prairies the sizeable towns of St-Eustache, St-Benoit, and Ste-Scholastique lay clustered amid scattered farmlands and patches of heavy forest. In both these regions trouble was certainly brewing, and there was the added danger in the Richelieu country of its nearness to the American border.

Midway along the Richelieu was the town of St-Denis. It was the home of Wolfred Nelson, a burly English doctor and a commanding figure in his region, who seemed to embody all its discontents. In Parliament and out of it he had always supported Papineau, and where Nelson was, there was the threat of violent action. St-Charles lay a little to the south of St-Denis and was another centre of disturbance. From each of these towns and from half a dozen like them a wave of increasing dissidence was flooding the whole valley. Tavern keepers were taking down their signs and replacing them with the American eagle. Printers were printing banknotes bearing eagles and *patriote*

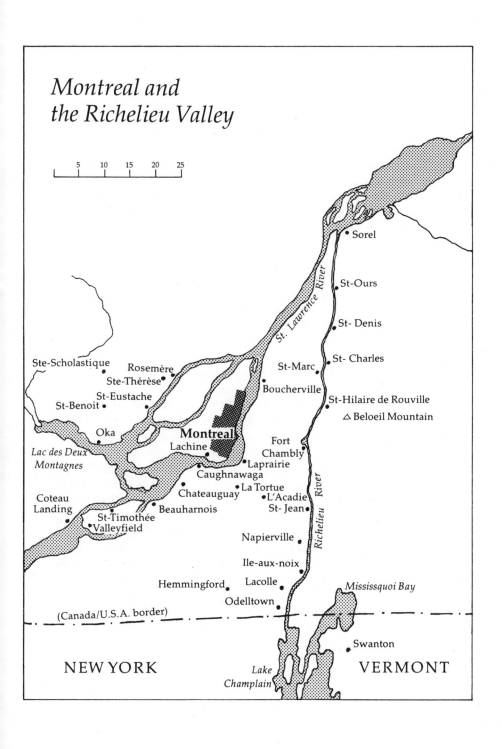

Montreal and the Richelieu Valley

5   10   15   20   25

Sorel

St-Ours

St. Lawrence River

St- Denis

Ste-Scholastique

Rosemère

Ste-Thérèse

St-Marc

St- Charles

St-Eustache

Boucherville

St-Benoit

St-Hilaire de Rouville

Oka

△ Beloeil Mountain

Lac des Deux
Montagnes

Montreal

Lachine

Fort
Chambly

Laprairie

Caughnawaga

Coteau
Landing

Chateauguay

La Tortue

L'Acadie

Beauharnois

St- Jean

St-Timothée

Valleyfield

Richelieu River

Napierville

Ile-aux-noix

Hemmingford

Lacolle

Mississquoi Bay

Odelltown

(Canada/U.S.A. border)

Swanton

NEW YORK

VERMONT

Lake
Champlain

slogans. At night there were marching men, their faces daubed with charcoal to preserve their anonymity, beating on drums and ringing bells for recruits. Terror and intimidation were part of the process, and there were stories of barn-burnings and house-burnings, and of horses with docked tails and shaved manes that left them to be maddened by insects and useless for any work. Weapons were being collected, country forges were melting lead for bullets, and there were endlessly repeated rumours of arms from the United States.

Committees of Liberty and Committees of Public Safety, self-elected by *patriotes*, were making their ominous appearance, and the situation to the north was even worse. From beyond Rivière des Prairies reports were telling already of a state of anarchy, with loyalists living in dread, loyalist officials chased out, and new officials "élu par le peuple" administering what law there was. But that region was isolated and it could wait. The centres along the Richelieu could be reached by an easy march when the time was ripe. The most pressing need for action, and the delay most irritating to Colborne, was in Montreal itself.

It was here, in this town that was now half-populated by the British and almost wholly dominated by British commerce, that Papineau made his home and all trouble centred. Much of its rebellious energy seemed to be channelled into the ranks of the "Fils de la Liberté," a new association formed by its young. Deliberately and pointedly reminiscent of the Sons of Liberty of the American Revolution, it was divided into a political section and a military section. Its proclaimed purpose was "to emancipate our country from all human authority save that of the bold democracy residing within its bosom",[2] and in the writing of the manifesto its French-Canadian organizers had enjoyed the services of Thomas Storrow Brown. He was a New Brunswicker arrived in Canada by way of the United States, and as he went bankrupt in the hardware business he had somehow risen to prominence on the lower fringes of politics. He was now General of the Society's Military Section and each Monday evening, under his leadership, the Sons of Liberty streamed through the streets of the town, filling them with band music, oratory and song. They were countered with equal enthusiasm by the Young Tories of the Doric Club who were beginning to carry axe handles, and had been another of the inspirations of Adam Thom. In the filth, uproar and confusion of Montreal the two organizations were now a principal feature, well watched by Colborne. "We must be prepared," he observed acidly to Gosford, "that if four or five hundred persons are allowed to parade the streets at night singing revolutionary songs, the excited parties will come into collision."[3] He was all for an immediate seizure of some of the excited parties, but the Governor held his hand. The civilian was still in charge; the General was required to wait.

2

The onetime Speaker of the Assembly was waiting too, while events moved beyond him. After the close of Parliament he had gone for a while to the pleasant seigneury at St-Hyacinthe where his sister lived with her husband. But there had been no rest there for the leader of the awakened people. Messengers and deputations had thronged in on him requiring Papineau everywhere, for the inspiration of his presence, for the call to arms at last. It had never quite come. He had travelled back by the Richelieu on the way to his own seigneury, and it had been a triumphal progress. Trains of carriages and wagons and hundreds of cheering marchers had followed him to his many meetings. They had been lifted up by his eloquence, carried away by his angers, stirred by the familiar catalogue of the people's wrongs. And he had passed on, to rest again in the house at La Petite Nation where the brown fields lay cropless and the patches of maple flared, glorious with autumn now. He had come back, passing through St-Eustache and the towns of the northern region, the idolized leader of a republic that seemed to be taking form. There had been no rest, no escape from the cheers, and the cry for arms was always a little louder. There were no arms and he had forbidden attempts to purchase them, but the unthinkable thought could never be quite put down.

As he returned to Montreal he had found the pressures mounting and the mood darkening. He had talked much with his cousin, Louis-Michel Viger, the dapper "Beau Viger", President of La Banque du Peuple. Arms would require money, and arrangements with the United States; there were no such arrangements. He was in daily demand at the house of Edouard Fabre, where the Permanent Central Committee held its meetings. There were always leaders there, many from the country districts, propounding new resolutions, bustling with hopeful plans. He held apart from them all; most of them he could not approve. Emissaries came from William Lyon Mackenzie, the Scot of Upper Canada. There was talk of a rising there, perhaps in early December; it would be wise to co-ordinate plans. He listened, advised, and hesitated; the plans would not take shape. His own son was in the streets now, marching with the Sons of Liberty, led by that Brown. He deplored the nightly parades and the threats of riot, but he let them go on. He could not stop them in any case, and they marched in Papineau's name.

The summons came from the Richelieu, not to be resisted or denied. There was to be a grand assembly of all the counties by the river, and from there the call would go out for a national convention. The proposal was Wolfred Nelson's, supported by those around him, but the national convention was Papineau's favourite dream. A gathering of chosen leaders, speaking for the aroused people, would lay down the ultimate challenge to British rule. It would depose the Constitution and decree another of its own, and the first step would be taken toward the framing of a new state. And then? — the dangers at the present moment were too obvious; there was danger even in this gathering that was meant to issue the call. It would be welcomed by every Tory as an act of open rebellion, and it would be attributed for every reason to Papineau's inspiration. And yet for every reason, at this meeting called to consider it, Papineau would have to be present.

St-Charles was the place appointed, and the date had been set for October 23. Edmund Bailey O'Callaghan, one of the great enthusiasts, was to report the proceedings for the *Vindicator*, and would certainly make the most of them. On the night of the 22nd Papineau arrived with O'Callaghan at the little village of St-Marc, directly opposite St-Charles across the Richelieu. Here he stopped, discouraged a demonstration, and spent the night in seclusion with some old and close friends. They found him uncommunicative, sombre, and pensive, and disinclined to discuss the next day's plans. The meeting, he said, was not his affair; he had only come in passing.

Next morning as he crossed the river the sky was a mass of racing black clouds, whipped by a cold wind. The pretty village of St-Charles, with the spire rising above its whitewashed houses, was somehow dour and subdued in the grey light. Yet the roads were alive with wagons and carriages and people on foot or on horseback, gathering from the counties of Richelieu, Chambly, St-Hyacinthe, Rouville, Verchères, and L'Acadie. Every rut was a quagmire from the eternal rains of the fall, there was a little snow on the ground, and there was mud everywhere. But there were banners everywhere too, whipped by the wet wind; the white banner with the death's head — "Death to the Legislative Council" — banners with the American eagle carrying a maple leaf in its beak, symbol of the new republic; banners with the beaver, and the tree of liberty, and the sword, and banners with the single star, "Our Future". There were long streamers of canvas with their legends picked out painfully by the women: "Fly, tyrants, for the People Awake" — "Liberty, Bread of the People, the Will of God" — "Papineau — principe de la liberté". For a while, with the dour O'Callaghan standing beside him, he watched the people come, chilled, muddy, and cheering, shivering with cold and excitement. There were already more than a thousand, perhaps even two thousand, but there had been six thousand expected.

The big plank rostrum stood in an open field, with its flags and streamers of bunting tossed by the wind. Before it was the tall, white-painted shaft of the Pole of Liberty, surmounted by a red cap, symbol of freedom and symbol of revolution. Around the base people were crowding in to read the inscription: "To Papineau — his Grateful Compatriots — 1837". Men and women were cheering, children were shouting shrilly, and spreading outward around them were the growing circle of watchers and the ranks of tethered horses and wagons and carriages. By noon, as the roads and footpaths emptied of their last trickles, it was time to begin the meeting.

As the delegates came to the rostrum they were led by Wolfred Nelson of St-Denis. Tall, authoritative, military as a grenadier, he had been an army doctor in the War of 1812. Though he had not been recently in the Assembly he had been most of his life in politics, and he had supported Papineau

55

under half a dozen governors. Now he was a rich man, a dis-
tiller as well as a doctor, and the unquestioned leader of
patriotes along the Richelieu. He was a fierce hater of bureaucracy and he was married to a French Canadian, but his French
was still uncertain. When his wild enthusiasms were roused or
his terrible angers came, he expressed himself badly; one was
never quite sure of his thought. One was never quite sure of
the man. For all his brusque certainties and the impression of
granite strength, there was sometimes something else, a loud,
officious emptiness, a hollow ring in the stone. He had fought
with total loyalty, but on the way to what? It rose as a troubling
question this cold morning.

The others followed him to the rostrum. Robert Nelson, his
brother, was a doctor in Montreal. A younger man than
Wolfred, he had lived in the other's shadow, and he was more
the man of medicine. He had a large practice and he cared for it,
and it kept him apart from the daily swirl of politics. Yet there
were seething angers darkening that hard face; this was a rash
man who could be a dangerous man. Beside him was another
doctor, Côté of L'Acadie; a man born for the stirring up of
crowds, for talk of fire and blood. Always near and always over-
shadowing him was his aide, Lucien Gagnon, lithe, powerful,
and truculent. He was sparing of talk, this one, but he translated
words to action. He would be ready for fire and blood if the
moment came.

Brown was here, the General of the Sons of Liberty, a little
uneasy among the greater leaders. Short, glib, quick-eyed, and
yet uncertain; the total impression was of shiftiness and
squalor. He wrote much, talked more, and politics had made
him bankrupt. Would politics lift him high in a new republic? —
there would always be such a thought for such a man. It would
not be so with Chénier of St-Eustache, still another doctor. He
was young, slight, dark-haired, quick and sure in his movements, and the sleeves of his heavy *capote* lifted and fell as he
talked. He was a guest here, not a delegate, but he would not
have missed this meeting, and he carried a banner in one of
those expressive hands. A compulsive talker, a banner-waver
and a leader, there was no mistaking that. Utterly sincere,
devoted; a man whose heart could be trusted to the death. But
that head?

Amury Girod, the swarthy, paunchy Swiss, as usual loudly

present. A soldier come from Europe – captain of what? He had owned a "model farm", raised a mountain of debts, married himself out of them, and seized on Papineau's cause. Posturing, shouting, pushing, thrusting in for the centre of every group, talking it to glares and silence, and thrusting on. A brass voice and an iron hide; the man could not be escaped. "A scoundrel, a dog, a sans-culotte, a rogue ripe for a ducking" – he had sued the author of those words for £3,000, and he had been awarded one shilling.⁴ A leader of a people's struggle – a general of *patriote* armies? – one looked away from Girod.

One looked with a new relief, a new warmth, at the other faces on the platform. Here were the real hope of *la nation canadienne*. They were of the new generation of doctors, lawyers, and notaries, grown from the seed of the first and shaped by Papineau. He had given them the hunger for proud and ancient roots, quickened them in strength and oneness. They knew it and they were grateful; his name rose in their voices and in the great throat of the crowd as he took his place on the rostrum. He had taught them, kindled them, given shape to their lives. He had led them all to this place, and to this work.

There was much space still in the frosty mud of the field – too much – but no more wagons were coming. The last stragglers were closing in on the fringes. There was a brisk approach of fifes and drums and bugles, and a lane opened in the crowd. Down the lane, wearing his old uniform with a pistol stuck in his belt and a sword at his side, came white-haired Captain Jalbert, a soldier of 1812. His company of fusiliers marched behind him, fifty lads in liberty caps and *capotes*, with their hunting rifles and shotguns and ancient French firelocks jolting on burly shoulders. They came on to the Liberty Pole with the quick, light step of youth, saluted it, and turned outward, moving to face the rostrum. Wolfred Nelson rose, chairman of the Assembly of the Six Counties.

He turned first to Papineau and the cheers billowed for the leader, a roar of hope and devotion. Then Nelson launched on his speech, long as always and fierier than ever before. The hope that had been reposed in parliaments was now spent. It was time for an aroused people – a people arms in hand – to gather its strength and put an end to tyranny. Nelson finished to a thunder of affirmation. Papineau rose and moved to the centre of the rostrum. Cheers surged more wildly, banners tossed in the wind, and muzzles flared and smoked in a *feu de joie*. One was lifted up, one was swept away by it all; one could hardly speak for the cheering and it was hard to think. Yet he was looking at the fifty firearms of the little troop before him, at the few scattered through the crowd, at the forks and sharpened sticks in other hands. They were the arms of this aroused people, and he had no more to offer. His words when they came were curiously soft and hesitant. The old wrongs were real, he was at home when he spoke of them, but beyond that he was a strangely diffident Papineau. It was a time now for all to pause and reflect. Much had been won by constitutional means, by parliaments and due process. There was still much more to be won, and by the same means. The great meetings would go on, the waverers would be drawn in, England would learn the force of this people's will. There would be more and stricter boycotts of British goods, there would be new elections and parliaments, but not this talk of arms. It was not yet time for arms.

"I differ from Mr. Papineau!" The words came at his side in the midst of a ragged silence. The cheers that had seemed to be faltering were suddenly lifting again, but they were responding to a new voice. Nelson had left his chair and was on his feet. He was thrusting in front of the leader, the stern red face suffused, his arms flung out to the crowd. "The time has come to melt our spoons into bullets!"[5]

For the next two hours the leader sat on the rostrum, graven-faced. The other delegates spoke, all in the vein of Nelson, all in the name of Papineau, binding Papineau to them. There had been Thirteen Resolutions prepared for the meeting, and they were passed with approving roars. There would be a national convention to replace a "nullified" legislature; soldiers would be raised and trained; it was the clear right of a people to change government at will. "Now," screamed Côté of L'Acadie at the end of his endless speech, "the time for speeches is past. It is lead we will throw at our enemies!"[6]

It had all grown from Papineau, and it was all built on him. There was no speaker who did not turn to him, no mention of his name that was not cheered, almost as much as before. He was swept down from the rostrum at the close of the meeting and led to the foot of the Liberty Pole, while the muskets barked in another *feu de joie*. A choir of young voices rose in a hymn to liberty, and the hundreds pressing about them closed in and joined. Côté, the self-appointed pontiff of the great ceremony, knelt at the foot of the column and offered it up to Papineau. The inscription was read aloud, and cheered deafeningly: "To Papineau — his Grateful Compatriots". One by one, led by Captain Jalbert, the men of the six counties advanced to the foot of the pole, placed their hands on its base and swore their oath, to conquer or to die. Ringed by the fusiliers, ringed by the crowd, the leader stood among them, bound in with his work. Then from the blackening sky the storm broke, in floods of rain that changed by night to a blizzard. Over freezing, water-logged roads on which the horses could hardly move, the crowd dispersed for its homes.

3

Next day from Montreal came the voice of the Church, condemning talk of rebellion. "Who dares to say," wrote Bishop Lartigue, "that in this country the totality of the citizens wishes the destruction of the government?"[7] Papineau returned to a city newly divided, and perplexed with mounting tension. The St-Charles meeting, duly reported and magnified in the *patriote* press, had been the last straw for Gosford. There were warrants ready now, awaiting only a pretext, a single overt action, and on November 6 it came.

That Monday was the occasion of the regular meeting of the Sons of Liberty. Papineau had advised against it. There had been one rumour, flying among many others, that a Liberty Pole was to be raised on Place d'Armes and that there would be more marching and oath-taking, following the example of St-Charles. Thom was screeching the word of it and promising blood in the streets. Lies, said Brown smoothly, all lies; there would be no march at all. There would only be a peaceful meeting, and it would be the last held till spring. With the approach of winter parades were being suspended. It was not quite reassuring and it did not dispel the rumours. The speeches were hardly peaceful as a hundred or so of the Sons gathered on Monday noon in the high, fenced courtyard of Bonacina's Tavern, facing on Great St. James Street. But there was no Liberty

Pole, there was no talk of a march, and outside the fence there were only a few stray watchers. Proceedings moved to a conclusion and it was almost time to adjourn when a shower of stones came arching over the fence. The crowd outside had grown and it now included a scattering of young Dorics, carrying their familiar axe-handles. They were much outnumbered by the Sons, and the young *patriotes* streamed out to herd them down St. James Street, into St. François-Xavier, and then along Notre Dame toward Place d'Armes. Here, however, the main body of the Doric Club was waiting in full force. The advance of the Sons of Liberty became a fighting retreat, with the force dwindling at street corners but stopping for many stands. For an hour the scattered skirmishes spread through the town, filling it with uproar, confusion, and the crash of breaking windows.

About two o'clock the Riot Act was read by a city magistrate, and an hour later the troops came, followed by light artillery. They had moved quickly but they could not be everywhere at once, and triumphant gangs of the Dorics had moved ahead of them. A house on Dorchester Street, identified as the headquarters and armoury of the Sons of Liberty, was broken into and ransacked, yielding three muskets and a banner. The office of O'Callaghan's *Vindicator* was turned inside out, and his type and presses were thrown into the street. Volleys of stones were spattering Papineau's house and a rush was just forming when soldiers arrived to stop it. They bundled away the attackers and cordoned off the premises, while for once *patriotes* cheered them. By nightfall a kind of order had been restored. Patrols moved through the streets, hospitals were busy mending broken heads, and the Sons of Liberty were mourning a wounded General. Thomas Storrow Brown lay in his room, carried there by his friends, with a bleeding gash in his forehead that was to cost him the sight of an eye.

There had been few seriously injured and none killed, but the time for waiting was over. By November 8 Colborne was recruiting and arming volunteers, directing the energies of the Doric Club into more productive channels. Another regiment of regulars was on its way from Halifax, travelling by the overland route. By November 12 troops had been ordered down from Upper Canada, all the colony could spare. Gosford still hesitated, delaying the fateful warrants, but everyone knew they would come in a matter of days. They were already in the hands of the authorities, with only the names lacking. Papineau's name was certain to head the list, and the friends came with their warnings and the pressures mounted daily. The indispensable man must be preserved.

By the evening of the 13th the rumour ran through the city: Papineau had left his home. Around noon of the 15th at Varennes along the St. Lawrence, one of the routes to the Richelieu, Amury Girod was called out from a convivial gathering in a tavern. "I found, first, O'Callaghan, trembling with cold, I think with uneasiness also — he wore a very elegant surtout, his head was concealed by an immense red shawl which formed a singular contrast with the paleness of his face; second, Papineau in a capôte but presenting a marked difference of appearance . . . he did not articulate a single syllable indicative of physical or moral debility. They required that I should go with them to seek a shelter from the impending danger." If they did so order, they were unsuccessful. In the unlikely conversation recorded in his journal Girod quotes himself: "I will not, I said, take the same road with you. Go you to Saint-Denis, see Nelson, be ready to procure arms. I will go to the north; from Grand Brûlé you shall hear from me . . . they eat something . . . our departure again became the subject of deliberation."[8] At last the departure took place, each man with a friend in a separate carriage. There was a night spent at St-Marc in careful seclusion, the river to cross next morning, and then the road by the Richelieu north to St-Denis. By the night of the 17th Papineau and O'Callaghan were the guests of Wolfred Nelson.

They were all wanted men now, and there was considerable other news. On November 16 twenty-six warrants had been issued in Montreal. That night, with six of the lesser leaders already in jail, the arm of the law had reached for two more. They were not particularly important, but they were easy to hand. In the town of St-Jean d'Iberville, an easy ride from Chambly, Doctor Joseph-François Davignon and the notary Pierre-Paul Demaray had been named as the principal disturbers. It had been decided to bring them in.

A troop of Montreal's newly formed volunteer cavalry, escorting a civilian magistrate, had crossed the St. Lawrence at Longueil, cantered down by Chambly, and set off to take the men. The arrests had been duly made and the prisoners bound and bundled into a wagon. Everything had gone smoothly for most of the return journey. Tired, sleepy, but complacent as they neared Longueil, the troopers had been riding along by an empty field, patched here and there with bush and with a low stone fence set well back amid its shadows. Suddenly the fence had erupted in a blaze of fire, followed by the whistle of musket balls and slugs. As the horses reared in panic, thirty or forty figures in bulky *capotes* had rushed at the volunteers. The horsemen had taken to the fields, leaving the overturned wagon, the spilled-out prisoners beside it, and a dead horse in the traces. By morning the troop was straggling back to the city, considerably the worse for wear, and pelted with eggs and snowballs by jeering *patriote* youths. One of the returning cavalrymen had buckshot wounds in his face, two had slugs in the leg, one had a gashed thigh, and one a hole in his hat. "Blood has been shed at last," rejoiced the Montreal *Courier* in its issue of Saturday, November 18, "by rebels who now stand unmasked and fairly subject to the worst penalties of the laws they have insulted."[9]

That same day Louis-Michel Viger, President of La Banque du Peuple, was quietly clapped in jail, charged with high treason. He would be "the better for a little hanging" said Adam Thom; the activities of his institution were well known.[10] On the next day, Sunday, Louis-Hippolyte LaFontaine, erstwhile lieutenant of Papineau, requested an audience with Gosford. The stocky, sober lawyer, whose resemblance to the young Napoleon was much remarked on, had been rarely seen with the leader for several months. He had not been present at the Assembly of the Six Counties, but he had read the omens clearly. "Papineau," he had said, "is lost and must be sacrificed."[11] If the Governor would recall Parliament LaFontaine was sure he could promise co-operation. The Governor declined regretfully; there were other wheels in motion.

4

Fort Chambly, the nearest garrison on the Richelieu, was now stirring with the arrival of regular troops. They were tired, muddy, and disgruntled from a march in ghastly weather, but they were a sizeable, businesslike force under a man who knew his trade. Leaving Montreal at around seven o'clock on the morning of the 18th, Lieutenant-Colonel Wetherall, with four companies of the Royal Regiment, a detachment of the Royal Artillery, and two field guns, had retraced the route taken by the Montreal volunteer cavalry. He was accompanied by some of the troopers and by two magistrates, and he was to recover the lost prisoners. In addition to that, he was to execute the warrants against Papineau and the principal leaders, who were known to be in the Richelieu country. He had passed by Longueil to inspect the place of the skirmish, and had found nothing but the overturned wagon, the dead horse, and some bloody tracks in the field. The grey, rain-beaten country had seemed to be empty of life, with barn doors open, cattle and livestock gone, and deserted houses everywhere, locked and barred.

Here and there, however, as the troops moved on, they had seen horsemen in the distance, obviously scouts. At the last bridge before Chambly they had sighted a body forty or fifty strong, seemingly prepared to give fight. It had scattered instantly as the head of the column appeared, and there had been nothing but a chase through the woods for running men. Wetherall had taken a prisoner or two, learned nothing from them, and entered the fort a little after dark. Here, after a brief survey of conditions, he had ordered his muddy troops to settle in. Fires and beacons were flaring up in the distance, the fort was seething with rumours of rebel gatherings, and the roads were almost impassable. He was bound north for St-Charles and St-Denis, but civilian arrests could wait. He dispatched a courier to Colborne and requested further orders.

Colborne approved of the pause when word reached him. There were more troops, and they were soon to be under way. By the 21st, with Wetherall waiting at Chambly, another force was preparing in Montreal. Colonel Gore, the deputy Quarter-master General, was to go by steamer to Sorel, at the junction of the Richelieu with the St. Lawrence, and march from there south. Wetherall would be reinforced and would move north. Midway between these forces, the two jaws of the nutcracker, were St-Charles and St-Denis.

On the afternoon of the 22nd Gore embarked. By six o'clock

he was in Sorel, landing a company of the 32nd Regiment, four companies of the 24th, an artillery detachment with a 24-pounder gun, and another troop of the Montreal volunteer cavalry. As he marched his men to the barracks square they were beaten by freezing rain, but he ordered them to prepare at once for a night march. By ten o'clock he was moving on St-Denis, south along the Richelieu, with eighteen miles of wooded road ahead of him. The tail of the column had hardly left the barracks before the men of the van were wading in knee-deep mud, the artillery horses were sinking in freezing potholes, and the rain was mixed with snow.

About an hour after Gore had marched, a calèche came slithering up to the barracks gate. Its lone passenger got out, tossed some money to the driver, and demanded to be taken at once to the commanding officer. His hands were shaking with cold and his drenched civilian greatcoat was splashed with mud, but there was no mistaking the manner or the man. Lieutenant George Weir, an officer of the 32nd, was soon explaining his mission to the barracks commander. He had been sent overland by Colborne with urgent dispatches for Gore, and because of the dangerous state of the country he had been told to dress as a civilian to avoid capture. Now that he had arrived, however, he wished to change immediately. His sword, jacket, and sash were with the baggage of the 32nd. Could he have them at once, please, and where was Colonel Gore?

Gore was an hour away, and the baggage could not be found. For "Jock" Weir it was a moment of rare disappointment in a generally light-hearted life. Twenty-nine years old, slight, and sandy-haired, he was a favourite officer in his regiment. He had been born near Edinburgh and recommended for his commission by the Earl of Lauderdale as "a young gentleman, heir to a large and good fortune" who would "make in every respect an excellent recruit". Now, fresh from a month on leave, burning to see action, he had no doubts about his duty and his inclination. He wanted to rejoin his regiment, he wanted his sash and sword, and he had to deliver his dispatches. Colborne was having afterthoughts about the state of the expedition. He was ordering Gore to delay and await the advance of Wetherall, or retire if he met resistance.

It was a dispatch that Gore would not see. Weir, after a frantic midnight search for a driver who would make the trip, at last got off on the road for St-Denis. Some ten miles down, however, as it twisted along through black and dripping forest, the road forked. One fork ran by the river through the little village of St-Ours, which was said to be infested with rebels. The Colonel, who was a better quartermaster than field officer, had decided to go around it. He was climbing away through deeper ruts and quagmires by a difficult little wood trail that was known as the Pot-au-Beurre. He was several miles from the main road and would only come to rejoin it at a bridge near St-Denis. Weir kept to the riverbank and was soon ahead of the army. Around two o'clock, as he came within a mile of the village, there was still no sign of troops. Instead, from the shadows beside the road, four men materialized in the homespun coats of habitants, two of them carrying firearms. They stopped the calèche and asked Weir to identify himself. Wet, anxious, and irritable, he answered with a little more than soldierly brusqueness. He was a civilian, a businessman with affairs in St-Denis; would they please clear the road?

They allowed the calèche to go on but walked politely beside it, two of them on either side. After a few minutes they stopped it again, abreast of a sizeable house. There were lights showing in the windows and much movement about it; many figures were coming and going in the rain. There seemed to be men in the distance at work with shovels; one could hear hammers on stone, a forge was bellowing and an anvil clanging somewhere. The gentleman was now at the home of Doctor Nelson. Would he have the goodness to come in?

Inside, the assumed guise of the businessman was dropped in a few minutes. It now seemed hardly necessary. The tall, gaunt doctor was obviously as disturbed as the gentleman by the unexpected arrival. He was overpolite, if anything, anxiously intent on ceremonial correctness. Restless, nervous, and abstracted, he was often called away; there was much whispering in doorways and discussion in other rooms. But an ample breakfast soon appeared on the table in the great, fragrant kitchen, and there was a comforting crackle of logs in the stone fireplace. The doctor ate little but he was solicitous for the needs of the guest. He sympathized with Weir's predicament, it was really awkward for both of them. There had been many rumours of troops advancing on the village and now they appeared to be confirmed. Weir was a British officer and he was

65

here on a military mission; was that not so? Weir admitted that it was. Very well; in the present state of affairs he must consider himself a prisoner, but he would be shown every courtesy. He was not among rebels here, the doctor emphasized that; he was among public men whose position had been misrepresented. There might yet be an accommodation with the commander of the advancing troops. In the meantime, at first light, Weir would be taken on to the town of St-Charles. He would be held there in safety and he would be expected to give his parole.

Toward daylight Nelson left, and a diffident young habitant stood awkward guard in the kitchen. A wagon pulled up outside, and an older man appeared. He was Migneault, the village postmaster, recruited to drive the wagon, and he seemed reluctant for the work. As he asked Weir to come with him, and tied the prisoner's hands with a length of strap, he was gentle and apologetic. They came outside into the chilly dregs of the storm and found Captain Jalbert waiting on horseback, the officer in charge of the party. He carried his sword unsheathed, resting over his shoulder, and a pistol butt protruded from his coloured sash. Another man, Maillet, got into the wagon, nursing an old French bayonet that was nearly two feet long. Weir followed him in, Migneault took up the reins, and the wagon moved off. The prisoner's bound hands were soon blue with the cold. Migneault glanced back and noticed it, and took off his own mittens. He motioned for Maillet to untie the strap and gave the mittens to Weir. Maillet glowered for a moment and then relented. He removed the strap from the wrists, tied it round Weir's middle, and kept the end in his hand.

Around them, as dawn broadened, there was a growing bustle of people and a sense of panicky confusion. Men went hurrying past them, making for a cluster of buildings at the northern fringe of the village. Women gaped from house doors, screaming at curious children, and huddled groups went southward, seemingly to escape the place. As the wagon jolted along over frozen ruts there were a few shots in the distance. The sound came from the north, and Weir lifted his head. But the strap tightened as he moved and he was pulled back to his seat.

Nelson had gone to the northern end of the village, where the road came down from Sorel. It was blocked with overturned wagons and lattices of heavy brushwood, but the barricade was still weak. There had not been time to gather the wagons and boughs. The largest of the cluster of buildings was an old stone coach-house and it would give command of the road; Madame St-Germain, the owner, had been moved out. The mallets ringing last night had cut loopholes in the walls, but there were hardly enough yet and there was no time for more. The two levels of the house were filling with men, most of them from the valley farms, but there were doctors and lawyers and members of Parliament also, wearing the grey *capotes* of the habitant and the bright toques and sashes. There would be perhaps two hundred in the house, and most of them had firearms of some sort and a good deal of shot and powder. Nelson's stone distillery was set back from the house, crowded with men too. It would be another strongpoint, if strongpoints came to be needed, but it had fewer men with weapons. Except for the skirmishers up in the woods ahead, and some others in the little houses along the road, there were no more men with firearms. The men with the chopped-off scythes and the forks and clubs were being urged to wait in the earthworks behind the church. They were complaining that the trenches were shallow, and so they were; the ground had been hard for digging. Many had come expecting to be given muskets, and some were slinking off.

Looking north, the road ran flat through the brown ploughing of the fields, slippery and icy-hard, flecked here and there with snow. The river ran close by the lower edge of the fields, glinting with a film of ice. For a mile or so in the distance there were houses and barns and fences, interspersed by patches of bush. Then the woods closed in and the road came twisting through them, down from the Pot-au-Beurre, cut by streams and creeks, crossed by a few small bridges.

Nelson had broken the bridges and set outposts near them, and it was from there that the shots were coming. Not many, but they seemed to be nearing, and they could only mean that the skirmishers were giving back. They would soon be appearing out of those woods ahead. And after them would be soldiers — British soldiers. There was too much shouting and confusion around Nelson, too much coming and going. Orders and counter-orders, complaints, cheers, panic. Questions everywhere, demands everywhere; he had no answer for any of

67

them. He looked around at the men going into the houses and the men drifting away from them. He felt the need of some food, a drop to warm him.

As he entered his own house, set on the riverbank half a mile from the distillery, Papineau and O'Callaghan were waiting. Talking. "On discutait toujours";[12] it summed up the work of the days since they had come. Planning and counter-planning, emissaries and more emissaries; always the litter of papers, the cloud of pipesmoke, somehow the stink of fear. The warrants were totally unjustified; there could be no accepting arrest. The people must now be organized, it was time to discuss arming. There must be new committees of resistance, the plan for a general convention would have to go forward; it had after all been resolved on. A circular had been prepared to call leaders to the convention; Papineau had slept the night on it and torn it up; it was tantamount to rebellion. Yet some copies of the circular were already on their way. Nelson had prepared a Declaration of Independence; Papineau had signed it. It was somewhere now in a drawer of the cluttered desk, with the letters from Upper Canada and the word of a rising there, set for December 7.

The talk this morning centred on other matters. Edouard Fabre, bookseller and director of La Banque du Peuple, had ridden in an hour or so ago. He was gone now, but the effects of his message lingered. Viger, the president of the bank, was held in jail. Some of the other directors were sought on warrants and all were under suspicion. Whatever their first intentions with regard to providing funds, they were cool and definite now. There would be no money forthcoming from the people's bank.

O'Callaghan had little to say. For five years he had said it all in *Vindicator*, flaying the oligarchy, calling the people to arms — an Adam Thom in counterpoint. The meagre, spectacled, waspish little man had lost his occupation with his type and his presses. He seemed to have lost his sting.

What Papineau said to Nelson, and Nelson said to Papineau, was to be affirmed and denied and lied about for longer than both would live. According to Papineau it had been agreed that Nelson should command the men who did the fighting. Papineau, as supreme leader, should not be made "repugnant" to British authorities by the shedding of any blood. He should hold himself apart, clear and beyond reproach, for later negotiations. Nelson, in the years to come, remembered differently. He had consented to fight the battle with the leader remaining behind him in the safety of the house. But he had expected that if he fell Papineau would be there to replace him.

"I demand that you go," he is quoted as saying to Papineau in other accounts. "You should not expose yourself unnecessarily. We shall have more need of you later."

"I might, perhaps, leave the village," Papineau is quoted in reply, "but it does not seem to be right . . . to go at such a time is to expose myself later, perhaps, to severe reproach . . ."

The stories twist and change but the facts remain. Whatever the words and thoughts of that bleak morning, a carriage left the village. It joined the stream of fugitives hurrying south, as women huddled in cellars with their children round them and the fighters with forks moved north for the stone houses. Hooded in their *capotes,* their faces turned from the watchers, Papineau and O'Callaghan removed themselves to safety.

There had been an earlier commotion on the road they took, but it was over now. If they passed bloodstained mud they did not see it. The wagon carrying Weir had come this way, and had stopped an hour before. There had been a renewed sound of firing from the woods to the north and suddenly, "like lightning" as Migneault was to say later, the officer jumped from the wagon.

He had forgotten Maillet's strap, and as it tightened he stumbled back, sprawling across the wheel, face up. Maillet struck with the bayonet and Weir fell in the road, blood gushing from his neck. He got to his hands and knees, screamed at another blow, and was under the rear wheels, with the guard stabbing through the spokes. Migneault hauled at the reins, but the frightened horses dragged the wagon along, dragging the man under it. Jalbert, who had been riding ahead with his sword over his shoulder, turned and came galloping back. A crowd was gathering from the street, people were running from houses, and still the stabbing went on, punctuated by the screams. The wagon moved clear of the writhing form under it, and the forks and clubs of the crowd began to come down. "Officer! Officer!"—this was a British officer, and panic and hate and years of desolate impotence had found a vent at last. Blood gushed from his back and groin and shoulders. Three gruesome fingers lay in the road. The mutilated hands were

69

over the sandy head, the face was hardly recognizable, and the screams were growing hoarse. Yet an old schoolteacher of the village was striking again and again with a heavy knife. "Finish him! Finish him!" — the cry came from Jalbert, or some said it did. A man with a pistol put it to Weir's head and pulled the trigger twice, and twice the weapon misfired. He swore at the damp priming, turning away to adjust it, and Jalbert's sword came down. Or some said it came down and some denied it; the story of that killing would come out in the courts later, as savage, confused, and meaningless as the death itself. But it was not without meaning then.[13]

The body was dragged, still breathing, to a space between two houses. There the crowd surrounded it and the last sparks flickered out. But the madness lingered in the men with forks and clubs, making for the shallow earthworks, the open door of the distillery, the loopholed mansion of Madame St-Germain. Nelson stood there looking off to the north, watching the troops appearing out of the woods with a gun moving behind them. He turned to see Jalbert at the head of the crowd, to hear the news and see the blood on the sword — or some said there was blood. His own blood drained from his face as he looked at the man on horseback. "You old fool — you don't know what you've done!"[14]

The loud, authoritative voice had become a shaken whisper. But the crowd was surging round him and the skirmishers were in from the woods. Breathless, mud-splashed, urgent, they were clamouring to give their reports. Nelson waved them off; the situation was clear. The weaponless crowd was disposed among the entrenchments. He followed the last with weapons into the gloom of the stone house. The doors closed behind them. Over a rustling quiet, with the slits of the loopholes giving the only light, he made his little speech, the parliamentarian again. The warrants were illegal, the expedition was illegal; he was resisting unjust arrest. He ordered no one to stay with him; any who wished might go. But the doors were closed, the friends and brothers watching, and no man moved.

He was looking out from a loophole now; it all seemed unreal. He had hoped for a parley, a chance to explain his position, gentleman to gentleman-officer. There was apparently not to be one. No white flag, no glittering scarlet rider; he was not sure now he was sorry. What could be said? Jalbert had changed all that. More troops from the woods; surely it must be all. No brilliant ranks, no lattice of pipe-clayed belts. That mass in the distance was as gloomy, muddy, and sodden as the day itself; spreading now, sprawling, and inching forward. The gun had stopped, the horses were out of the traces, and it was swinging round to position. Men bustled beside it, and were abruptly blurred by smoke. A roundshot clanged shudderingly against the stone wall of the house, and there was now no more to be said.

FIVE

"Nos têtes sont en jeu maintenant . . ."

The day had turned bitterly cold, and the strong east wind was carrying flakes of snow. On the upper floor of the stone house the men were steadying again after the first blow of the roundshot. It had struck at the lower level, where the walls were four feet thick, and had obviously done no harm. Perhaps it had done good. In the mutter of talk round Nelson there was a new and hardening note.

Whatever the state of their weapons, many of the men at the loopholes were huntsmen and crack shots. There were others as good behind them, ready to take their turns. Some were biting nervously on stubby pipes, a few were fingering rosaries, but all were intent and waiting. Nelson's neighbours, most of them, all of them Nelson's friends. Old Captain Blanchard—he had worn the King's red jacket in 1812, but the years since had changed him. Now he was like the others in the grey homespun coat, the bright toque and sash that had come to be a kind of uniform. Louis Pagé here too, a prosperous merchant and a good businessman, already with a family to care for. A man who might well have sought to avoid all trouble, to enjoy an easy life. Something had been lacking in that life; he was fondling an old musket now, patting the wadded paper that his wife had given him for a breastplate. David Bourdages, son of Louis Bourdages, the great old deputy who had carried the fight in the Assembly for more years than Papineau and died with the fight unwon. Grandson of Raymond Bourdages, the dispossessed Acadian. David himself a man of thirty-seven, heir to that bitter legacy. It had brought him here, and it had lined that stony face.

Too many of the other faces were fresh and young, hardly beyond boyhood. Habitant faces, most of them; these were the farm boys led here by Nelson. The weight of that work lay heavy on the leader. Yet there were the others, too, somehow lightening the burden; these men thought for themselves. Ovide Perrault, lawyer and parliamentarian at twenty-eight, knowing the odds, accepting them. The wit, the flashing charm, the reckless, exuberant gaiety frozen in a new stillness. He looked set and strange in this light, somehow withdrawn; a man with a premonition? The two Cartier brothers from across the river, Henri and George Etienne. Hardly a mile away, smoke would be threading up from the seven chimneys of the big, comfortable house where they had been born, signalling the lost peace, the lives set in the balance. For what? They seemed to know. All here seemed to know. The confusion of comings and goings that had marked the early morning had settled to this hard quiet. It was the same in the fields outside, beyond the roadblock. Men were still on the run, muskets were snapping sporadically, but it was only a general retirement of the last skirmishers. They were making their way purposefully, across the front of the advancing British, toward the barns and houses and woodpiles that lined the road. Silence enveloped them too as they disappeared, an ominous, waiting silence. The battle, if there must be a battle, would not be decided by any wave of panic.

Colonel Gore had come to the same conclusion. He had led his three hundred men on a gruelling night march for which the only justification had been the hope of surprise. That hope, if there had ever been one, had been gone since first light. Skirmishers had appeared from the woods along the road, harrying his column and breaking the bridges ahead of it. He had been heralded by church bells all along the river, sounding the warning tocsin. As he came in sight of the village and displayed his force, he had fired a ranging round from his single cannon. It had bounced back from stone, accomplishing nothing. There had been no white flags, no deputation of peasants, caps in hand. The town lay before him settling to silence as the last skirmishers vanished along his front. Bells in the distance still went on with their clamour and across the river to his right, less than a mile away, there were men and boats gathering.

Gore now moved forward with the rough ground dipping ahead of him into the shelter of a small coulee. Here he halted again and went up on the forward slope to survey the prospect. Ploughed fields ran to his right along the river and there were still woods to his left, thinning to clumps of brush as they neared the town. There was a barricade across the road to his front, a large stone house behind it, and a clutter of other buildings flanking the approach. Beyond these, topped by the spire of the church, the straggling village ran southward, everywhere hugging the river. There was no hope of encircling it by a march along the bank, and the view to the left was hardly more attractive. There was cover for the defenders everywhere, in houses and barns and outbuildings, in patches of wood and bush and behind the sodden hayricks and the formidable stone fences. The heart of the defence, however, was obviously the stone house, and it would be the first objective. He ordered the gun forward up the lip of the slope, and sent it across the ploughing toward an old barn on his right. It would be well in range of the house there, and the angle of the barn would offer a little shelter.

A company of infantry moved ahead of the gun, with the men slithering and falling in the iron-hard ruts of the field. They were met by a ripple of fire as they neared the barn, and they dropped flat to their bellies. Then they were moving again, going in with the bayonet, and the barn's defenders were on the run for the town. As straining horses fought at the mud-clogged wheels, the gun and the ammunition wagon rocked up to position. The barrel swung round, the gun was unlimbered and trained, but it was spattered with slugs and bullets now from the slits in the stone house. Three of the gunners dropped, one after the other, before the first round went off. When it did go it proved to be a lucky shot, piercing an upper window; but as three more followed it they clanged against solid stone. The walls of the lower level could not be smashed in; the house would have to be taken. Gore looked over at Markham, his best officer, a captain in the 32nd. He could spare him three companies. These glum men in the coulee, freezing in their drenched uniforms, with their Canadian moccasins in ribbons and their numb fingers stiffening around their muskets, would have to go in and take it.

Three times, with his force of about two hundred, Markham made the attempt. By noon he had cleared the buildings on the approach to the barricade. By one o'clock, after a fierce mêlée with bayonets, he was into a house across from the main fortress. But he had been twice wounded in the neck, he had a shotgun slug in his leg, and there were dead and wounded strewn in the fields behind him. Helpless himself, his men were helpless too because they were caught in a blistering cross-fire whenever they tried to move. It came from the stone house, from the distillery behind the house, and it was growing from the direction of the river and from along the road to the south. The boats from the other side were crossing now, and there were new arrivals by land. The whole dismal countryside seemed speckled with running men. They were fanning out around him, dodging from shelter to shelter, threatening to cut him off.

He decided to withdraw his troops and was carried with them, jounced along in a stretcher. By two o'clock the force was back in the coulee. Markham was out of action, there had been several other casualties, and Gore was still at the point from which he had started. The fire on his front slackened, while off to the right his gun went slamming on, accomplishing little or nothing. It seemed to have damaged the upper floor of the house; there was no fire from there, but the lower level had not been pierced at all. The direct assault had failed, and there was one recourse left. The tired men moved out again, edging around the landward side of the town to encircle it from the left.

They stumbled across ploughing, groped their way through bush, and began to move forward among a thickening tangle of outbuildings, some of which were ablaze. Then they went to their bellies at a sudden spatter of fire. There were shallow earthworks in front of them, masked by patches of scrub, and they seemed to be filled with men. There were in fact nearly five hundred, but this was the "fence-post brigade", with pitchforks and clubs and hardly a dozen firearms. The troops, however, could not measure their enemy; the advance lost its momentum and the pause was just too long. Nelson, an hour before, had sent George Etienne Cartier across the river to gather the last resources of men and weapons. He was back now, and he had done his work well. From boats at the river's edge came nearly a hundred fresh, well-armed men, driving at the right of the troops. At the same moment the doors of the stone house opened. Black with the smoke and deafened with the roar of five hours of fighting, the men in the house had caught the scent of victory. They surged forward jubilantly, following the reinforcements, and the fence-post brigade came welling out of their trenches. Taken in front and flank, the troops gave way and were soon on the run for their starting-point through the shelters they had just cleared.

Once more the force was back in the coulee, while the town seethed in front of it with a mass of new fighters. They were scattering out to the fields now, beginning to threaten the gun. From every hayrick, fence, and woodpile there seemed to be fire coming, and it was always edging closer. Gore, watching the comings and goings, estimated the strength of his enemies at fifteen hundred. It was double the real number but there had been other reports as high as three thousand, and he was in no mood to discount them. He had three hundred sleepless men, soaked, exhausted, and hungry. It was three in the afternoon, there was more snow in the wind, and the ammunition was low. Of the sixty-six rounds he had brought along for the gun, six only remained, and he had ordered it to cease firing. He could not mount a new assault, he could not hold on where he was, and he could not face retreat by the Pot-au-Beurre. One bridge remained, connecting with the lower road along the river, and it would not be standing long if he did not use it. As grey-clad shapes in the distance worked round toward his rear, the bugle sounded retreat.

An hour later, with some of his wagons and wounded left behind, Gore was still battling to hold the approach to the bridge. The infantry straggled across but the gun remained, anchored in frozen mud. As a rearguard spread before it, harried by marksmen streaming out from the town, the gun-horses gave up. The officers' horses replaced them, and sank exhausted too. Then it was lines of infantrymen, hauling on long cables. They inched the gun to the bridge, across the bridge to the road, and began to fall in their turn as the clogged mass sank in mud. The medical officer made his way to Gore; another half-hour of this would finish them all. Gore watched grimly as the gun was spiked and abandoned, and the rearguard crossed the bridge. The force limped into column and was on the march for Sorel.

It reached St-Ours at midnight, halfway along the road. The village was black and quiet, with every window and every house door barred. But there were no shots and no enemies to be seen. The ragged files tramped through, with only the sucking of torn moccasins in mud and the dull clank of equipment. A mile or so on, among the barns and outbuildings of what had once been a prosperous farm, Gore called a halt. The men had to be rested and they had had no food since dawn. Officers scouting the root cellars discovered a cache of potatoes and distributed three or four to every man. They lighted fires and roasted them and fell asleep as they munched, with their icy backsides stiffening and their faces glazed with the heat. At dawn, as they moved off, they were startled to hear the tramp of men ahead. It was an infantry company with two guns that had been ordered down from Sorel. But the reinforcements had come a day too late. After a brief council on the road the newcomers turned about with the beaten troops. At eleven o'clock in the morning they reached Sorel, carrying their six dead and some of their ten wounded, and with six men missing. The rebel losses, thought Gore, "must have been about one hundred".[1]

He was over-hopeful. In the stone house three had been smashed to pulp at a single blow as the second roundshot crashed through the upper window. One had gone at the loopholes, and several more in the open. As Nelson faced the morning, after a night of wild rejoicing, he had watched Ovide Perrault die, making the twelfth man killed. Four had been badly wounded, three lightly, and on the whole the price seemed small for what had been gained. The word of the victory was spreading far and wide, growing as it travelled the valley to Montreal. Floods of jubilant strangers who had come late for the battle were alight with other plans for the mighty rising. It would sweep the valley of the Richelieu, it would overwhelm Montreal; the frightened city was girding itself already.

Papineau had not gone far and would soon be back, with convoys of arms from the Americans, at the head of American armies. Perhaps, Nelson agreed, perhaps in good time. But his eyes were sombre, he would not look at Jalbert, and he spoke more of strengthening the town's defences. "Nos têtes sont en jeu maintenant," he said to some of the shouters and quieted the plans with a single brusque word, "Attendons."[2]

There was not long to wait. On Saturday the 25th, the burial day for the dead, the flag-draped bodies came to the door of the church. There they stopped, deprived not only of the sacraments but of burial in consecrated ground. The unrelenting curé, who had always opposed the *patriotes*, considered the men who had died outside the faith. His vicar, Abbé Lagorce, a man of different stamp, had remained throughout the battle as priest and comforter. But he would not defy his superior; he could not be persuaded to say mass for these dead. One after the other, amid a storm of anger and heartbreak that almost threatened their lives, the priests walked down to the river and were rowed away from the village, taking all comfort with them. Unblessed and in sombre silence the bodies went to the earth, and all through the dismal ceremony heads were turning to the south. There was a sound of gunfire coming up from St-Charles.

2

From Saturday the 18th to the night of Wednesday the 22nd, Colonel Wetherall at Chambly had waited for a break in the weather. He had had little information from Montreal and no new orders; he suspected that Colborne's couriers might have been taken. But his original orders stood, he was to move north for St-Charles. Speed was certainly called for; a night movement might offer some hope of surprise, and the rains of the past four days had slackened to a chilly drizzle. At dusk on the 22nd he crossed by the Chambly ferry to the right bank of the Richelieu and started his march north.

He had a force of six companies, with another company held in reserve at Chambly, but he was not in very good heart. The black country around him was alive with sinister stirrings, he knew he was watched everywhere, and the column was moving at less than a mile an hour. On the frightful, washed-out road, the two guns were sinking and the gun-horses were floundering, while artillerymen groped ahead of them with lighted lanterns. Wagons overturned and had to be righted. The cursing files of the infantry, knee-deep and hip-deep in the oozing yellow clay, sometimes sprawled on their faces as they struggled to free their legs. At three in the morning Wetherall called a halt and when he moved again at daybreak it was only to St-Hilaire, halfway along his route. By noon his force was at rest, with the officers billeted in the manor house and the troops in the barns and outbuildings of the seigneur Hertel de Rouville, a moderately loyal realist who was accommodating and polite. He was also exquisitely uncomfortable under the loom of Beloeil Mountain, which overshadowed his seigneury and was thick with *patriote* patrols.

Here Wetherall remained through the next day, waiting for news of Gore. It came to him around midnight. The northern force had been defeated and was plodding back to Sorel. There were the usual reports of huge rebel gatherings, with thousands at St-Denis, and even more at St-Charles. He discounted some of the rumours, but not all. The lights and watchfires winked at him from Beloeil Mountain, and the surrounding country was certainly up in arms. His best move, he suspected, was to retire on Montreal, but he had no orders to do so. In any case, he would need his reserve company. He did not know, as he sent a courier galloping off for Chambly, that orders for his retirement has been twice sent out by Colborne and twice captured by rebels.

By daylight next morning his own courier was back. He had reached Chambly but there had been a lively chase each way by *patriote* horsemen, and when the reserve troops followed they came floating down the Richelieu in two scows. They were a welcome sight, but the news they brought was bad. They had come by water because they dared not march by land, and behind them ice was beginning to form in the river. The ferry at Chambly would soon be out of action, and when that happened it would cut the line of retreat. Wetherall would be lying marooned in enemy country, on the wrong side of the river, and out of communication with Montreal. He waited fretfully for orders through the rest of the 24th, but he was also readying his troops. On the 25th he moved.

By nine o'clock in the morning the column was on the road, well fed and rested and with much of its mud scraped off. The weather was still cloudy, but it was turning dry and fine. Relieved of the rain the men were in good spirits, which Wetherall hardly shared. He had decided to continue north since he had not been ordered south, and St-Charles was his first objective. It was reputed to be even stronger than St-Denis, and he would be faced, he thought, by perhaps three thousand men, in a well-defended position. He had two guns, some three hundred and fifty men, and the awesome reputation of British regulars. He intended to make what he could of a bad dilemma, but he did not like the odds.

He liked them less as the morning wore away. The bridges were broken at every creek and streamlet, and felled trees and roadblocks delayed the march. Whenever the column moved in sight of the river there were shots from the other side. He could see clusters of men and then a scattering of boats, crossing to land ahead of him in the woods on the near bank. By one o'clock there were shots coming from the woods, and from the occasional barn or house set back from the road. He deployed skirmishers, rushed the buildings and burnt them, but there was no clearing the woods. There was no counting the figures pacing the march, scurrying from tree to tree and knoll to knoll, but they were well-directed guerillas and they knew what they were about. For another hour, as the force approached St-Charles, it was harried and often stopped by spatters of fire.

Then it was out in the open before the village, with the river close on the left and the woods thinning to the right. Wetherall had been faced thus far by the *patriote* outposts under Bonaventure Viger, a distant cousin of the banker and a man born for war. But Viger's work was done now and his men were retiring on the fortress, which was the work of General Brown. Wetherall surveyed it carefully, and perhaps a little incredulously, after his fears of the early morning. There was a rampart of logs and branches coated with frozen mud, which the guns could batter down in half an hour. But that would hardly be necessary. The low wall came curving up from the river to cross the road, with a manor house marooned on its right flank. Neither protected the other and both were dominated by a hill that rose behind them, obviously undefended. The landward flank of the rampart dwindled into clumps of bush, but there was open ground beyond it and the way was clear for the guns to reach the hill. The whole position was a trap, and instead of three thousand men behind those ramparts he could make out barely a hundred.

Beyond the rampart, less than a mile away, were the clustering houses of the village, the tall spire of the church, and the road continuing on to St-Denis. There were stragglers hurrying north along the road and others scattering in the fields, but he could see no bodies of fighters. There was no rising of earthworks and no glint of weapons. He ordered his troops to deploy with the two guns before them, their left flank on the river, their right bent toward the hill. Then, with his strength displayed, he sent for a prisoner, an old man who had been taken on the way north. He was to inform the town's defenders that the British were passing through for St-Denis. There would be no injuries or reprisals if they were given peaceful passage.

The messenger disappeared behind the rampart, but he was long in finding Brown. The General was not there, he was somewhere down in the village, calling out reinforcements. He was not sure, he had hardly been sure for days, of where he should be at all. With his head broken in the riot and a warrant out for his arrest, he had started from Montreal for the United States. But he had been stopped by *patriotes* asking ominous questions: "Why do our leaders all desert us now?"[3] He had found himself in St-Charles, and somehow, unbelievably, in command. Puny and frail as always, with his jawbone dislocated and the sight of one eye gone, he was hardly able to talk or sit a horse. But he was still the man who had led the Sons of Liberty, and better men than Brown were impressed by that. Their faith had inflated him, and he had somehow managed to impose himself on them. For almost a week now he had been issuing lofty orders, confiscating grain and cattle, proscribing suspected loyalists, and building the fortifications that faced Wetherall.

In the flush of new authority his health had seemed to return. He was much in touch with Nelson, and his confidence had soared skyward as the fighters of St-Denis told of their victory. From north of St-Ours to as far south as Chambly, and on both sides of the Richelieu, *patriotes* were on the move. It seemed to Brown to be the stir of an assembling army. Men flowed into St-Charles, moved on to St-Denis, and scattered about the country in search of provisions and weapons. The results were lean as yet and the numbers actually in the village were always changing. There seemed to be around three hundred when he tried to count them, and a hundred of these had firearms. It was not much, it was even a little frightening when one paused to think, but by the night of the 24th he was still confident. Winter was closing in, roads were breaking up, ice was thickening on the rivers. The British would not move in such weather. He would have months to arm, and build his command to thousands, and complete those fortifications. Later that night it seemed they might not be needed. The word came in that Wetherall was in retreat, hurrying back to the safety of Montreal.

Next morning scouts had come in from along the Richelieu, dispelling that bright hope. Brown had adjusted slowly to the first alarms. As shots were heard from the south, and the outposts tumbled in, all his ailments seemed to be coming back. The British were moving northward after all, there was much confusion everywhere, he felt confused himself. He delegated many tasks, ordered men to the ramparts, and galloped back to the village at the first glimpse of the troops. He had to rally the people, there was corn to be ground at the mill. There were a thousand things to see to; he hardly knew where to begin. When the messenger from Wetherall reached him he hardly knew what to say, but the words somehow came out. If the troops wished to pass they must lay down their arms in the road.

The messenger started back with Brown's reply. The General himself followed the messenger at a distance, expostulating with some of the villagers who were reluctant to go to the front. There had been considerable delay, however, and it proved to have been too long for the British commander. Suddenly from ahead of Brown there were flashes of flame, and musket balls came singing around his ears. His horse reared, spilling him onto the road, and when he mounted again he seemed to have lost direction. He was somehow galloping north, racing back through the village, and then he was out on the road again, bound for St-Denis. There in the dismal twilight he was confronted by Wolfred Nelson, and only saved by the doctor from the hands of raging *patriotes.*

As his time limit expired Wetherall had moved forward, with his left and centre closing in on the rampart and his right swinging wide around it. Then he had halted again, hoping for a white flag, or at least the return of the messenger. He was met instead by defiant shouts from the rampart and then a blaze of fire. The troops of the centre and left went to the ground, fixing their bayonets as they waited. The men on the right went forward in a wide sweep to clear the hill for the guns. In fifteen minutes it was taken and the guns were in place and trained, firing roundshot and shrapnel into the trapped men below. In effect the battle was over, but the killing had only begun.

"Them fellers fought well," was the comment of a soldier later, "they waited too long to run." As the roundshot smashed their shelter and the shrapnel tore among them, the hundred or so defenders, with a few additions from the village, waited for the bayonet charge. The guns on the hill fell silent and the charge came on, through great gaps opened in the wall of logs and mud. The *patriotes* met the regulars at every gap, fighting them hand to hand. There was no escape except by way of the river, and some were killed as they tried. Some gave back along the road that led to the village and fought from house to house. But the troops were hard after them, the houses were soon blazing, and in an hour the last of the firing died away. Wetherall and two of his officers had had their horses shot under them. Three of his men were dead and he had eighteen wounded to care for. Of the rebels, he did not know how many died in the river or the burning houses but he was able to report to Colborne: "I have counted fifty-six bodies and many more were killed."[5]

That night, wrote one of the British officers, "In the great dusk of the church a fire was lighted, around which groups of soldiers were eating and drinking. In the thick darkness a single candle threw a feeble light. Before the altar were extended the bodies of soldiers and in the sacristy were the prisoners, for the most part kneeling in silent and solemn prayer."[6] Outside, musket barrels, powder flasks, and cartridges were exploding all through the night, and the battlefield seemed alive as fire flickered across it. The singed grass had ignited, and it was burning away the woolly *étoffe du pays* that clothed most of the dead. There was the sickening smell of roasted flesh every-where. On Sunday morning, before the mass burial, relatives picked their way about the field, seeking their own. They were often courteously guided by British officers, and there were sometimes shots ahead of them. Soldiers were firing at pigs which had escaped their pens and were nibbling the naked corpses.

The curé from St-Denis had come to St-Charles. Wetherall sent for him after the battle was over and ordered him back to his parish. He was to see that his people returned at once to their homes, or the town would be destroyed. The warning was stern but vague, and Wetherall made no attempt to follow it up. He was still worried about crossing the river at Chambly, and there were new reports of rebels gathering in his rear. On Monday the 27th he took to the road south. On the 28th, as he neared the Chambly ferry, he dispersed a ragged attack with a dozen shots. By Thursday, November 30, he was marching through Montreal with thirty haggard prisoners and the Liberty Pole of St-Charles, topped by its red cap.

3

That same day Gore was in motion again. He had come to Montreal to report to Colborne, and he had found barri-cades at the suburbs, a city in near panic, and a disapproving commander. As Wetherall began his victory march Gore was reboarding the steamer *John Bull,* with more infantry and more guns to add to the force at Sorel. When he arrived at dusk he embarked the troops he had left there, intending to continue south at first light. But as dawn broke there was the gleam of thickening ice on the Richelieu River, and the *John Bull* gave up after taking several hours to make a mile. By early afternoon eight companies of infantry, with a battery of four guns, were tramping south by the too-familiar road.

St-Ours was quiet that night as the troops arrived and halted. There were lights in some of the houses, a few barn doors stood open, and there was the occasional gleam of a lantern where cows were being milked. In a macabre and stealthy fashion daily life had resumed. As the force moved on next morning the road was empty, and scouts came back perplexed at the condition of St-Denis. There were some new barricades and earthworks that had apparently been just begun, but they were standing uncompleted. There seemed to be no defenders in the big stone coach-house. An occasional boat could be seen leaving by the river, and scattered groups were making off for the woods. Beyond that, there were no other signs of life. Gore moved on warily, but except for the tramp and clank of the long column the silence remained unbroken. At the bridge before the village, where the abandoned gun still lay with its nose in the mud, there was a downcast group of men with a white flag. They announced that all the fighters had left the town, and that those who remained were asking only for mercy. They were ordered to return to their homes, with cold comfort. The innocent would not suffer, but innocence remained to be proved. The property of every rebel would be destroyed. The march resumed, with the emissaries watching dolefully, and the column entered the town.

With cool order and efficiency the troops broke up into search parties and began to ransack the houses. Officers stalked behind them from door to door, chalking up the number of men to be billeted at each place. In the late dusk families began to creep back across the fields, some of them to homes they were not allowed to occupy. Innocent or not, they had decided to risk return rather than freeze in the woods; and along with them came local friends of *bureaucrates* who had had barns burnt, horses stolen, and had suffered various indignities at *patriote* hands. They were out now for revenge, and were soon assisting and egging on the troops. Nelson's house and distillery were already ablaze. Madame St-Germain's fortress was blown apart with gunpowder and then put to the torch. All that night and all through the following day Gore's fire parties and their assistants went stolidly on with the work. By the end of that smoky Sunday there had been fifty buildings burned.

On Monday, December 4, with five of his eight companies and two of his guns, Gore moved south to St-Charles and from there on to St-Hyacinthe where Papineau was said to be. The force arrived late, in the midst of a heavy snowfall, and was met by crowds of habitants with the parish priest at their head, offering information and protesting loyalty. The pause was reassuring but the speeches were long, and perhaps diverted Gore from his main purpose. It was almost midnight when a young Lieutenant Lysons, heading a line of sleighs, drew up to throw a cordon around the home of Papineau's sister. It was a large manor house with many barns and outbuildings, and many places of exit. As the troops took up their stations surrounding the place, the Lieutenant went to the door and knocked politely. He was received with equal politeness by a dignified elderly lady who was surprised by the purpose of his mission but eager to be of help. For an hour she led the Lieutenant through every nook and cranny of the huge old house. At the last chest in the last garret Lysons became suspicious, but it was too late by then. Convinced that the quarry had been there, and was now certainly gone, he returned to report his failure.

The next day Gore marched back by St-Charles to St-Denis. On the sixth he left for Sorel and arrived that night, with garrisons left behind him in both villages. On December 7 he landed in Montreal, with his battered reputation somewhat restored and his lost gun recovered.

4

There was a rough pine coffin prominent among his baggage. At St-Denis on December 4, while Gore himself was marching into St-Charles, the troops he had left behind him were completing another mission. The search for the body of Lieutenant Weir of the 32nd had gone on from the first hour of the return, and every soul in the town had been sternly questioned. It was obvious with some that knowledge haunted their eyes; it haunted the whole village, but for a day and a night there had been a blank wall of silence. Then, on the morning of the 4th, a letter was brought by a boy to Lieutenant Griffin a brother-officer of Weir.

The body would be found, the letter said, in the tanyard back of the house of Madame Ayotte. Here Griffin began the search, with Doctor McGregor the medical officer, a work party of the troops, and a few conscripted habitants. The yard was long and ran down to the Richelieu, which was open again that morning after four days of ice. There were pits and mounds that might have been made by digging but none seemed to be recent. The ground was coated with snow and frozen hard, and the men's pickaxes and shovels could hardly break the surface. After a laborious hour some of the watching habitants, who were standing without tools, began to drift toward the river. One of them came hurrying back to whisper to Griffin; he could see something in the water.

Griffin followed him down to where some roughly piled stones jutted out a little from the bank as a kind of pier. Below him he could make out something waving to the ripple of the current. It seemed to be a shred of cloth; and there was a sprawling mass under it, almost covered with stones. He ordered the stones removed, and the mass tilted upward stiffly. Bare feet broke the surface, then the trousered legs. The trunk followed, wrapped in a heavy greatcoat with the arms fast at the sides, pinioned by a leather strap. The last stone came off, freeing the shoulders. A matting of yellow hair began to lift, and swirling about it with the disturbance were scraps of bone and brain. Griffin had seen enough. The face was quite unrecognizable, but he knew the "lion skin" greatcoat. He ordered the habitants off, "as I was afraid of some of the soldiers coming down and seeing the body."[7]

There was no hope that they would not, and some of them would have to help. As Doctor McGregor took charge, the rigid form was stood bolt upright for a moment, and then hurried to the house of Madame Ayotte. Fires had to be stoked and kettles of water boiled before the solidly frozen clothes could be taken off. The watch fell out of a pocket as that was done. The body was not blue, the doctor noted, it was dead white; it had bled to death before it reached the water. He began his partial inventory of the work of that savage morning, eleven days before: "On the right side of the neck below the ear, a large sabre wound . . . it cut all the vessels of the neck as far as the bone . . . another wound met it at a right angle and exposed the windpipe and the bones of the shoulder . . . a wound dividing the scalp . . . the skull and brains and bones on the back of the head a complete pulp . . . a gunshot wound in the shoulder-blade, a gunshot wound in the groin . . . his left hand had three fingers cut off . . . on the other hand one of the fingers was cut up the middle . . . two or three other sabre wounds on the head . . . I do not know how many wounds on the body . . .".[8]

By the afternoon a coffin had been prepared. It lay in the officers' mess, holding the shrouded body, when Gore returned from his march. On December 6, as he left again for Sorel, all of the 32nd went back with him. He could not leave those men who had known Jock Weir to garrison St-Denis. But there were a company of the 24th and two of the 66th remaining behind, and they were there for a long, grim winter. The "poor, deluded habitans" had become the murdering French, subject to the full rigours of an army of occupation. And it was not the end of the affair.

5

The odyssey of the departing leaders had now begun, relieved only by a skirmish some three miles from the border. Doctor Côté of L'Acadie, with his aide, Lucien Gagnon, had been among the first to cross to Vermont. There, at Swanton, to the south of Mississquoi Bay, they had been joined by other fugitives and had been welcomed by French Canadians already settled in Vermont. They had also been heartened by many native Americans who were eager for a sister republic beside their own. There was no doubt that Vermonters thought like Canadians, and they were liberal in promises of aid. For the most part, at the moment, it amounted to a handsome flag, sewn by the Swanton ladies, but it helped to restore morale. Lucien Gagnon the fighter, though he had been swept south in the first flight with Côté, had no need of such help.

Within a few days of his arrival he had coolly recrossed the border into Canada, and was gathering men and weapons. He was hardly welcomed but he was not betrayed, and he made his way back to Swanton with sixty-six recruits. With these added to the *patriotes* already there, and with a few additional Vermonters, the force in Swanton rose to about two hundred. It had too many ex-politicians but there were also hunters and woodsmen, and it was comparatively well armed. By the evening of December 6 it was invading Canadian territory, with the town of St-Césaire as the first objective. The place lay on the Yamaska

River, about thirty miles to the north, and the latest rumours put Wolfred Nelson there, establishing a new base.

There was no Nelson at St-Césaire, and there was no base. Gagnon, moreover, in the course of his first return, had managed to alarm loyalists in the whole region to the north of Mississquoi Bay. They were far from defenceless, since they had been assembled in volunteer companies and provided with arms by Colborne, and they were now alert to danger. As the *patriotes* crossed the border and began the tramp north, they were met at Moore's Corners by fire from many directions. The place was a little crossroads between St-Armand and Philipsburg, two border villages, and volunteers from both towns had been hurrying to set an ambush. They had not all made it by the time the enemy appeared, but they fired from wherever they were. In the snowy darkness, with both sides totally confused, it seemed to be a battle of thousands and the invaders gave way first. Within ten minutes they were on the run for the border, leaving one man dead behind them, five taken as prisoners, and seventy of their precious muskets. For this winter, the war in the Richelieu valley had come to an end.

It had not quite ended for Papineau with his flight from St-Denis. On November 23, the day of the battle, he had made his way to his sister's home at St-Hyacinthe but he had not been able to stay there. For ten days, restless and ineffectual, he had ridden about the countryside, haunting the embattled towns. He had met Nelson and conferred with the other leaders, listening to rumours and spreading them and planning nothing. It was Papineau who had told Gagnon of the base that did not exist at St-Césaire. With O'Callaghan as his constant shadow he had come to Brown at St-Charles, and had left again before the British arrived. He had been across the river at St-Marc, still with O'Callaghan beside him, on the day the British came. Sitting his horse on the riverbank, clouded by drifting smoke, he had seen St-Charles destroyed.

There had been a last conference with Nelson and after that O'Callaghan had disappeared, to reappear in Vermont. Papineau himself had returned to his sister's home, and had lingered there till the night of December 4. He had only moved when the sleighs drew up with the troops. When the knock came at the door and Lysons began his search, Papineau was crawling off through a snowy ditch, making his way to some

89

woods back of the farmyard. He had reached friends, found a sleigh and a guide, and driven as near as he dared to Mississquoi Bay. Then there had been miles on foot through marshy woods, a search for a boat as he came to the shore of the bay, and finally a last malevolence as he reached safety. Crossing the rough water to the southern shore in Vermont, he had fallen hard while getting out of the boat and had entered the United States with a sprained ankle.

Nelson had clung on, after the disaster at St-Charles, watching his own town empty itself away. By the morning of December 2, with Gore on the march from Sorel, there were hardly a hundred people in St-Denis. There was no food, there was almost no ammunition, and there was nothing to be learned anywhere that offered a ray of hope. The seething, rumorous countryside knew more than Nelson now, and the flush of the first victory was long gone. Those who could were huddling into their homes, and the homeless were taking to the roads in search of safety. There was no safety in the homes of St-Denis; everyone knew that now. Even the woods were better than the doomed village, and the few remaining families wanted to be gone. They wanted Nelson gone; perhaps without his presence there would be at least something spared.

Half a dozen of the leaders were still with him, and some had come from St-Charles. There were the two Cartiers and Bonaventure Viger, and there was Jalbert and there was always Brown. They gathered in a last council on December 2, and by noon they were plodding south. It was fifty miles to the border and the country between was thick with loyalist patrols; in a few hours the party decided to break up. The Cartier brothers went off, to winter in a friendly farmhouse on Canadian soil. Jalbert was soon captured. Bonaventure Viger, the expert woodsman, was taken close to the border. So were several of the others. Brown managed to cross, arrived in Vermont half dead, and recovered to continue south as far as Florida. For ten days, with the help of an Indian guide, Nelson fought his way down through swampy woods. He was taken by volunteers on December 12, exhausted by cold and hunger after ten fireless nights. Bound fast and bundled into a wagon, he was hauled first to Mississquoi and then to Montreal, where jeering crowds paraded him on to jail.

"Nos têtes sont en jeu maintenant..."

At Quebec, on December 5, LaFontaine had again asked Gosford to recall the Assembly. He had been told to frame a formal request in writing. On December 16 he submitted a petition signed by fourteen members, and it was declined the next day. Few noticed by that time, for the talk of papers and parliaments had been drowned once more in gunfire.

SIX

The Grand Brûlé

"In the county of Two Mountains," Colborne had written the War Office on December 7, "the *habitans* are still in arms, and I shall not be able to send a force to occupy the villages of which they have taken possession till the season is more advanced."[1] With the Richelieu valley quieted he was looking to the northwest, and here the winter freeze-up had become the key to his movements. He intended to march by rivers and he wanted solid ice.

The two mountains, Calvaire and St-Joseph, were low, wooded hills rising from the north shore of the Lake of the Two Mountains, which became the Ottawa River a few miles to the west. On the northeast the lake narrowed again into the Rivière des Milles Iles and flowed on, some twenty miles to the northward of Montreal, to empty into the St. Lawrence. Beyond this line of water, and enclosed by one of its curves, lay a triangle of rich land that sloped gradually upward into the foothills of the Laurentians. Much of it was still uncleared and one of the stretches of forest around the mountains had become known as the "Grand Brûlé", from a fire of years before. There had been seigneuries here, however, from the days of the French régime, and a cluster of large villages had been mellowing for half a century.

To the northeast of the triangle, just below the first rising of the Laurentians, there was Ste-Thérèse-de-Blainville, and Lachute was to the northwest, on the North River. The town of St-Eustache, nearer the Two Mountains, was the largest and most distinguished. Twenty-five miles from the Ottawa and the boundary of Upper Canada, it lay along the banks of the little Rivière du Chêne which meandered down from the northwest to empty itself, under the shadow of the twin bell-towers of the church, into Rivière des Milles Iles. It was surrounded, like all the villages, by thick woods and served by abominable roads, but it had grown leisurely and well. The fur brigades had passed it in the old days of the trade, making west for the Ottawa and the *pays d'en haut* beyond. Many of the early loyalists had come this way, and some had stopped nearby. There were British settlements in the region, and a few families in the village, and they had got along with the French. Religion and language had posed the eternal barriers, but there had been a living for all. For years the fine church and presbytery, standing with their backs to the river and facing a well-paved square, had looked out over prosperous farms and orchards and acres of good pasture. In addition to two private schools and a newly completed convent, there were flour mills, sawmills, carding mills, and a profusion of substantial homes. St-Benoit, eight miles to the northwest in the heart of the Grand Brûlé, and Ste-Scholastique, fifteen miles north, had also been centres of comfortable rural affluence.

They were hardly that now. They had their cholera cemeteries, and they had suffered like the rest of the province from the years of poor crops. But it was the war between *patriote* and bureaucrat, and the proximity to Upper Canada, that had been of most effect. The Ottawa ran too near and Britishness lapped across it, creating disturbing currents. The land-grabbers and the placemen had done their work here, shrivelling up the first goodwill of the region. Seigneuries had changed hands, and the new master of the habitant had become the Tory squire. The prosperous French Canadian, wishing to remain prosperous, had become more and more British. It was the same with the office-holders and the seekers after office. There began to be the Chouayens and the *vendus* — the sellers-out to the conquerors. The resentments of lesser men hardened them into *patriotes* and as reform became republicanism the rebel-haters developed.

Division had been slow to come, and it was never total. There had been English, Scotch, and Irish fighting with the French against bureaucracy, bad government, and the hard hand of Torydom. There had always been French upholders of the established order, wishing to keep what they had. Yet little by little the ground of politics had shifted, changing the geography of battle and re-dividing the people. With each stormy election of the past five years, the mass of the British had parted from the mass of the French. From the English and Scotch settlements and the settlements of Irish Orangemen, and even from Glengarry County across the Ottawa, the club-swingers and the stone-throwers had appeared in support of *bureaucrates* who had managed to equate their cause with that of the King. The French had met them with stones and clubs for Papineau, and the rancours had not healed with the post-election bruises. Each side had committed the occasional outrage with a barn-burning or a house-burning, and raids and threats and reprisals had begun to divide the region into sullen camps, always rubbing together and always hostile. The miasma haunting the countryside had thickened over the villages, and it had closed down in its fullness during the tumultuous summer of 1837.

Papineau had come this way in early June, with the last session of Parliament still ahead of him and the wave of fury building over Russell's Ten Resolutions. He had visited St-Eustache and St-Benoit and had gone on to a great meeting at Ste-Scholastique, enriching the memory of thousands with the flags and banners of the procession and with the angry music of his voice. There had been other voices too. It had been an occasion arranged by Jean-Joseph Girouard and William Henry Scott, the two deputies to the Assembly for the county of Deux-Montagnes. They had ridden beside the leader that sunny day, the one tall and grave, with the dark, commanding authority of an Indian chief, the other shorter and slighter and a fiery, flaxen Celt. "This man," wrote one of Gosford's informants, reporting to him on Girouard, "is a Rousseau in principle and a man of much influence and talent. He is one of the most dangerous men in the province and may do infinite mischief in his closet, but he will never take the field."[2] Scott, to the same informant, was "a wicked little fellow who would fight if required".[3]

They were descriptions given by an enemy, and were not known in this place. The men were. Girouard, at forty-two, was a notary of St-Benoit, an intense and brooding dreamer with the deft hand of an artist. Amid the tumult of the times around him he was to produce some notable sketches. He was the son of a widowed mother who had served as housekeeper to a long line of curés, and had brought him up in presbyteries. She had not quite made him a man of the Church. With a passion for education and a lust for freedom, he had found the faith difficult and the bureaucracy unendurable. Yet he had remained a friend of priests, and he had been no enemy to the English. Drawn inevitably to politics and inevitably to Papineau's side, he had sought to tear down *bureaucrates* by the quiet voice of reason. If he looked beyond that downfall to a state without a king, it was to be achieved by due process and the work of dedicated men. Yet it was certainly to be achieved. He did not burn barns and did not advise their burning, but he was not to be turned aside by such excesses. The truths conceived in his study must prevail.

It was the same with Scott, the merchant of St-Eustache. He was thirty-four years old, and he had settled with his parents in the town while he was still a boy. He had prospered among the French, been accepted by them for all his stubborn Protestantism, and had found his own resentments a part of theirs. He had fought the monopolies and land-jobbing and the social and family cliques that ruled the region, and it had led him on to Parliament and again on to Papineau. He was not to be shifted away, this adamant little dogmatist, with any of the other shifters. Right was right, and the resolutions of Russell were clearly wrong. What a British Parliament had done it must be made to undo, by that ever-faithful instrument, the voice of an aroused people. On the rostrum at Ste-Scholastique he had spoken as bitterly as Papineau — more bitterly than Girouard — and he had been cheered by the aroused people from its fifteen hundred throats. All the leaders had been cheered, and been lifted high by the sound. They had left, inspired and inspiring, at the end of that great day, and gone on to other rousings while the fruit ripened behind them.

"I have resided for eighteen years in the said parish," deposed Duncan M'Coll of St-Benoit on July 11, 1837. "We have always lived in the greatest peace and harmony with our Canadian neighbors until the time when a certain political meeting took place at Ste-Scholastique. Since that meeting our Canadian neighbors have even ceased to speak with us . . . and indeed with all the inhabitants of British origin. My brother Donald is a blacksmith; he formerly had very good custom from the Canadian farmers; since that meeting he has had only two jobs from two Canadians, and these two, for having employed him, have had the manes and tails of their horses shaved . . . my brother John is a grocer . . . the Canadians or those who call themselves patriots have withdrawn their custom from him . . . no Canadians are allowed to remain in our service . . . I verily believe that spies are set over us . . . Louis Bourguignon, yeoman of this parish, said that I had better go over to their party, *qu'il né arriveroit malheur* . . . I verily believe that the said Louis Bourguignon conspires with divers others to drive out my father and brothers and all the English inhabitants . . . I therefore demand for us justice and protection."[4]

It was only one of the demands, in French as well as English, that were flooding the desks of authority in Montreal. There were no reports from the other side of the quarrel, and they were not sought. By early autumn the refugees were coming, flying from their barred-up houses, bewailing their lost possessions, demanding instant vengeance. The Grand Brûlé and the villages lying round it had extended their leaders' teachings and were well beyond the leaders. They were divesting themselves of the loyal now, without regard to tongue. They had deposed magistrates, defied warrants, and sent Gosford's bailiffs packing. With their own elected officials they were now a republican commune, assembling their own army. Scott the angry deputy had become a protesting Colonel, "élu par le peuple" against his will. Girouard of St-Benoit, with his spacious home a headquarters flying the death's-head flag, was presiding over a revolutionary committee, with what mixture of emotions no man knew. Jean-Olivier Chénier, the doctor of St-Eustache, seemed now to be the man who was leading both the leaders, and mid November had brought them Amury Girod. Strangers came to the village by every road, and in the frozen fields around them there was always drilling and marching. Bands of armed men, continually on the prowl by night, were stripping the farms of cattle and the houses of men and guns. Where donors proved reluctant there were stones and shots through their windows, and hesitant recruits were marched off with the patriotes, *qu'il né arriveroit malheur*. There was no measuring the strength gathering in the villages; it melted away each morning and grew again at night. But it reached out, or it might reach out, from its centre in the Grand Brûlé to the Laurentian foothills and as far east as the Richelieu. It remained a thorn in the side of Montreal. As the latest refugees came in with their stories they were creating an edge of panic.

Colborne was not in panic, but he knew what he meant to do. To the west of the Grand Brûlé were Chatham and Grenville, centres of angry English. To the southwest was St. Andrews, bitterly loyalist too. In the Gore, north of Lachute, were the ever-to-be-trusted Orangemen and to the south across the Ottawa were the highland Scots of Glengarry, always the King's men and already itching to march. It was an ominous ring of loyalism and it would not be without support. At Carillon, the meeting-point of the Ottawa with the Lake of the Two Mountains, there was a detachment of regular troops under Major Townshend. They had been part of the force brought down from Upper Canada, and Colborne had stopped them there.

Townshend would march when Colborne gave the word, with his small detachment of regulars and the volunteers from the settlements. The Commander himself would move from Montreal. He had edged forward already to the Rivière des Prairies, and was holding a bridge at the village of St-Martin. Beyond that was a ten-mile march through treacherous, wooded country to the Rivière des Milles Iles. He would be expected there and he would not find bridges standing; he was almost sure of that. But he would .rrive, when the weather served him, not quite as expected.

2

On November 15, after parting with Papineau and O'Callaghan at Varennes, Amury Girod had set off for the

Grand Brûlé. He had left, according to his journal, with the stately injunction of his wife ringing in his ears: "Go to thy duty and think not of me. I would prefer to see thee dead on the field of battle, than to see thee abandon the cause of the country."[5]

In mid afternoon, en route to the field of battle, he had stopped for refreshment at a tavern "where I found people dancing. After having danced I threw myself down to rest till six o'clock, and at nine I set off."[6] An hour or so later he had reached the village of Ste-Rose, the principal crossing-point of the Rivière des Milles Iles. It was served by a substantial bridge and the Grande Côte road was on the other side of the river, winding along beside it to St-Eustache, just ten miles away. Girod, however, had apparently felt the need of further rest. He had stopped on the near side and quartered himself for the night with Father Turcotte, the parish priest. Here he had found another visitor, not particularly congenial, who was to loom large in his future.

The Abbé Jacques Paquin, curé of St-Eustache, was a bulky authoritarian in late middle age. He was distinguished for learning as well as for his great obesity, and along with both went a considerable sense of humour. Waddling about the parish under his broad shovel hat, or more often travelling in state in a handsome carriage, he had been able to laugh at himself along with his people. The confident arbiter in politics as in all the village's quarrels, he had leaned for a while toward Papineau, but he had stood firm for order. The decision of public questions was to be made by due process, under the authority of a state that had always protected the Church. Little as he liked the *bureaucrates* of his flock, he had applied the rod impartially when *patriotes* went too far, and he had become the subject of ribald *patriote* hymns:

> "Ce gros ventre, joufflu, bouffi,
> Poussé par le mauvais esprit,
> Craignant pour sa dime et sa clique,
> N'ayant pas d'autre politique,
> Trompant ses pauvres habitants
> Qu'il voulait vendre à leurs tyrans."[7]

It had all been tolerable and part of the life of a priest, who was usually kicked by the sheep he kicked toward heaven. For the most part they had followed his guidance still. The familiar ranks of officialdom had held fast with the Church serene above them. The tall red pole, standing on a well-kept lawn, had denoted the home of the local militia commander, always a substantial citizen and usually allied with the curé in keeping peace. Now it was all changed, and there was little left of the Abbé's sense of humour. Papineau had gone mad, and was being sought for high treason. Girouard and Scott were making revolution, or were having it made for them. The poles were all chopped down, or they were flying rebel flags. Meetings of village hotheads, who had long been too well known, were swollen with strangers now from God knew where. They were holding elections and legislating chaos. Peace had departed the parish, the peaceful were leaving with it, and the curé was powerless and isolated. He had come to discuss his worries with Father Turcotte, and he did not welcome the arrival of Amury Girod. This *soi-disant* soldier, brandy-reeking and truculent, was an all too obvious sign of what was coming.

The conversation was acrid and was soon cut short. The Abbé returned that night to his presbytery in St-Eustache. Girod followed next day, announcing himself to the village as the commander sent by Papineau. Here too the welcome given was not effusive, for he was little known to the multitude and too well known to the leaders. But he had blustered his way through tougher men than these, and he was soon exuding orders. Jean-Olivier Chénier, now possessed of a sword, remained as talkative as ever and a little jealous of authority. But he was utterly loyal to Papineau, and he obeyed in Papineau's name. Scott, the reluctant Colonel, who had been pushed beyond his depth, could not believe that Girod was Papineau's choice. But he had less faith in himself in his present role, and somebody must command. Girod at least was a soldier, or was said to be a soldier.

The soldier rode on that night to St-Benoit, and inspected the camp there. It was seething like St-Eustache with restless men, carrying clubs and forks and demanding guns. He promised them guns, ordered them out to the country to fetch men and provisions, and "commenced drilling the elected officers". On November 18, after a day in St-Benoit, Girod returned with Girouard for a general council of war in St-Eustache. The farmers, notaries, and medical men, who were all elected officers, debated for five hours. Proceedings were often punctuated by the arrival of sweating couriers, there was much marching in the streets, and there were reports on new contingents who were expected from neighbouring regions. In spite of it all, Scott remained gloomy and dour. He was depressed by the lack of legality and more by the lack of arms, and he suggested consulting Papineau as to the next course of action. Girod was firmly opposed; he was here to speak for the leader. Chénier was fretful and difficult, and inclined to the making of speeches that had all been made before. He dissected his enemies in the parish, stormed at the firm hostility displayed by Abbé Paquin, and was for instant rigorous measures against the waverers and the weak. But he had little else to propose in the way of action, and there was a steady drop in the temperature between himself and Girod.

Girouard discussed the warrants that had now been issued, for himself, Chénier, and Scott as well as Girod. Bailiffs might soon be expected, perhaps with troops in escort, and for his part he was ready to accept arrest. Events had strayed from their due and proper course, and must be put back in perspective. The only intent was peaceful agitation, and it was directed to lawful ends. There were no rebels here, and he was not a leader of rebels. He could establish that, he believed, by his own submission. He was instantly shouted down; the proposal could not be thought of. It would destroy confidence, it would put an end to recruiting; it would invalidate all the elections of the past month. If bailiffs and soldiers came they would be chased off, as others had been before them. The might of an aroused people would determine its own intent.

Girod hastened to agree with this consensus. He was far from being accepted, either as politician or soldier, but he was the man fresh from Papineau. He could impart the broader reasoning that lay at the heart of affairs. Political pressure on the government had become military pressure, though it might not lead to war. Papineau was on the Richelieu, and the army there would soon be master of the valley. There would be arms and men and munitions from the United States. It would be the same here when the army of the north was built. The garrison in Montreal, threatened from two directions, would capitulate without a shot. The frightened government in Quebec would soon give way, and the Canadian republic would be a fact by spring. He dismissed the thought of danger from British troops;

there were not enough to defend the Richelieu valley. Here in the north, behind the barrier of the river, there would be time for arming and training the coming thousands. Recruits must be hurried in, provisions piled up, and spies and traitors weeded out of the ranks. In the meantime, he suggested, all boats on the south side of the river should be brought across, and the bridge at Ste-Rose destroyed.

3

Some boats had come, but the bridge was still standing, when a message arrived that put it out of mind. It was Papineau's circular, issued from St-Denis, calling for a national convention on December 4. The leader had destroyed the original and forgotten the escaped copy, but it clanged here with confidence and the ring of the old times. On November 23, the actual day of the battle at St-Denis, the elated chiefs of the north discussed the summons. The place set was St-Charles, and Girod was ready and eager to go as delegate. Girouard, however, was the man chosen by his colleagues, and he left the following morning, relieved and hopeful. There were to be high politics again, then, and debate and resolutions, instead of this whirling talk of guns and bridges.

He was hardly well on his journey before he was summoned back. The greater news had arrived, and it was military; the die was cast for war. A British force had attacked at St-Denis, and been routed and driven off. There were a hundred and ninety-seven British dead, an unknown number of prisoners, and at least three field guns among a mountain of other spoils. The reports grew more exuberant as later messengers came. The retreating troops were throwing away their weapons, deserters were melting off; there was hardly a British soldier left in the region. For Girod, who had been elected to "command the forces" while Girouard was away, there was no relinquishing of title as the politician returned. He was now firmly in the saddle, growing with every rumour, and the decisive letter arrived from Montreal. It was written by Robert Nelson, Wolfred's brother, and it told of a city in panic with almost no defences.

"So," records the journal of the commander of the forces for the night of the 24th, "I determined upon going the following day to Montreal, to storm it."[8]

The tocsin rang in the morning and all roads, now beginning to be sprinkled with the first snow, were thick with arriving men. They brought with them, however, some sobering considerations. The stripped farms had produced few new weapons, and "as everyone commanded and no one obeyed, the arms fell God only knows into whose hands."[9] There were no sleighs or wagons arriving from the Richelieu with the fruits of victory there. A few cattle were being driven in for slaughter, the tavern doors were swinging and there was much clanging of anvils and melting down of lead. But there was little powder for the bullets and hardly a man in ten was equipped to fire them; the only supplies that were plentiful were beef, whisky, and rum. The council of war that morning chilled the General, and his jubilation faded. His march on Montreal became a raid, three nights later, on the Indian mission at Oka, by the Lake of the Two Mountains. He left with Scott and Chénier at the head of four hundred men and returned the following morning with a total of twelve shotguns and a keg and a half of powder. He had also sobering words from the Indian chief. "Brother," said the tall Iroquois, "you come upon us at a moment when our young men are away hunting. But they will return for revenge, I promise you that."[10]

Even before this there had been other news for Girod. He did not dare to believe it, and he could not allow it to spread. But it was trickling out already as a first scattering of fugitives began to appear from St-Charles. There were rumours of great defeat around the General, blotting out all the confidence he had built on St-Denis. They could only be blustered down, galloped over, as he drove his foraging parties about the country. He was more insistent now that the bridge at Ste-Rose be destroyed. He was more afraid of spies and the spreading of rumour. Pillage became more necessary as the cry for arms grew louder. There was much pillage, and much dragging in of men, a re-ransacking of houses and more raids on the farms. Yet in spite of patrols and picquets the camps gathered in the villages began to dwindle. The dragged-in men slunk out. The walkers on roads at midnight were usually walking away. The word came in from other towns that had promised large contingents; they could not be expected now.

The General mustered reviews and bellowed orders, bellowing rumour down. The bad news from the Richelieu was all false; it was being spread by spies and traitors. Arms would come; they were certainly on the way. There must be more order; there must be more discipline, for weaker folk were sick of the army's ways. An end must be put to pillaging without official sanction. He spoke from a fine new saddle on the back of a splendid horse, one of the many now retained in his stable. He himself "lived like an emperor and demanded service like a pasha",[11] but there would be chains, flogging, and hanging for lesser men who stole. For the good men and the fighters there would be the wealth of the new republic. There would be a choice of the best lands, there would be no more tithes to the Church, no more dues to the seigneur, no more fear of the English. For himself, he said, he would be glad if the English did attempt an attack; he would be master of Montreal a day later.

Yet he was seen less often now in St-Eustache. St-Benoit lay to the north, farther away from the river and Montreal, hidden in thicker woods. It was nearer, perhaps, to the hostile English settlements, but they were the lesser danger. Their volunteers, if they came, would have a long march through woods, and there were entrenchments dug in the bush round St-Benoit. Before St-Eustache there was only the open river, already filmed with ice. If a blow fell—and a prudent man must think of it—this camp to the north would be the healthier place. It was the healthier place now. In St-Eustache there were only Scott and Chénier, the one suspicious and hostile, the other a babbling fool. In St-Benoit there was always Girouard waiting, though he no longer knew for what. There was also another presence, the Abbé Etienne Chartier, a vivid, comforting contrast to Paquin of St-Eustache.

The curé of St-Benoit, Chartier had been a lawyer at twenty-seven, and according to his own account a man of the world. He "had not been brought up in a shoe, and he had seen the girls."[12] At twenty-eight he had forsaken law and the girls in favour of the priesthood, and in the nine years that followed he had been rapidly in and out of six parishes. He had also served as director of a classical college, and had been dismissed for anti-Englishness and his novel methods of teaching. Since 1835, when he came to St-Benoit, his rich voice, rolling out from the pulpit and dominating public meetings, had been first a recruiter of *patriotes* and then a call to arms. It was not to be silenced now, even by his own bishop, and the word from St-Charles had only added shrillness. Never at peace with authority, always at war with the English and now at odds with most of his brother-priests, he had burnt too many bridges to retrace his steps.

The men Girod could depend on were becoming more valuable now, as they became scarcer. Scott was no longer one of them, and even Girouard seemed to be growing strange. The one man fully trusted by all the village, he remained an enigma wrapped in his own brooding. There was still that urge to surrender himself, to place his neck in a noose, as if the pull of a rope could make a peace. He was curt with Girod and often at odds with Chartier; he could see no armies forming and he would not invent them. He was afraid of volunteers from the English settlements, of troops from Montreal. He was dreading fire and slaughter, as who was not? The thought was growing even in General Girod.

The General's musings circled that nightmare now, more and more. It swam in through the brandy haze, and chased him across the country. But there were other fears too, and they were nearer shapes in the flesh. They were around him at every march, each review, clouded in acrid smoke from stubby pipes, wearing the long-tailed toques, the rough coats, the great hide boots and mittens. There were still many of them yet, these farmers, hunters, and woodsmen, drifting from camp to camp, following and believing rumour, awaiting the arms that would make the new republic. They were big men, simple and angry men, with their pouches of homemade bullets and their forks and chopped-off scythes. They had been promised much and they were eyeing the promiser now; it would not be easy to escape them. Better to lead them still, wherever it led.

The Abbé Paquin remained in St-Eustache, harbouring his own thoughts. Through the last weeks of November he had worked with one aim: to empty the town of every soul who would go. He had thundered warnings from the pulpit, his presbytery doors had been open night and day, and the stacked treasures of the departed filled its rooms. The carriages and wagons and sleighs had streamed off, with the walkers plodding along among them, clutching the hands of children, bent under bags and bundles. Each day there had been a few more doors and windows boarded up, a few more empty benches at morning mass, and the sick quiet in the streets had grown more ominous. Yet each night there had been the tramp of returning *patriotes*, marched back by Chénier. It was Colonel Chénier now, setting his guards at crossroads, raiding the distant farms, herding his shouting strangers into the halls of the new convent.

It had been the Abbé's latest achievement and greatest pride, this just-built school to be filled with teaching nuns. The quiet voices would not be heard there now. Chénier had taken it over on December 1. He had stalked into the presbytery and snatched the keys from his priest, against Paquin's flat refusal to hand them over. On that next evening, Saturday, December 2, Chénier had come to his final break with Scott. He had been standing in front of the convent with sixty or seventy men when Scott had appeared to urge them all to disperse. Convinced at last by the rumours welling from the Richelieu, Scott had abandoned hopes of armed resistance. The men should make for their homes or take to the woods, they should be anywhere but here. Chénier had shouted him down, Scott had shouted back, and though the brawl closed with darkness it had resumed the following morning.

On the church doors that Sunday as the congregation came out from high mass, there had been a proclamation from Gosford enjoining peace, and another listing the rewards offered for the heads of rebel leaders. The vicar had read them solemnly for those who could not read, and Scott had climbed the steps to repeat his warnings. He had been dragged down and hauled to the convent doors, to be ranted at and belaboured and threatened with clubs and guns, and to remain as stubborn in his fears as he had once been in his hopes. He had escaped at last from the tumult, a despised and broken man, but many who kicked and cursed him had later drifted after him. Only Chénier remained, ranting and still unshaken, surrounded by a dwindling remnant, and keeper of the fortress now.

That evening, Sunday, December 3, Father Turcotte of Ste-Rose arrived at the presbytery. He had come with news from St-

Charles and it was final: the *patriote* cause on the Richelieu had collapsed in total ruin. Paquin listened to the end, and sent for Chénier. His vicar, Father Desève, went off for others. By the time Chénier arrived, sword in his belt, there were Scott and several of his friends with the three priests in the room.

Scott counted for nothing now; he was only bent on escape and he had said so. The lesser men were wilting as Turcotte repeated his news. Paquin looked at Chénier; he had married the man and baptized his one child. He had respected him as a country doctor, deplored him as a politician, and fought with him and prayed for him as an errant son of the Church. Chénier had been unimportant among older, cleverer men. But he was important now, for the cleverer men were going, or they sat blank and bewildered as they saw the end of the road. There was only this man left with what had made him, the will to live of oneself, the iron, instinctive purpose that had somehow survived the Conquest. It was eyeless, angry, and desperate, it had come to this absurd sword; and it would still survive this ruin. The old priest, looking at the young man, was warmed by the long thought. But there was no other warmth here. The face set as he pleaded; the answer came with the old, wild rush of words. The news from St-Charles was false; Chénier had heard of a victory. Even if it had been defeat, there would be arms and money yet. Papineau had not been heard from because he had gone to the United States; he would soon be marching back with thousands of men. The priest was a traitor now; there were spies and traitors everywhere, turning the people away. As Scott and the others prodded at him, driving their facts home, Chénier dissolved abruptly into racking sobs. But he rose to his feet again with the sword drawn, striking the familiar attitude — "one might as easily bite the moon as change his mind."[13]

4

By the morning Scott was gone. The Abbé Paquin, with a frightened crowd in the presbytery, was packing for Montreal. There was nothing he could do here; he might, perhaps, do something with the authorities there. He had only the one word to those who begged for advice: "Go—now. Go while you still can." On the steps outside there was a ragged tramp of men, and Chénier appeared at their head, sword in hand. He had allowed Scott to go and there would be passports for all these others, the weak men and the fear-spreaders, the women, and the old and helpless. But the priest would have to stay—he was the head and heart of this parish.

Paquin stayed, and the Vicar Desève stayed with him, semi-prisoners now. They drove out each night, through the riot and confusion of the town, to sleep at a nearby farm owned by Paquin. Each morning they returned to the church to say mass, and to open the doors of the presbytery to hungry, frightened visitors. On December 5 the first alarm came. There were the red coats of a cavalry patrol on the far bank of the river. By ten o'clock they had vanished and at eleven Girod came, swept along with the men from St-Benoit. They stormed in on a milling crowd in the square, recovering from near-panic. Chénier had left them leaderless in a search for more recruits, and as he came back he had high words with Girod. But the church-bells sounding the tocsin were falling silent, and danger seemed to have passed. The assembled army melted into the taverns, and the General rode the wave of confident relief. There was a re-inflation of authority and a new assertion of command. The priests had left for the farm at the sight of the troops, they had urged the people to follow them, and much of their other conduct was not to Girod's taste. That night a hangdog trio arrived at the farm, with orders to bring Paquin to the General's presence. Paquin refused the summons, the three returned with the refusal, and were at once sent back to shoot him. It proved to be a night, however, for forgetting orders in taverns, and the firing squad dispersed with its work undone. Girod himself seemed forgetful when he called the following morning, oozing assurance and charm. Soldiers in the heat of battle were given to harsh words; he begged the priests to forgive him, he trusted in their support.

On Friday the 8th, the feast of the Immaculate Conception, the church was packed to the doors. Somehow, gauntly, desperately, the parish clung to its ways. The roads filled for the Holy Day, the people came to town. But they found Chénier's recruiting squads on watch by the church steps, and some of the men were bustled into the ranks. Many were gone by morning and went quickly back to their homes, but the lesson was well learned. There were soon families hiding in camps in the woods, and at mass the following Sunday the church was almost empty.

Monday the 11th brought the second alarm, followed by a surge of confidence that ran about like a fever. As a cavalry patrol appeared, apparently testing the ice, the tocsin began its summons and couriers spurred away for St-Benoit. The square in front of the church began to fill, and Chénier mobilized fifty men with arms. At the head of these he crossed to the far shore, and though the patrol vanished ahead of them the *patriotes* remained for the night. They advanced on the 12th to seize a crossroads tavern and establish a post there. On the morning of the 13th, with Chénier striding ahead of them, most of the force came back to St-Eustache. They had met no enemy soldiers, but they had recognized some of the horsemen chased away. They were not British cavalry. They were only the frightened Tories who had deserted St-Eustache, the *chouayens* and *bureaucrates*, hiding under red coats. Girod received the news sitting his tall white horse, and around him now there were fifteen hundred men.

They had followed him from St-Benoit or materialized from other camps, and they were becoming a little frightening. The weather was growing colder, and the winter was closing in. It was harder to live on a country that had been almost scraped bare. The mittened hands were tiring of homemade weapons, and the ears under the toques had heard enough. There would have to be fulfilled promises or there would have to be better promises, and in the General's situation there was only the one choice. The men were cheering the word from Chénier's patrol; Girod himself was much cheered up by the noise. His voice soared out, guttural and thick as always with its German-and-Italian French. Over the demand for guns, the shouts for action, he appraised the situation and propounded his latest view.

It was now clear to Girod that there had been no victory for the British along the Richelieu. There had been rumours of nearer troops at St-Martin; they were false too, or almost as good as false. The bridge there, halfway along the road from Montreal, was held by the dressed-up *bureaucrates*, who patrolled and ran away. Montreal itself was lying open behind them, defenceless and disaffected. The time was therefore ripe for the great attack—Girod would urge his views on the council of war—and the voices rose over him, shouting all counsel down. As dusk closed in on the evening of December 13, a third of the fifteen hundred had drifted off. But a thousand were left to march in grand review, sated by fiery speeches, quickened by fiery liquors, and headed by drums and fiddles. There was to be a march tomorrow night on St-Martin, and from there the force would advance on Montreal.

Girod, as usual, returned to St-Benoit, followed by most of his men. There would be much mustering tomorrow in the northern region, and many matters to see to. The Abbé Chartier, however, remained behind, unchilled by a freezing welcome at the priest's farm. Usually a rare visitor in the Abbé Paquin's parish, he had been much about the village for the past two days, everywhere making speeches. He had spoken this night at the side of Girod and Chénier, and he was still buoyed up by the cheers. For Paquin's acid comments on the lack of weapons he had only an impatient shrug. There would be weapons enough, and glory enough, when Montreal was taken. He had another shrug for the interdict of his bishop. If he was now to be deprived of ecclesiastical authority it would give him greater courage. He retired a little hungry, for the farm had been stripped of almost all its food. But he went with a sardonic smile for his fusty colleagues, who would not be sharing the fruits of the new order.

About eight o'clock next morning the priests drove into the village. Desève said the only mass in an almost empty church. By nine the few faithful were hurrying away to their homes, and the priests sat down to a lean and cheerless breakfast. Outside the presbytery couriers were galloping off and men who had been billeted in the convent emerged yawning and stretching. There was a first trickle of arrivals along the roads, Chénier appeared in the square before the church, and three or four hundred of the *patriotes* were soon gathered around him. It was a good day for a mustering, clear and cold, and there was no particular hurry. The march, if it took place—and it began to seem unreal in the morning light—would not begin till dark. It was about eleven-thirty in the morning when distant bugles were heard.

They were answered by the tocsin from the belfry, and bells in the distance began to take it up. Once more there were red-coated horsemen across the river, filing along by the ice. The sight, as usual, created confusion in the square, but this was the third alarm. Chénier's voice rose confidently over the babble; it was only another patrol to be chased off. He called for men and started down toward the river, with a hundred or so following. In a few minutes they were well out on the ice, filtering among the islands that obscured the view. Shots began to be heard. They were desultory and there were long silences, and nothing seemed to be happening. The patrol had either gone off or it was hidden by the far islands, and Chénier's men were vanishing among them too. There was a snowy pounding of hooves along the road from St-Benoit, and Girod came galloping up to the crowd in the square. There were no men following him, but he readily explained that. St-Benoit, he said, had been warned of a coming raid from the English settlements, and his men might be needed there. They would not be needed here; he was all confidence. The affair would be over in an hour.

The Abbé Chartier had come on the run from the presbytery, and heard the words with relief. Among the houses of the town, half empty as it had seemed, there were shutters and doors opening and horses being led from stables, but the first anxious shouts were settling to quiet. The men in the square were joking edgily now, and some were moving to join those on the ice. Then there was another murmur; shots were crackling again.

Chénier's men were beginning to reappear, breaking out from the islands, stopping to fire, and turning and running back. There was red following them now, the coats of a file of horsemen, threading among the islands and lengthening as it came. The men in the square who had been starting down for the ice stopped short and watched. Then there were other shouts and they were turning away and pointing. They were looking to the northeast, along the near bank of the river, where the Grande Côte road came twisting down from Ste-Rose. There was not much to be seen there, among the thin woods and the snowdrifts, but there was a heavy stir of movement and suddenly a hard, flat sound. A field gun had barked and there was a roundshot skidding on ice, plunging among Chénier's men. The men were breaking back, scattering along the riverbank, and most were running for the square.

The gun barked again, and there was a growing rattle of fire from mid river. The file of horsemen was inching raggedly forward, fed from the far shore. There were bugles now on the left, from where the sound of the cannon came, and the last houses of the village were emptying themselves of people. There seemed to be so many still, in spite of every warning; the old who would not move, the young who had stayed with parents, the wives who had not persuaded stubborn husbands. They were all persuaded now, they were frantically hitching horses into sleighs, while shouting people on foot went hurrying past them. The men in the square watched with the tocsin jangling above them, and abruptly most of them broke to join the rush.

Chénier came from the riverbank, trying to stem the flight, leading a few and driving some before him. Girod circled bellowing, sitting his splendid horse, beating at running men with the flat of his sword. He was urging them into the houses around the square; they were all stone, every one was a fort. There were men running for the convent, and Chénier was pointing at the church. The Abbé Paquin and Desève came by in their sleigh, shouting for all to follow them or scatter for open country. Girod turned on them and cursed them, and the sleigh went on for the farm. Suddenly the Abbé Chartier was racing after it, his cassock hauled to his waist. He did not catch the priests, but another sleigh drew abreast of him and he made a grab as it passed. There were half a dozen children crammed in the low-slung box and two women on the seat, whipping a lone horse on. He caught it up and was into the box, piled on top of the children. But, true to himself, he did not stay there long. The horse was poor and the children seemed very heavy; he was soon making better time on his own feet.

Girod glared round at the tumult, his mouth still spouting orders, as the rifles cracked from the river and the gun smashed from the road. There were two guns now, he recognized the second sound, and behind the guns was an endless blur of red. Muskets and burly greatcoats, horses and plumes and wagons; the woods were disgorging horror. There were still a few men about him, yelling for guns, for help. Fists waved, hands tore at his saddle, and he was suddenly beating them off. He was reining the horse round, settling into a gallop, knocking the screaming stragglers out of his way. The screams rose, bullets came whistling after him, but he was hunched well down in the saddle and making hard for the north. The square behind him, littered with cast-off clubs and trampled snow, had become almost empty. There was only Chénier with his rusty sword, beating the last men ahead of him into the church.

5

Around noon on the day before, Wednesday, December 13, Colborne had ridden out from Montreal, accompanied by a sizeable staff. Riding in escort with him was a troop of eighty horsemen, some of whom had been seen a few days earlier along the Rivière des Milles Iles. They were, as they had been reported to be, *bureaucrates* and friends of *bureaucrates* from the county of Two Mountains. Having left the region as much-discomfited fugitives, they were returning now as loyalist volunteers. Their captain, the seigneur Maxime Globenski, was a descendant of Polish fur traders who had settled in St-Eustache and prospered there. Long at odds with the *patriotes,* he had been one of the dispossessed when trouble came. His comfortable manor house, the largest home in the village, was now a rebel headquarters, and he was not sweetened by the thought. Most of the men under him were reflecting on similar losses and shared the captain's mood.

There was ground too for the reports of agitation in Montreal. The city was almost stripped of regular troops and a daily crop of rumours grew in the streets. The quiet in the Richelieu valley seemed too much to believe, a descent from the Grand Brûlé was considered always imminent, and the latest alarm had bred in another region. The northern rebels, it was reported, were sweeping around the city, joining with men who were coming up from the border, and preparing to attack Lachine. All day, after Colborne's going, there was a zestful mobilization of volunteers, who had been armed and left behind. The bearskin-helmeted squadron of the Lachine volunteer cavalry had galloped to hold its post along the river, conveniently located beside Laflamme's Tavern. At sunset, crossing the water in a file of Indian canoes, came the warriors from the reservation at Caughnawaga, with their long-unheard war whoops filling the evening air. On Place d'Armes that night, in the heart of the city itself, four thousand official and unofficial volunteers stood waiting the call to action. They stood down in the morning, however, their services not required.

Colborne had spent the night at St-Martin, some ten miles northwest. Here, around his bridgehead on the Rivière des Prairies, he had established most of his troops from Montreal and reinforced them with others as they returned from the Richelieu valley. By dawn of the 14th the camp was melting away. Files of infantry and cavalry and lines of wagons and guns mounted on runners were emptying into the snowy road for the bridge. By eight o'clock the first of the brigades was across, commanded by Colonel Maitland of the 32nd, with three hundred and fifty men of his own regiment and as many of the 83rd. The second brigade followed, commanded by Colonel Wetherall, with a battalion of the Royal Regiment and most of the artillery and cavalry. On the far side there was a pause in the frosty sunlight, as cursing teamsters were cursed into position and the troops muttered and stamped under the cloud of their own breath. Then, as the shouts and orders began to dwindle, Colborne cantered down to the head of the column. His staff joined him, and the force was under way, some eighteen hundred strong. With the six guns and the rocket troop, the ammunition and baggage wagons, the blood-red ambulance wagons, and the sleighs with timber and tools and stores and rations, it rippled along the road for two miles.

There would soon be another column, thirty miles to the west, moving on a converging course. It would not be as crisp and military but it would be as large or even larger, and whatever it lacked in discipline it would make up for in zeal. Major Townshend at Carillon, in charge of the volunteers from the English settlements, had been finding it hard to hold his men on leash. His troubles were now over, for they had been ordered to march today.

The usual route to the north was by way of the Ste-Rose bridge. It was only slightly damaged, patrols reported, and it could be repaired in a few hours. Colborne ignored the reports and the bridge alike. The column was grinding along through fresh snow, among scrub woods and a scattering of deserted homesteads, by a market trail that linked up the back concessions. It was called La Petite Ste-Rose, it wound northwest to the Rivière des Milles Iles, and it was served by no bridge.

113

When the first troops reached the bank about ten o'clock they were faced by a glaring sheet of empty ice. But they were just three miles downriver from St-Eustache, and across was the Grande Côte road.

There had been a detachment of horsemen sent off an hour earlier. Globenski's volunteers, separated from the main force, were working their way to the river by other trails. When they emerged from woods, as they had on earlier patrols, they would be directly across from the village and highly visible. They were meant to be; they would provide useful diversion.

As the main force came up, the crossing of the river began. Colborne had moved promptly and accepted an element of risk, for the hard winter freeze-up had only begun to bite. But he was totally unopposed, apparently not even sighted, and there was ample time for the work. The cavalry walked across, each man at an interval of ten paces and each leading his horse. The infantry threaded out in single file, well-spaced and breaking step; and behind them, all unhitched, came the artillery horses and wagon horses, led by gunners and teamsters. The guns themselves, and the vehicles, were hauled over by ropes. The only mishap of the crossing came as shots were heard in the distance. Globenski's men had been sighted from St-Eustache, and there was a first burning of powder. It was too much for an elderly artillery major who was still waiting with horses hitched to his wagons. He started across at a gallop, ordering the tumbrils after him, and there was a thundering rush of action in the best style of his youth. It was broken in mid ice by a decisive crack, and a wagon with its rearing horses and its cursing, lashing drivers began to settle into the river. The major hurtled to safety on the far bank, and was shrivelled by a glare from Colborne. Within a quarter of an hour, however, men lying flat on the ice and hauling on long cables had recovered the wagon and saved the men and horses.

On the Grande Côte road the first brigade was already re-formed and moving. By noon the head of the column was approaching St-Eustache. There was more firing ahead, and it was from the ice in mid river; Globenski's patrol was doing its work as planned. As he came in sight of the village and could see the skirmish on the ice, Colborne ordered a halt. He was still covered by woods, but they were beginning to thin out. The road ran straight for the village, opening off to the right on snowy fields and with the river close on the left. He had a clear view, broken only by a cluster of little islands, of the rebels now engaged with the volunteers. He ordered two of the guns to the head of the column, and roundshot roared away. Within ten minutes, as they screamed over the islands and slithered and plunged in ice, they had put an end to the fighting. Groups of rebels were stumbling back toward shore, and there were splashes and strings of red on some of the islands. The volunteers were establishing themselves to prevent escape by the river.

The surprise, such as it was, was now over, and the column advanced into full view of the town. There were scattered shots as a few men ran from the ice to attack the vanguard, but they were quickly swept aside. As Colborne halted again, and the second brigade closed up, there were only the distant church-bells and a confusion of distant voices. He could see people in flight by all the roads, there were some running in the fields beyond the little Rivière du Chêne, and a few were out on the ice of the larger river, scattering from the volunteers. Most of the houses seemed to be standing empty, with no smoke from the chimneys and snow thick on the roofs, a sign of no heat inside. But the tall spires of the church rose in front of him, a mile or so to the west, dominating the little avenue by which the road entered the town. He could see the square in front of it and the cluster of houses and buildings near about, all of them large and strong. There was certainly commotion there, and it would have to be dealt with. The church looked away from him, facing north, toward the main street of the village and the road to St-Benoit. He meant to close that road. He dispatched Maitland's brigade on a long march to the right, with orders to throw a cordon around the town. Wetherall was to follow Maitland, with two guns. Fire would be opened meanwhile, with the four remaining guns, on the houses around the church in the central area.

The enormous Congreve Rocket was also to assist the guns, and it provided a brief diversion. It had been an eccentric weapon in the Peninsular War, and again at Waterloo, and the elderly sample that had been stored for years in Canada had not improved with age. As the match was applied to the fuse the rocket took off, with instantly disastrous results. From its first lift it went into a sudden dive, barely skimming the top of a

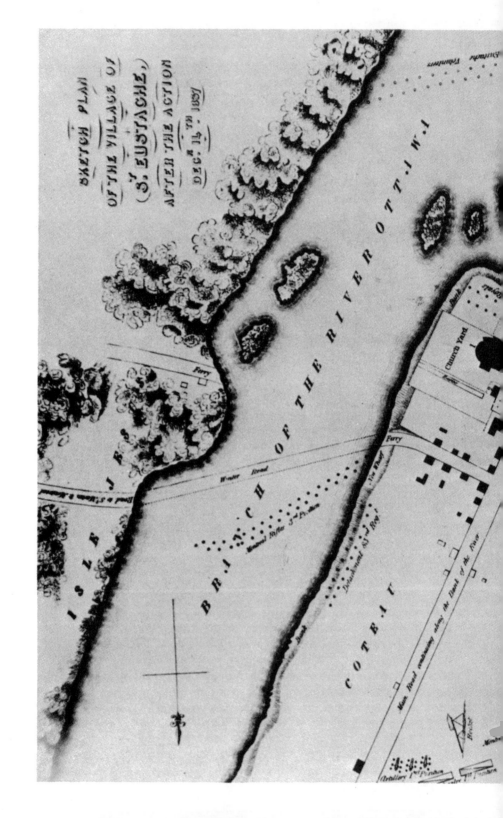

SKETCH PLAN
OF THE VILLAGE OF
(S.ᵗ EUSTACHE,)
AFTER THE ACTION
DEC.ᵃ 14.ᵀᴴ 1837

British Volunteers

ISLE JESUS

BRANCH OF THE RIVER OTTAWA

Road to S.ᵗ Martin & Montreal

Ferry

Water Road

Montreal Rifles 3.ᵈ Position

Detachment 83.ᵈ Reg.ᵗ

The Wharf

Ferry

Bank

Church Yard

Main Road running along the Bank of the River

Artillery 1.ˢᵗ Position

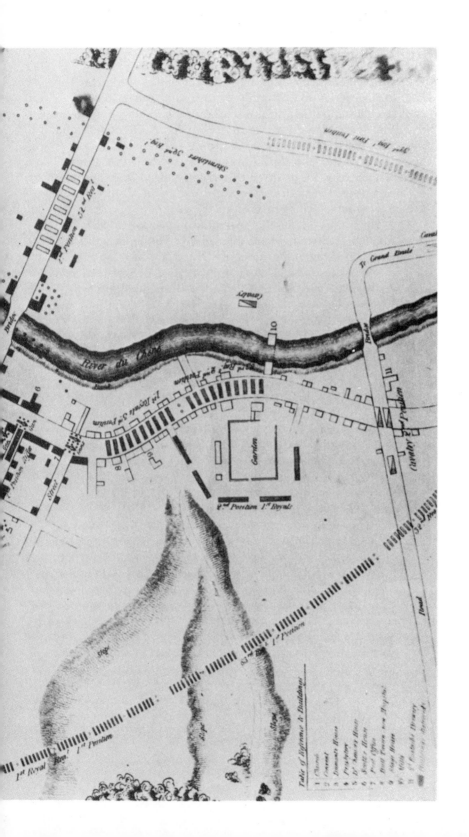

wooden fence and shearing away its tail as it passed over. The head spun down to the ground, still very much alive, and circled a ploughed field to come tumbling back. It roared in on the headquarters staff, scattering them in all directions, and then proceeded in chase of a volunteer. The regulars watched, fascinated, as he dived in a snowy furrow and the monster sizzled over him to go up with a final bang. When the man resumed his running it was in the direction of Montreal, and few of the troops blamed him.

The guns opened as the interlude came to an end and Maitland's brigade moved off, followed by Wetherall's. It was a long and difficult circuit around the fringe of houses and barns at the village limits, and the men struggled over fences and across streamlets and bridges, often plodding along in waist-high snow. The bombardment roared behind them and the smashed houses to their left were disgorging rebels, some of whom straggled out to fire on the troops. But most of them were soon scattering to escape the closing net. By noon Maitland had crossed the road to the north, sealing off St-Benoit. By one o'clock he had worked his way down Rivière du Chêne to its junction with the Milles Iles, and St-Eustache was surrounded.

The guns had stopped by now and there was a smoking silence over the target houses. Most of them seemed deserted as the acrid, grey-black clouds drifted away. Wetherall's brigade, close on the rear of Maitland's, was stopped by new orders as it reached the road at the northern end of the town. Wetherall was to turn left, following the main street, and proceed down toward the church at its southern end.

As he came with his two guns, his infantry broke away on either side and skirmishing parties entered the battered houses. They were all empty and the careful advance moved on, approaching a jog in the street that prevented a direct view southward. The guns came round the elbow and Wetherall stopped them. He was facing the church at musket range now, and he could see that the doors were barred. The glass had been broken out of the upper windows and wood nailed across, leaving only slits for firing. The building appeared to be occupied and to be made ready for defence, and there were similar signs in the presbytery and in the convent on the other side.

He gave the order to fire a warning round, and the reply was prompt and devastating. As slugs, bullets, and buckshot

118

whistled about them, the infantry took to cover and the guns were hastily withdrawn. From the comparative shelter of the little angle in the street, Wetherall sent a courier racing off to Colborne who was waiting on the Grande Côte. The report was hardly necessary, for the General had heard the firing. As the two guns re-opened from behind the elbow, the four at the entrance to the village joined in. For the next hour, supplemented soon by withering blasts of musketry, roundshot crashed and rebounded against the stone walls of the church.

The infantry worked forward again, picking their way as before from house to house. At the same time Maitland's troops closed in. There was almost no opposition, except from the church, the presbytery, and the convent, and in all the buildings facing them the riflemen were soon established. They were pouring fire into barred and smoking windows, but they could not get across the square. At every sign of movement barrels poked out from the narrow slits in front of them and bullets and buckshot swept the open ground.

The stone walls of the church had only been gashed by the roundshot. The great oak doors, though they had been battered apart and separated, were still standing in place. They were blocked on the inside by two of the church's heavy iron stoves and by a mass of wooden benches. In the great vault of the interior there were seventy or eighty men. A few were at the side windows on the lower level, facing east and west. Most were in the galleries and choir loft, looking on the main street. Some of them had broken already and some were now breaking under the steady thunder of shot and whistle of lead. "We have no guns!" some of them had screamed at Chénier as he herded them in through the doors. "There will be dead soon," he had given them the grim answer, "you will be able to use theirs."[14] There were dead now, and there were men using the weapons they had dropped; not all of them were breaking. Shut in their stone trap, beaten mad by the guns, they were fighting still with the man who had led them there. He was keeping the pledge himself that he had made long before. He had been one of the minor speakers on that far-off bright June day at Ste-Scholastique. "What I say to you," he had said, "I believe and I will do. Follow me, and you may kill me if you see me run away."[15]

Outside, the crash of the musketry was rising to a new pitch.

The volunteers, on the ice behind the church, had been working their way forward and had begun to attack the presbytery, which was connected by a covered way with the church itself. It had very few defenders, and as the volunteers closed in on them they leaped through windows facing away from the river. It was a sign to the regular troops in front of the building, and they broke forward and entered. Lieutenant Wetherall of the Royals, the son of his commanding officer, was the first man inside. He dashed for the iron stove that heated the big front room, kicked it over on its side, and spilled out live coals. As he piled on mattresses and blankets flames licked up toward the walls, and in five minutes smoke from the blazing building was drifting across the square. The face of the church was masked and there was no view from the windows.

Wetherall's father was quick to seize his chance. In the buildings facing the church men broke out from their cover, and infantry advanced at the double along either side of the street. Some of the platoons swung left to attack the new convent and it was soon ablaze and cleared. Its last fighters, out on the ice of the river, were dodging among the islands with the volunteers in chase. The flanking buildings were taken, the troops had forced their way to the edge of the water, and only the church remained.

The young Wetherall by now, with two of his brother-officers, had come by the covered way to the back door. They battered it down and found themselves in the sacristy. There was still firing from the main body of the church, and now a commotion of axes smashing timber. All the *patriotes* had retired to the galleries and choir loft and were chopping the stairs away. Wetherall and the two officers, followed by a handful of troops, pushed on from the sacristy and around the back of the altar into the gloom of the lower level. At first they could see nothing, for there was hardly any light from the barred windows and the interior was filled with smoke. Then they made out beside them the statue of St-Eustache, the Christian warrior, tall and strange in the dimness and standing quite undamaged. They moved on past the statue, and a rain of shot from the galleries drove them back. Sheltering behind the altar, they began to smash at the woodwork and heap up splintered sticks. They added vestments from the sacristy, sprinkled them over with gunpowder, and struck flint to the pile. Then, with the fire well started, they turned and ran from the building.

Outside in the smoky twilight the church was now ringed round. The volunteers with other squadrons of cavalry were closing in from the river. There was a solid mass of infantry distributed along the front. The ground by the presbytery was held, and on the other side among the gravestones of the little cemetery that lay between the church and the convent there were lines of waiting men. They were standing or kneeling there with fixed bayonets and many of them wore the insignia of the 32nd, Jock Weir's regiment. The word was already running along the ranks, "Remember Jock Weir."[16]

From the church, as the dry wood of the interior began to blaze, came the glow of fire and the screams of desperate men. Some were leaping from the windows, or hanging over the galleries to drop to the lower level. Many who dropped were trapped in the flames beneath them, and those who went out by the windows faced steel and flying lead. A few escaped in the smoke and gathering dusk, but there was no quarter for the others. They dropped to rise to their knees with arms upraised, but the guns blazed in their faces and the bayonets drove home. It was too much for the officers and they fought to control the troops but the cry rose over their voices, "Remember Jock Weir!" Chénier's voice was the last heard in the church, calling for some to follow him as he slipped through the narrow window of the Virgin's chapel. He was trying to make for a ditch behind the cemetery, but he was hit as he touched the ground. He was found under the window about six o'clock that evening, with a musket ball in his heart. To a British soldier, who took the stock from his neck as a souvenir, he seemed "a genteel looking young man about twenty-four years old".[17] Battle and death apparently had not aged him, for he was actually thirty-one.

Firing had almost ceased by five o'clock, and as dark fell there were only a few stray shots from middle river. There were volunteers on the ice there, still in pursuit of *patriotes*, but most of the horsemen were galloping about the town. Some had discovered their own houses burning along with others, and some were in search of well remembered rebels. It was a night for settling scores, rooting out men from cellars, and chasing the last shocked stragglers who flitted from street to street. The roof of the church fell in at six o'clock, and smoke rose till morning from the gutted wreck of the interior. There was smoke everywhere at dawn as the Abbé Paquin and Desève returned from the farm, guiding their sleigh carefully around the puddles of reddened slush, the smouldering masses of cloth and charred timber, and the bodies and parts of bodies. They discovered Father Turcotte, who had been there most of the night ministering to the wounded, and for a while they joined him in his work. From there they went on to the prisoners, huddled in icy barns, and from there again to the church to probe the ruins. There was little left to be sought for, and the little would have to wait, for the stone shell was a furnace and the embers were red hot.

The shrouded body of Chénier lay on a counter in Addison's Tavern, opened by British surgeons to discover the cause of death. There were seventy other dead, not so distinguished, and the wounded were receiving treatment as they were found. It was slow work and long work and it was left not quite completed, for at eight o'clock the bugles sounded assembly.

At nine the force moved off for St-Benoit. There was a barricade on the road, which was brushed aside, and a ditch that had been dug beyond it was bridged in a few minutes. As the vanguard approached the village Colborne ordered a halt. Fourteen men were standing in the road ahead of him, holding a white flag. They were, they said, a deputation of the town's principal citizens and they had come to request peace. All the houses behind them were hung with white flags, and there was now no thought of resistance. Colborne asked for Girouard and the other rebel chiefs, but was told they were all gone. He ordered the fourteen back to those who had sent them, carrying grim instructions. Every species of firearm was to be collected and given up. The people were to assist his officers in the search for wanted men. If there was one shot fired, he warned them, the village would be destroyed.

He slept that night in Girouard's house, and ordered it burnt in the morning. There were a few other houses, identified now as belonging to rebel leaders, that were also marked for destruction. The ransacked cellars of the town had produced guns and men; probably the bulk of all that remained in hiding. With his work done, Colborne ordered his troops to prepare to march.

But there were other helpers now, fresh from the west and north. Major Townshend had joined the day before, with his one company of regulars and his two thousand volunteers, the English and Scotch from Chatham, Grenville, and St. Andrews, the Orangemen from the Gore, and the tall Glengarry Scots from across the Ottawa. They were fired by a long night's work of search and scouring, all were bellowing with loyalism, and most were roaring drunk. The General left them there, in possession of the helpless town, and did not look back at the smoke that rose behind him. The pillage began as the rearguard filed away, and the last stripped house was a mass of flame by night. The ruin sprawled in the morning, a black blot on the countryside, with its church befouled and desecrated, its ashes still smoking, and clusters of vague-eyed homeless picking among the ruins. Wearing the church vestments, riding the stolen horses, high on the loads of plunder, and driving the cattle ahead of them, the volunteers went home.

Colborne returned with Wetherall's brigade by way of St-Eustache. On the 17th he arrived in Montreal. He had stopped en route to meet the Abbé Paquin, and had granted a gracious interview. He would order reprisals by loyalists to be stopped in St-Eustache, and would leave officers and troops to see that the order was obeyed. As to St-Benoit, he was regretful and philosophical. "It is scarcely possible to suppose," he was to write later to the War Office, "that the loyal and peaceful subjects whose property had been pillaged and who had so recently suffered from the outrages committed by the rebels of the Grand Brûlé ... could be prevented, on being liberated from their oppressors, from committing acts of violence."[18]

Maitland's brigade, on leaving St-Benoit, had been detached on a northern route. It came with its stern panoply first to Ste-Scholastique and then to Ste-Thérèse, and was met with white flags everywhere and with humbly submissive greetings. There were loyal protestations from former rebels, and in Ste-Thérèse from one recently converted there was word of W. H. Scott. He was hidden, the man said, in a farmhouse near the town, and when Maitland dispatched a cavalry patrol the informer proved correct. Scott went on with the force, chained in a baggage-wagon, to be displayed as one of its trophies when it entered Montreal. "The measures taken by Your Excellency," Maitland reported to Colborne on December 20, "appeared to me to have the most beneficial effect in restoring good order and tranquillizing the minds of the people."[19]

6

By that time the dead of St-Eustache had gone to earth, unblessed and unforgiven. "Sans cérémonie, les corps sont jetés au cimetière des enfants morts sans baptême."[20] New civil magistrates were assuming neglected duties throughout the region and restoring the forms of law. Lesser rebels sat in the country jails, while others left in consignments for trial in Montreal. Meanwhile, for others still, the search went on, and across the Lake of the Two Mountains, forty miles from his home, Girouard was living out his days of freedom.

On the morning of the 14th, as Colborne's troops were approaching St-Eustache, Girouard had been concerned for St-Benoit. There had been many warnings from Carillon of the approach of volunteers, and he was sure it was now imminent. He had gone off on a long patrol through the woods, and had seen enough to confirm all his forebodings. Girod had left in the meantime, summoned to St-Eustache, and by the time Girouard returned he was galloping back. The guns could be heard behind him, and he was blubbering of death and slaughter. He had obviously run from one battle and intended to continue running. At the word of volunteers from the English settlements he had dissolved in hopeless panic.

Girouard had cursed and threatened him but had allowed him to gallop off, a bloated wineskin shrinking down in his saddle. There was no help in Girod and there was no help in himself, either for the friends around him or the friends in St-Eustache. He could not lead men to a hopeless, useless massacre, and he had now no way to save them. He could only stay and die. Yet the friends still clamouring around him would not have it; they were not prepared to die. With the volunteers on the one side and an army coming on the other, there could be no more thought of fighting. It had not been Girouard's thought, they said; he must make that clear to the authorities.

He must escape and reach authority for the sake of all his people. Somehow, somewhere, he must find them a way to peace.

He had let them bundle him off. He had spent that night in a house of frightened women, not five miles away. He had watched next night from the woods outside the town, and he had seen the peace he found them. He had wandered on from the burning, day after blank day, finding a friend everywhere and never finding comfort. He had crossed the lake to Vaudreuil, and there had soon been patrols following. He was twenty miles southwest of it now, freezing in a friend's sawmill near the village of St-Polycarpe, and once again he was offering up his life. Wherever he came, he said, he brought danger; there was no point and no hope in continuing. The friend was a poor man and the reward was high; Girouard wished him to have it. There was no such bargain struck and there never would be; on Christmas day Girouard walked alone to an English magistrate and gave himself up.

Girod had come to his end a week before. As he galloped away from the church in St-Eustache he had risked a stop for brandy on the road north, and he had found the tavern dangerous. There was smoke and gunfire rising in St-Eustache; why was the General here? He had slithered out of the tavern and made for St-Benoit. He had slithered away from Girouard and kept on pounding north. But he had encountered suspicious *patriotes* marching south, and they had turned him round to lead them. There had been a pause at another tavern, with the firelocks all laid down, and he had gone off to relieve himself and scuttled through an open window.

With his horse gone, he had come in a stolen sleigh to Ste-Thérèse, and from there to Pointe-aux-Trembles below Varennes, close to the wife who had sent him off to battle. He was not to see her face, if he ever sought it. Everywhere he came the word had come before him; there was no safety at home, there was no safety with friends. There were no friends; "On me fuit comme la peste."[21] By the 17th he was at Rivière des Prairies, begging for help or shelter or a guide across the ice. There was no help, and the ice was thick with patrolling volunteers. He was back that night at a house in Pointe-aux-Trembles, and before dawn there was word of patrols again. They had been roused up by one of the old-time friends, and they were combing the little village house to house. The General crept through the streets dressed as a beggar, but the disguise did not serve long. As he edged away for the river there were horsemen cantering after him, and as he broke into a run there were more ahead, spreading on either side. He stood in his rags and tatters, watching the ring close. His sword was gone with his horse now, but he had managed to keep a pistol. There was a last, heartfelt cry, according to legend, "I don't want to die in prison like my father!"[22] Then he put the pistol to his forehead and it barked once, stilling that last fear.

He was taken to Montreal to be buried in the public way, in accordance with the grisly law of the times that governed deaths by suicide. The place chosen was the crossing of Sherbrooke Street with St. Laurent, and a stake lay across the body as it sank in the hacked-out pit. The frozen clods were shovelled back on top of him, and one of the watchers gave his epitaph: "It's all he deserves, that dog."[23]

SEVEN

"Une sorte de César sans emploi"

By December 22 the word of rebellion in Canada had reached England, spoiling the young Victoria's first Christmas as Queen. To the Whig government of Lord Melbourne, itself divided in factions and faced by the militant Tories of Sir Robert Peel, it posed a question of survival. "This is a fine occasion," wrote the acid diarist Greville, "for attacking the government and placing them between two fires . . . the radicals abuse them for their tyrannical and despotic treatment of the Canadians, and the Tories attribute the rebellion to their culpable leniency and futile attempts at conciliation."[1]

As usual, he added, neither of the claims was true. The easygoing Melbourne, who had succeeded Earl Grey as Prime Minister after the passage of the great Reform Bill in 1832, was as little inclined to despotism as he was to culpable leniency. He had had enough of reform, more than enough of radicals, and his main attribute, so far as colonies were concerned, was a total lack of interest. Whatever had been done in Canada under his régime had been done largely by Lord John Russell and Lord

127

Glenelg, the Colonial Minister. It seemed to have worked out badly and there would have to be changes made. They would probably have to be drastic, they would require a strong man, and they involved the question for Melbourne of how to save his government.

It was allied inescapably with the question of the radicals in his cabinet. They, no less than the colonies, would certainly have to be quieted. And looming beyond them was the shadow of the Earl of Durham, who was presently out of the cabinet but even more to be thought of. For two years, to Melbourne's intense relief, he had been far away from London as British Ambassador to Russia. Now, however, he was back, "une sorte de César sans emploi," as he was to be described later, "à qui il ne manquait qu'un champ assez vaste pour déployer ses grandes qualités de gouvernement."[2] Melbourne would not have used the flattering terms, but he recognized the abilities and the dangers of leaving them idle. "What to do with Durham" was again a political problem of the first moment.

John George Lambton, first Earl of Durham, was one of the richest peers in England and the son-in-law of Earl Grey. He was also, as he said of himself in his own inimitable manner, "one of those who see with regret every hour which passes over the existence of acknowledged but unreformed abuses."[3] He had led the fight for the Reform Bill of 1832, and it was largely because of Durham that the rotten boroughs were now abolished, the middle classes enfranchised, and the power of entrenched Torydom shaken to its very roots. He was cheered as "Radical Jack" by the great unwashed masses, and no politician could doubt the power of the nickname. He was a potential prime minister who had not yet reached for the heights, but who threatened the place of every man who held them. Anathema to all Tories, he was quite as abrasive to many Whig detractors, among whom Melbourne ranked high. Out of the cabinet or in the cabinet, haughty, sickly, rigid, and autocratic, he was equally unpredictable and equally dangerous.

He had returned to England from Russia two days after the accession of Victoria, and the first ceremonial act of her reign had been the investiture of Durham as Knight Commander of the Bath. The great sword of state had been too heavy for the little seventeen-year-old girl, and Melbourne had had to steady it as she laid it on the Knight's shoulder. With what he knew and what he expected of Durham, he might well have inclined to another use for the weapon, but forbearance promised rewards. If there was any Whig in England with a chance to succeed in Canada, it was probably this Durham. In any case, if he could be made to accept the mission, he would be three thousand miles from London. Melbourne summoned Parliament for January 16 and commenced the stalking of his man.

2

As the debate on Canada opened in the House of Commons, later dispatches began to arrive from Gosford. The troops, he reported, had now returned to their barracks, leaving garrisons in the restless centres. Armed resistance was quelled. "All the newspaper organs of revolution are now no longer in existence . . . Loyal Addresses are daily pouring in on me from the French Canadian population in all parts of the province."[4] In the United States President Van Buren had issued a proclamation enjoining neutrality and forbidding American assistance to the cause of rebellion. The Governors of New York and Vermont had done the same. Of the rebels taken in Canada, 112 had already been released and there were now just 169 remaining in the jails of Montreal and Quebec.

If the impression was reassuring, the actual conditions in the province were somewhat different. Gosford's statistics on prisoners did not include the thousand or so who were held in the rural regions, to be leisurely processed by magistrates and subjected while they were waiting to the sweets of local revenge. Even in the cities themselves, where the hunters-out of rebels were still at work, no friend of a *patriote* could consider himself safe. There were new charges flying and new searches inaugurated every day. There had been martial law in effect since December 5, the suspension of habeas corpus stilled the courts, and with the organs of revolution consigned to silence there was little but the press of the oligarchy, thundering for ropes and scaffolds. Montreal was a great armed camp through most of December, with a third of its men in uniform and parading as volunteers. Toward the end of the month, as Colborne disbanded some of them, they reluctantly surrendered their warm greatcoats, fur caps, and 2s. 6d. per day, but the amateur touch was only replaced by the professional. Three regiments of regulars, hurried up from New Brunswick in a bitter overland march, had arrived in Quebec and were moving to Montreal.

On December 24 a warrant was issued for Louis-Hippolyte LaFontaine, snapping the last tenuous link between the French Party and the government. By the 28th LaFontaine was out of the country, much to Gosford's relief. He was said to be bound for England to plead his case, and the Governor wished him well. Gosford, who had long since asked to be recalled and was daily expecting his summons, had as little enthusiasm for the arrest of LaFontaine as he had for the daily bellowings of the loyal press. The constitution under which he had governed the country was of no effect now and was soon to be formally suspended by an act of Parliament. The British party in the province was flatly assuming the end of "French domination", by which it meant the end of popular government. Gosford could imagine the result, and he could admire LaFontaine for risking a trip to England. He would certainly have agreed, if he had known of them, with the words that the French Canadian wrote to a friend: "Our adversaries move heaven and earth to deprive us henceforth of an Assembly . . . they may succeed if we are not watchful. In that case, at one blow, we should be true Acadians."[5]

LaFontaine had not been quelled with the quelling of armed resistance, and neither had others like him. In the Richelieu and Two Mountains regions the hopeless, leaderless people lay stunned and impotent. But the smoke of the burning villages had drifted far, and it had brought more than terror. Aroused by official savagery there was a new rage at officialdom, spreading in mute parishes under the froth of loyal addresses. It was deeper and far more bitter than the ripple of old resentments, and it needed no politicians to stir it up. It ran from mouth to mouth, farm to farm, washing around the garrisons and seeping under them. It was not blotted out in the cities by all the red of the troops. There were French-Canadian judges and French-Canadian magistrates who had held apart from Papineau but were not apart from this. Etienne Parent, the great editor of *Le Canadien* in Quebec, had been as steady an opponent of rebellion as any man in the province. He was as steady now in

Matthew, Baron Aylmer was one of Wellington's generals sent to govern Canada. By the time he left in 1835, the colony had been decimated by cholera and drought, and the British overlords had done nothing to provide relief. *H.W. Pickersgill*

Archibald Acheson, Earl of Gosford, governor 1835-37. His mission was reconciliation, but government paralysis forced him to suspend the Assembly and govern by decree. *T. Phillips*

Sir John Colborne was the general in charge of the defence of the colony. He led the military forces that quelled the rebellion and took over as Provisional Administrator in 1837. *Richmond*

The governorship of John George Lambton, first Earl of Durham was shortlived in 1838 but his 1839 report became a controversial and long-remembered document. Durham pressed for the union of the two Canadas and insisted that the last hope of *la nation canadienne* must be brushed away. *T. Phillips*

Thomas Storrow Brown was a New Brunswicker who had come to Lower Canada via the United States. He helped write the manifesto of the "Fils de la Liberté" and was general of the group's military section.

Wolfred Nelson was a burly English doctor and an ardent supporter of Papineau and his party. He commanded the volunteers who defeated the British troops at St-Denis. *J.-J. Girouard*

Captain Jalbert led the party moving a captured British officer from St-Denis to St-Charles and was present during the officer's brutal murder. When Nelson saw the blood on Jalbert's sword, he knew he had no other choice but to stand and fight. *J.-J. Girouard*

Jean Olivier Chénier, commander of *les patriotes* at St-Eustache—"What I say to you I believe and I will do. Follow me, and you may kill me if you see me run away!" *J.-J. Girouard*

Gosford's government spies told him that Jean-Joseph Girouard was "a man of much influence and talent. He is one of the most dangerous men in the province and may do infinite mischief… but he will never take to the field."

The same spies told Gosford that W.H. Scott was a "wicked little fellow who would fight if required." But when it became clear that the cause was a losing one, Scott earned the hatred of his followers by urging the rebels to disperse and save themselves. *J.-J. Girouard*

Patriotes had defeated a company of British regulars to the north at St-Denis, leaving Colonel Wetherall and his government troops to make their way through hostile countryside to St-Charles without hope of support. (above) They launched their attack on St-Charles on November 25 and overpowered the defenders in the town. (below) *C. Beauclerk (above and below)*

In mid-December 1837, Colborne moved troops and volunteers on the town of St-Eustache, northwest of Montreal. The town was surrounded and the road north to St-Benoit was sealed; at day's end the town's defenders were trapped in the burning church. (above) By the next day, the town had been reduced to a charred ruin. (below) *C. Beauclerk (above) P.J. Bainbrigge (below)*

Colborne's troops marched north to St-Benoit where the residents sued for peace and surrendered their weapons. After an overnight stay, Colborne left the town in the hands of 2,000 volunteers—English and Scottish—from Chatham, Grenville, St. Andrews, Gore and Glengarry. By nightfall every house had been stripped and burned to the ground. *J.-J. Girouard*

Odelltown, just north of the border with New York, was one of the scenes of renewed fighting in 1838. Rebels who had fled south regrouped, led by Wolfred Nelson's brother Robert, and once again attempted the liberation of Canada. Volunteers loyal to the British crown were better equipped and routed the attackers. *Dr. McCallum*

Dr. Jean-Baptiste-Henri Brien took part in the 1838 attack on Beauharnois at the start of the hoped-for revolution. While awaiting trial in 1839, he penned a confession that won him his freedom, but sent others to the scaffold. *J.-J. Girouard*

Originally condemned to death in 1839, Francois-Xavier Prieur survived internment in Australia and returned to Canada in 1846. At his death in 1892, Prieur was the Superintendent of Prisons for the Dominion of Canada. *Wiseman*

Chevalier de Lorimier, a Montreal notary, had been part of the first rising in 1837, taking refuge south of the border and returning to recruit and command in 1838. He was hanged on February 15, 1839. *J.-J. Girouard*

Louis-Joseph Papineau had been a member of the Assembly at the age of 25, and was its Speaker at 32. As leader of the French Party he had waged a tireless battle against the privileges of the *bureaucrates* and by 1837, he was the rallying point for all who demanded responsible government. Exiled after the 1837 rising, he returned home and to the Parliament of the United Canadas in 1845.
Napoléon Bourassa

Louis Hippolyte LaFontaine, a supporter of Papineau, was imprisoned twice during the uprisings, but soon returned to public life. Shocked by Durham's report, LaFontaine determined to overcome its purpose. He forged a partnership with Robert Baldwin of Upper Canada that set the course for the building of the nation.
J.-J. Girouard

attacking its real roots. He was speaking out, in the face of the rule of the bayonet for a return to the rule of law, in the face of triumphant Englishness for the unwon claims of the French. And around Parent and growing was the acid skill of the satirists, flicking the bayonet-wielders with a deft hand. The little humorous news sheets had begun to appear, almost too light to draw official thunder, but driving their needles home. "We are told," said one of them, "that Christmas day about four o'clock in the morning three old ladies came to the gate of the city at the end of the faubourg of Quebec. They came for the mass at dawn, armed with their rosaries and prayer books. They were held long enough to miss mass . . . but . . . persisted in their claim that they had no intention of taking the city."[6]

Colborne, who was soon to replace Gosford as Provisional Administrator, was thoroughly aware of the real mood of the province. But he was faced by other and more immediate problems. On the borders of the Richelieu country, in New York State and Vermont, there were hundreds of fugitive rebels from Lower Canada. They were clustering in large communities, returning in night-time forays to meet friends and maintain old feuds with enemies, and generally creating chaos along the line. The line itself had almost ceased to exist for practical purposes, since there were five American sympathizers for every Canadian exile. Worse still, the boisterous welcome to patriots was now extending west. On December 5 rebellion had duly come in Upper Canada. On December 7 it had ended in almost bloodless farce. William Lyon Mackenzie, leading the friends of democracy against the rule of the Family Compact, had achieved complete fiasco in an attempt to take Toronto. It was something else, however, as he became a leader in exile.

Arriving in Buffalo, New York, on December 11, he had immediately commenced recruiting among the American friends of his rebels. There were thousands of them along the whole line of the frontier, cherishing long memories of the War of 1812, impoverished by bad crops and hard times, inflamed by the wrongs of the patriots and even more by their prospects. The word was abroad that for every deliverer of Canada from British rule there would be three hundred acres of land and a hundred dollars in silver. It filled halls to welcome Mackenzie's coming, and it emptied listeners out of them as swaggering volunteers. On December 13, just two days after his arrival on

American soil, Mackenzie returned to Canada at the head of an invading force.

The objective taken that day was Navy Island, on the Canadian side of the Niagara River, within three miles of the Falls. It was obviously an excellent base for attacking Toronto or Kingston. The word that the rebel was here, with five hundred armed followers who were soon rumoured in thousands, was a torch in Upper Canada. The principal results of Mackenzie's first adventure had been a swell of blustering loyalism, a mustering of volunteers, and an inflow of regular troops. The result of the second was action. It was inspired by the high Tory loyalist, Sir Allan Napier MacNab, transformed from a politician to a commander of volunteers, and it was done with a burly Britishness that smacked of the long ago. On the night of December 29 a party of Upper Canadians under a Royal Navy captain crossed over to American territory, set fire to the steamer *Caroline* that had been used to supply the rebels, and set it adrift to sink just short of the Falls. Within a few days, as the roar of outrage travelled to official Washington, pin-pricks along the border had grown to be a threat of war.

For the invaders on the island itself, after the raising of the banner of Mackenzie's provisional government and the first magniloquent promises, there were lean rations, no pay, and steadily dwindling prospects. By January 15 the Americans had gone home, and volunteers from Canada had restored the Union Jack. But the cause of the *Caroline* flared along the border, politicians were bellowing, and restless soldiers of fortune were rattling swords for Mackenzie. There was new strength and impetus behind the hopes of real invasion. Not only in New York State now, but in Pennsylvania, Ohio, and on to Michigan, there was a roar of patriot recruiting and a clash of new-found arms. They came from the local gunsmiths and the shops of friendly merchants, and some were rumoured to have come from militia arsenals. There were even reports to Colborne from as far away as England, hinting that arms from Birmingham were to be landed in Alabama and smuggled north. How many guns there were, or how many men to use them, no man knew for sure. But Mackenzie's American generals were raiding Canadian soil, and the bumbled attempts of January were only a promise of more. By February 26, when Gosford finally took his departure for England, there was trouble or the threat of trouble from as far west as Detroit to as far east as Maine.

3

So far as Lower Canada was concerned, it centred now around the person of Robert Nelson, brother of Wolfred. The man was a brilliant surgeon and had always been a friend of *patriotes*, but he was a cranky, difficult autocrat who moved in his own ways. He had applauded the victory of Wolfred at St-Denis and been cast down by St-Charles, but he had stood apart, in rather besmirched innocence, from outright acts of rebellion. It had not quite saved him when the end of rebellion came. Hauled away from his practice, deprived of his boots and braces, he had spent some three or four days in a crowded jail. Though the stay was soon terminated for lack of substantial evidence, it had been long enough in his case to produce fanatic fury. "The English government," he had scrawled on his cell wall, "will remember Robert Nelson."[7]

It was becoming conscious of him now. Making his way to Albany through the crowds of *patriotes* seething in the border villages, he had quickly discovered Papineau, and despaired of what he found. The leader had come to rest in the state capital under the pseudonym of "Mr. Louis". He had been warmly received and was now being coolly avoided by high American officials. There were no armies visible and there was no talk here of arms. The great loans to be raised from American banks were not forthcoming. Papineau had been to Washington and to Philadelphia and New York, and had come back with nothing. He had been rebuffed by the French Ambassador to the United States, and he had failed to interest Russia in a war for the new world. He had no interest himself in the tumult of the upstate towns, or the plots of quarrelling exiles or the cheers of their Yankee friends. Doctor Côté was one of the principal leaders now, with Gagnon still assisting him, and others of similar stripe. Papineau distrusted their proposals and offered none of his own. He would not lend his countenance to their raidings along the border. He would not approve their program for a republic free of the Church, free of seigneurs and tithes, free of the claims of property. The abolition of seigneuries, said Papineau the man of property, would be pure and simple theft. He would not lead, he would not follow, and he would not change. He had nothing more to promise. Nelson had turned away from him in loud disgust, and was soon the first of the activists around the head of Lake Champlain.

By Sunday, February 25, 1838, he was reaching out decisively for a grip on the leader's place. "Papineau has abandoned us," he wrote to a *patriote* in Canada that day, "and this through selfish and family motives regarding the seigneuries . . . we can do well without him and better than if we had him, a man fit only for words but not for action."[8] Nelson, the man of action, was employing the Sunday well, and the letter went on to inform and instruct his colleague. There were high hopes and plans already in train, concerted with western exiles and with a sublime faith in William Lyon Mackenzie. "According to agreement," Nelson loftily reported, "M'Kenzie, with a large force and well provided for war, took up his march on Thursday evening last towards Upper Canada . . . last evening a slip from Montreal came to hand saying he had taken Kingston." With that firmly assumed, and with other developments in prospect, Nelson himself was moving. "Our force is abundant for our purpose, so if you can possibly co-operate our success will be easier of attainment. I would advise you to make your way with all possible speed to Three Rivers if you have men enough, when we shall by rapid movements join you after having rescued Montreal . . . we have the most positive assurance of a lively and cordial reception on our arrival."[9]

On the next morning, Monday the 26th, word came to General John E. Wool, commanding American forces in New York State and Vermont, that the militia arsenal in Elizabethtown, New York, had been looted of a thousand rifles and three cannon. As he began a search with his handful of regular troops, the weapons were moved to Alburgh Springs, Vermont. From there, on the night of the 27th, they went on to the Canadian border in the hands of Nelson, Côté, Gagnon, and three or four hundred *patriotes* and friends of *patriotes*. On the morning of the 28th, in a train of forty sleighs, the new army of invasion made its crossing. It advanced a mile from the border onto

Lower Canadian territory, and came to a solemn halt. A proclamation was read to the snowy fields, a Declaration declared the new republic, and Robert Nelson signed it as first President.

Some two hundred miles to the west, however, a wing of the far-flung plan was already drooping. The "slip" that had come to Nelson from Montreal proved over-optimistic. Mackenzie's force of invasion, numbering about five hundred and commanded by his latest acquisition from the unemployed Napoleons of the United States, had not quite reached its objective. Its nearest approach to Kingston had been desolate Hickory Island in mid St. Lawrence, just within Canadian territory. Here, through the freezing, snow-blown afternoon of February 22, General Rensselaer van Rensselaer, "a gin-sling, sottish-looking genius of twenty-seven",[10] had called for volunteers to march on the city. To the first call 83 had responded, but 12 had withdrawn at the second call and 48 at the third. By nightfall, with Kingston unassailed and reluctance become unanimous, the whole army of deliverance had been back on the American side.

At the Lower Canadian border, on the morning of the 28th, the halt of the *patriote* invaders became protracted. General Wool and his regulars appeared on the other side. Wool had established good relations with Colborne, and was aware of the latest developments in Upper Canada. Though he could not cross the line, he sent a messenger to Nelson, advising a prompt return to American soil. His advice was soon supplemented by Nelson's own emissaries who had been scouting the roads north. The lively and cordial reception was certainly coming, but it would be provided by tough, well-armed volunteers from Mississquoi Bay and by regular troops from St-Jean. The mile south to the border began to seem long to the men, and the country beyond it irresistibly attractive. By nightfall all had succumbed. The army had surrendered its weapons to General Wool, and Nelson, Côté, and Gagnon were bound for an American jail.

They were not to remain there long, and there was not much promise of relief. Colborne, now promoted to the rank of Lieutenant-General and Knight Commander of the Bath, had become Provisional Administrator as Gosford left the country. He much disliked the post; he was sick to death of Canada and had asked for recall for himself. On February 26, in response to

135

a hopeful suggestion by the Bishop of Quebec, there had been a day of public thanksgiving for the restoration of peace. It was followed a day later by a proclamation from Colborne continuing martial law. By the end of April he had selected the Special Council through which he was to rule the country. It was of the same mood and much the same composition as the earlier councils. The old men were still there, more rancorous now than ever and hated more. The old clamps were fastening again on the country, habeas corpus stood suspended, and prisoners waited in jails for trials that could not be held. They would have to be jury trials, the juries would have to be English and French Canadian, and there was no hope that any of them would agree on a verdict. It was too early for thanksgiving, too murky to see the way, and everything waited, in any case, for the coming of the new redeemer.

4

He arrived on May 27, coming upriver to Quebec in the frigate *Hastings*. The harbour was jammed with warships sent before him and the city was filled with newly debarked troops; power to support authority. There was a great booming of guns and manning of ships' yards to salute the arrival, and then a two-day wait. Officials and delegations boarded *Hastings*, but only silence came forth. It was the morning of the 29th before Durham came to be seen in the streets of Quebec, tall on a white horse, surrounded by a train of equerries, with Colborne riding beside him and followed by marching troops. Forty-six years old, spare and olive-skinned, with the grave and beardless features of an ailing saint, he was "High Commissioner and Governor-General of all Her Majesty's provinces on the continent of North America and of the islands of Prince Edward Island and Newfoundland",[11] and he looked every inch of it. "I owe protection to all, justice to all,"[12] he had told the House of Lords as he left England.

In the carriages following the Governor rode the twenty-two members of the party that had come with him in *Hastings*. It was of high status, and of mixed omens. It included Lady

Durham, daughter of Earl Grey, the man who had accomplished reform in England but had not done much for the colonies. The piquant Janie Ellice had come with her husband, Edward, who was one of Durham's secretaries and a nephew to Earl Grey. In addition to these connections his roots ran deep in Canada, since he was heir-apparent to the seigneury of Beauharnois, one of the richest in the province. His father, "Bear" Ellice, had enlarged a family fortune built on the fur trade and retired with much of it to England. There he had married a sister of Earl Grey and begun a career in Parliament while he maintained his interests in the colony. The Bear was regarded on both sides of the Atlantic not only as a merchant prince but as a political *éminence grise* whose advice no man ignored. He was well known, and hardly favourably known, to Canadian *patriotes*. He was not loved by his tenants of Beauharnois. He had been a prime mover in the attempt to unite the Canadas years before, and he remained unchanged in his views. He had been close at the side, more recently, of the men who had chosen Durham, and the fact was not forgotten by the French, who watched his son. "To those accustomed to public demonstrations in England," wrote Lady Durham in her journal at the end of that day, "the cheering might have seemed faint."[13]

British merchants and bureaucrats, also watching the procession, had equal cause for doubt. They saw in that brilliant entourage, coming as Durham's advisers, some of the foremost radicals and brightest minds in England. Charles Buller had a name for himself in Parliament, and he had made it at Durham's side. His brother, Arthur, though somewhat less distinguished, was quite as much a radical and as unbeloved of Tories. Edward Gibbon Wakefield and Thomas Turton had outraged British society by their lively marital experiences, and disturbed British politics with their lust for colonial reform. If they were to have free rein in Canada they evoked frightening prospects. There was change or the promise of change in all those carriages, breasting the slope of Mountain Street behind the man on the white horse. It was sensed as the procession ended at the drab Castle of St. Louis and the tide of newcomers swept along the halls, glittering with many orders, bristling with brains and authority. Lady Colborne, according to Janie Ellice, "seemed very much alarmed at us all. To say the truth, we are altogether a formidable party."[14]

Over them all, most formidable of all, towered the Governor himself. His first act, as he assumed the reins of authority, was to defy ancient tradition by dismissing Colborne's council. The old men glared and stuttered in furious disbelief, but the arms waiting as usual to enfold the new-come ruler had been brusquely lopped off. That done, with a council of five to serve as a rubber stamp, Durham began his work.

It was to be done, as he did everything, with a regal disregard for the common way. His magnificent dinners were served in a different style, and there was a new grace as there were new guests at his many splendid receptions. He rode abroad among lines of scarlet outriders, where Gosford had slumped in a carriage. He would have only eggs that were warm from the nest for breakfast, and no man spoke to his lordship till his lordship spoke first. Moody, sick, and irascible, he was bound for an early grave, and there could be a gravestone chill and dullness to an hour spent in his presence. He had no light talk, his attempts at humour appalled Janie Ellice, and at Durham family evenings one sat in paralysed silence or whispered behind one's hand. Yet for others on other occasions there was charm and fire and excitement, and a sense of new worlds. This man who towered in the present world would change it before he left. Or he would die making the attempt.

Charles Buller was closest to him, and the man most of his mind. Never, he believed, "did men embark in any public undertaking with more singleness and honesty of purpose. During the long period of our voyage out we read over all the public documents connected with the subject of our mission, and the dispatches, instructions and other papers with which the Colonial Office had supplied us; and very fully did we discuss all the various and difficult questions which it appeared to us that we should have to solve. . . . And I think I may also say that we had very few prejudices to mislead us."[15]

Only on one point, soon resolved, had there been a measure of difference at first between pupil and master. Buller had boarded the frigate thinking of rebellion "as having been provoked by the long injustice and invited by the deplorable imbecility of our colonial policy. But Lord Durham from the first took a far sounder view of the matter: he saw what narrow and mischievous spirit lurked at the bottom of all the acts of the French Canadians; and while he was prepared to do the individuals full justice, and justice with mercy, he had made up his mind that no quarter should be shown to the absurd pretensions of race, and that he must throw himself on the support of the British feelings, and aim at making Canada thoroughly British."[16]

It was thus and in this mood, "with very few prejudices to mislead us", that Durham released his advisers on Lower Canada. Their innumerable commissions of inquiry were to search out each malaise, and produce the facts for a cure. Fearlessly and without favour, no matter what the wreckage, they were to drag evils to the light. They were to build the plan of another day without them. Nothing was to be left neglected in the program of total reform, and all was to fuse at last into a new system of government. A people remade — and remade in the lord's image — was to rise in North America to command of its own affairs.

5

In the meantime, there remained the dregs of rebellion to clear away. The burnt villages could not be raised from their ashes, and there were hard questions from England about the need for some of the burnings. They would have to be answered by Colborne in the best way he could. There was no immediate remedy for the troubles along the border. But in justice tempered by mercy and administered with a high hand, there was hope of one solution of one problem.

The number of rebels still held in prison had by now declined to 161. Though he had released many others, Colborne could find no pretext for ridding himself of these, and they could certainly not be disposed of by way of the regular courts. British juries would hang them, French juries would free them, and mixed juries would never agree on a verdict. There remained, above all juries, the Governor General himself. He was much besought by the British party now, and had conceived a vast distaste for its loudest members. To the snubbed Tories of the bureaucracy he was adding Tory merchants, as colonial manifestations of all he meant to change. They bellowed for law on rebels and he would have to give them law. But it would be law of his own making, and it would be applied with his own hand.

Of those now reposing in the new prison at Montreal, completed just in time to receive rebels, seventy-two were classed as principal offenders. The élite within this group could be narrowed down to nine, with Wolfred Nelson and Girouard as the men standing at their head. They had come to the prison shocked, despairing, and exhausted, and there had been little within the walls to repair their mood. Colborne had gradually lightened the worst rigours and had permitted occasional visits from friends and families, but there had been lean comfort in that. The doubts overhanging him overhung the captives, and he had had little hope to offer them even if he had wished to do so. For almost six months, as men who were facing a charge of high treason, they had lived in the gallows' shadow. Toward the end of May, however, within a week of Durham's arrival, the climate began to change. The shadow retreated a little, there were discreet glimpses of sunlight, and the prisoners were quick to sense the warming rays.

Major-General Clitherow, the officer commanding in the District of Montreal, became a visitor to Wolfred Nelson. Mr. Simpson the magistrate, who had accepted the surrender of Girouard, began to drop in on him. Other dignitaries visited the other men. There was a new care for their comfort, and there were long discussions of the ills that plagued the province. It might well be the ills themselves, the visitors agreed, that had forced reluctant men to attempt rebellion. Their actions could not be countenanced but they could be better understood, and the new régime in Quebec was sympathetic. Lord Durham was well aware of the many causes, and intent on finding a cure. He was not disposed to revenge, he was disposed to clemency, but he required a confession of guilt from the nine leaders. With that given, there could be a proclamation of amnesty for all the others, excepting only Papineau, the rebels active in exile, and ten additional men accused of murder. For the nine who signed the confession there could be no official promises, but there were strong official hints. The prospect raised was exile, but it was exile only to Bermuda, and when conditions improved in Canada they might return as free men.

Everything turned on the "voluntary" confession, and it was

two weeks in coming. In the Castle of St. Louis at Quebec, with the Governor close at hand, Buller and Turton formulated the proposals. They were conveyed by the lesser emissaries, and at first rejected as they came. The nine were prepared to write, they were eager to write interminably, but they were not prepared to confess. They were all of them bitter men who had lost much, and they had had six long months to reflect on it in discomfort and degradation. They were most of them politicians, with a conscious eye on the record. There was much to explain to those they had brought down with them, and they did not choose to explain it to the satisfaction of Durham. He asked for a confession of rebels and he received a lecture by *patriotes*, dilating on all the evils they had sought to cure. The letter came back to the jail, not accepted, but the men who brought it remained persuasive and warm. There was much truth in the statements, but perhaps more than necessary. The real acts of rebellion had not been quite avowed. A revised letter was suggested.

It came to the Castle of St. Louis on the 14th of June, signed by eight of the nine. Girouard's name was missing; he had refused to join with the others, and had written his own letter. It was still unsatisfactory and was irritably dismissed by Buller as "an extravagant avowal of heroism and patriotism".[17] Nelson and the other seven, while remaining heroes and *patriotes*, admitted to "ambiguity" in their first statement and referred with as much more to their acts as rebels. It could only be called a confession by straining language, but the weary lawyers in the Castle were prepared to accept the strain. On June 24 the sun of clemency rose with a general amnesty, and on the 28th the sword of justice fell.

It was wielded by Durham with slight recourse to law. The eight signatories to the letter, at his suggestion, had thrown themselves on his mercy and prayed that there should be no trial to disturb the public peace. He had replied with an Ordinance of exile that consigned the eight to Bermuda, and with a proclamation of amnesty that freed all other prisoners but for the few specially excepted.

Both Ordinances were issued on his own authority, and neither was actually effective until it was approved by the British cabinet. But he would not abide delay, and he meant to assume approval. There was no legal precedent for a sentence of exile

141

passed without trial, and it could be construed by distant liberals as an act of outrageous tyranny. On the other hand, to high Tories in Canada, punishment would seem to have resolved itself into a stay on a pleasant island for eight bloodstained rebels. There was danger on either side for the noble lord but he was acting with a cool head, he was acting in the cause of peace, and he meant to act at once. He still had a measure of trust, though it was now dwindling, in the high-placed friends who had sent him out to Canada. He would appease many French with the basic clemency of the measures, and there was a growing mass of the British who would accept them if they brought quiet. The exiles would go to Bermuda, they would remain there at pleasure, and they would have to be seen to go. For the loud-shouters of both camps there remained the theatrics of departure, with a suitable show of rigour producing its due quota of martyrs.

On the afternoon of the 28th the grim stone jail on the waterfront was surrounded by huge crowds. They filled the streets, jostled along the wharves, and almost blocked the gateway. Stern-faced squadrons of cavalry rode them back, a double line of infantry extended down to the river, and the steamer *Canada* lay waiting beside the dock, also bristling with troops. The prison doors opened, guards marched out to form in a double file, and between the files the state prisoners appeared, manacled two by two. There had been a sharp discussion of manacles the day before between Clitherow and Wolfred Nelson. If they were to be used, Nelson had claimed, there should at least be due regard for his own height. Clitherow had seemed to agree, but the agreement had not been kept, and Nelson walked with a stoop now, chained to a shorter man. The doctor glared at the General, who was watching in some embarrassment, and offered a half-salute. For the benefit of nearby listeners and the pages of later history the martyr's voice rang out. "By what authority do you chain us like felons?"[18] There was no answer, and the clanking line moved on to pass through the gates. The ironbound arms were lifted to the watching crowd and there was a long groan from the French, drowned by cheers from the British. The prisoners entered the wagons that were to carry them down to the ship, and emerged on the Horseboat Wharf to climb the gangway. Again they lifted their arms and again the cries rose, in dissonant competing symphonies.

Steam belched from the funnel, paddlewheels began to turn, and the exiles moved downriver to the next stop at Quebec.

Here, after similar paradings in public, they boarded the frigate *Vestal*, where the air changed. The Royal Navy captain welcomed them to his immaculate decks, not as felons but as respected passengers and patriots who had chanced to differ with his government. He was curious about their reasons and asked Nelson to explain them, which was to produce another statement in the course of a leisurely voyage. In the meantime the irons were struck from their wrists by the ship's blacksmith, who politely hoped to meet them all in heaven. Nelson consigned him to hell and declined to meet him there, and he had equally black rejoinders to the offer of creature comforts. They were an insult, he said; he would live on the prisoner's rations of bread and water. If he did, there was much he missed. Charles Buller appeared, suave, affable, and regretful, to see to the exiles' needs. He was followed by bulky crates of expensive provisions and a stock of excellent wine. Through Mr. Simpson, the magistrate, came a draft for £500 which was provided unofficially to ease life in Bermuda. By July 4, as *Vestal* towed from harbour and set off down the St. Lawrence, there was the exhilaration of martyrdom with some of the fruits of victors.

In another three weeks there was the comforting additional knowledge that they remained a problem of state. On the 24th they arrived off Hamilton, Bermuda. On the 25th came word from the Governor's residence that they could not be allowed to land. They had been tried by no court, they were under no official sentence, and Durham's authority in any case did not extend to Bermuda.

For three days, with the exiles duly enjoying it, the portentous squabble went on. *Vestal*'s captain had carried out his orders; he had brought the men to the island. They could not be thrown into the sea, and he would not carry them back. The Governor was equally difficult about having them come ashore. Rumours came to the prisoners of the high debates in council as to how they might be accepted, where they could be allowed to go, at whose expense they would live. Along with the rumours, and bringing them, came groups of the island notables, eager to see the strangers and discuss the affairs of Canada. Tradesmen added their welcome with offers of goods and services, and even offers of credit. With the sun bright and warm on the blue

143

sea, only squirming officialdom maintained its fretful chill. On the 28th the Governor at last capitulated, with a worried explanation to Lord Glenelg. Bermuda, he said, was not a penal colony, but he had no desire to embarrass the Governor of Canada. The prisoners had been allowed to land and to give parole. They were to enjoy the freedom of the island, except for the garrison areas, and they would be installed in suitable quarters of their own choosing, "it being taken for granted that they have the means of maintaining themselves."[19] It would be less than two months, comfortably covered by Mr. Simpson's draft, before the thunderbolt fell that brought release.

5

It came on Durham out of a September sky, dispatched by the hand of Melbourne and carried in a steam packet. With no prior warning, and in flat contradiction to the views it had first expressed, the British Government revoked the Ordinance of exile. It rejected Durham's solution and overturned his work. Every political problem was returned to its old chaos, the Governor's act was swept away and discredited, and the effect on him was clear. "All weight, all real power is taken from my authority . . . nothing remains but military force."[20]

He had done much with authority while he had it. The jails were almost emptied of the last rebels, and the courts were functioning again. They were not functioning to his taste, for the mixed juries were unreliable as ever, but he had watched the acquittal of men excepted from amnesty and had coolly let them go. He had freed the stubborn Girouard, unrepentant, and had not repented the act. He had waved aside vengeance and diluted malice, with a chill contempt for both. From Quebec's subdued bureaucracy he had gone to the hostile merchants of Montreal, and had almost won them over. There was no dream they dreamed for this British country that the Governor did not share, that he was not bent on fulfilling. But it would be in his own way, and on his own terms. He had cut a swath of state through Upper Canada, and the lordly rites of the progress had not obscured his view. There would be as short shrift for venerable western autocrats as there had been for eastern *bureaucrates*, and the Family Compact felt the tremors of doom.

He had faced the threat of war with the United States, and he had faced the threat down. He had spoken to official Washington with charm and grace and statesmanship, and with a new note of respect. Yet he had used every occasion, and he had manufactured occasions, to exact respect in return. At Niagara Falls, the terminal point of his Upper Canadian progress, he had staged a grand review of his British troops, the pick of some ten thousand who were now assembled in Canada. He had invited his American neighbours to cross the river and see them, but at the same time he had provided neighbourly cheer. There had been a great dinner in the evening for a hundred or so of the most distinguished visitors, and the glitter of lamps and silverware had balanced the show of iron. He had spoken to every guest, charmed every guest, while suave, imperial magic played around them. Burned ships and border raids had dwindled to insignificance, and raucous politicians had enlarged on the joys of peace. They had gone home replete, dazzled by marching redcoats, warmed by the hand of friendship and bubbling with high goodwill. "A million pounds of money," wrote the ever-admiring Buller, "would be a cheap price for the single glass of wine which Lord Durham drank to the health of the American president."[21]

He had come back to Quebec and to the work of his bright young men, readying their briefs and findings. They had gone out, in the light of their own Englishness and the light of the Governor's views, to untwist a knotted tangle of discontents. They had studied the problems of owning and granting land, the problems of immigration and education, the problems of British commerce and of every level of government. They had dug deep and they were dragging the roots up; the patterns of mighty change were coming clear. They were shaping in Durham's mind by the end of that lively summer of 1838, after a bare ten weeks in Canada. "The time is fast approaching," he wrote in his dispatch to Glenelg on August 9, "when I shall be able to bring these measures under the consideration of Her Majesty's government."[22] In the meantime, and even with the measures pending, he observed around him a kind of sultry

145

peace. "The exercise of the very extensive powers placed in my hands seems to have operated as a sort of charm, like oil poured upon troubled waters. At this moment all is still."[23]

That the quiet was a false quiet he knew well. "Even the children, when they quarrel, divide themselves into French and English like their parents."[25] The old enemies waited to spring at each other's throats, and they were none of them friends to him. He had outraged British bureaucracy, the merchant princes of the oligarchy remained cold and watchful, and he had not won over the French. He had not tried to win them; he had given them British justice. He had given them Adam Thom, their most detested enemy, who sat among Durham's friends now on one of the high commissions. There were few men less like Durham than the dismal little Scotch bigot, and the Governor had chosen the man hardly knowing him. But with that one appointment he had paralysed French goodwill, and he had been moved by no pleadings to attempt a redeeming gesture. While Thom came and went in the inner offices of government, there were only the outer rooms for LaFontaine.

The one-time friend of Papineau was now no longer a fugitive, but he was a tired and angry man. He had arrived in Canada a little after Durham, returning from a frigid welcome on the other side of the Atlantic. Though he had gone as an accused rebel he had risked a stay in London, and had presented himself and his case to Bear Ellice. The Bear had listened stolidly to the man with a warrant over him, and had not suggested arrest. But he had had few other suggestions of which a French Canadian could approve, and he had been much relieved when his visitor left for Paris. He had even provided some letters of introduction, but they had not proved very helpful and some had been wrongly addressed. For two months, tramping through strange streets, knocking on strange doors, often returning sick to his cheap hotel, LaFontaine had measured the hopes of aid from France. There had been no hope there. He had been lifted up by the word of Durham's appointment, and had turned from rebuffs in Paris to the thought of London again. A clipped note from the Bear had changed that. He would probably not be arrested, Ellice said, but "unless you have business here I think you will do as well to return to America by the Havre packet."[25]

He had been back in Canada within a month of Durham's

arrival, and he had occasionally met the Governor. But he was consigned to Buller and Turton and the other lesser figures, always received politely and always damped by the reception. He could not be quite ignored, for his steady courage was obvious and he was obviously a growing leader. He was also stubborn and insistent. He had fought for the rights of prisoners who had not been freed by the amnesty, and for his right to represent them. He had offered to care for Wolfred Nelson's children, and he had influenced the long debatings that led to Girouard's release. He had obtained much, including the cancellation of the warrant against himself, but there had been no rapport with Durham. LaFontaine in the eyes of the Governor remained one of the French, a man to be heard in the anterooms but not in the high councils. There could still be no quarter for the absurd pretensions of race.

During the first weeks of September 1838, the calm along the border began to break. The burnings and runnings-away had stopped with summer, but there were now more ominous stirrings that belied the seeming quiet. There were troublesome men in movement along the American border and many frontier villages were sites of restless camps. On both sides of the line and in both Canadas there was talk of a secret, newly building strength. For all the Governor's efforts, the province was tense and threatening, and its condition added urgency to his need for support from London. Parliament was now debating the Ordinance of exile, and though he had no fears for its approval he was irked by the long delay. He was doubly irked by the distant accusations, of tyranny and misgovernment, of sentences without law, of justice set aside by his own hand. They were made by ignorant fools or by the old familiar enemies, and they were not to be taken seriously. Melbourne was sure of that, and even the soft Glenelg; and for once they were both right. The disposition of the exiles had been the only possible course, and it had brought what peace there was. It was not to be set aside by cheap politics; the pin-prickers and the fault-finders had troubled the Governor enough on lesser matters. On this he must be upheld; it was the basic act of his reign. He was sore and sick with impatience as he waited for the final word, but he was confident of vindication. Nothing else could be thought of; he would be nothing without that.

"A day I can never forget!"[26] wrote Lady Durham in her journal for September 19, 1838. She had been out for a drive along the sunny heights of Quebec, laughing with some of the children and the ever-present escort. They had seen the smoke of a steamer down the river and had recognized the New York packet, bringing the official mail trans-shipped from London. They had hurried home to greet it but it had docked when they arrived, and the Governor was already shut away with his letters. When he reappeared it was to greet his wife in their dressing-room, and his face told the story. He had a letter from the Prime Minister and a letter from the Colonial Minister, profuse with congratulations. He had been wise and right in his disposal of the exiled prisoners. He was told to "go on and prosper."[27] But he also held a copy of a London newspaper, sent by way of New York in a faster ship. It was dated later than the letters and had overtaken them, and it told of the final phase of the great debate. Outfaced by the opposition, Melbourne had caved in. The Ordinance was disallowed.

With that, in Durham's opinion, his influence was totally destroyed. Nothing remained but the military force "which I cannot wield so well as an officer, and would not if I could."[28] On the status of the men in Bermuda there was almost total confusion, and there would be no attempt to resolve it. By late November they would be landing in the United States, from a schooner hired by themselves, to be welcomed and fêted and allowed to scatter there. In Quebec, as word of the disallowance reached the public, there was the shock of impending loss. There was a flood of loyal addresses and a wave of baffled protest, even from the men who had fought the Governor's rule. From the Governor himself there was an angry proclamation, and there were bitter letters home. They changed nothing and improved nothing. Caesar, stabbed in the back, was again out of employment. The great reign ended, hardly well begun.

On November 1, down either side of Mountain Street from the Castle gate to the docks, the long lines of the troops took up their stations. The man who had climbed the hill riding a white horse rode down now in a carriage, a man marked for death. The young men of the commissions were left behind him, still completing their work. The great report would be written and its influence would remain, for good and ill. But Durham himself was gone. With the weary business of salutes and ceremony ended, the frigate *Inconstant* towed out of the harbour. She lurched down the river under a cold November sky, starting a luckless voyage with a dangerous fire on board. There was to be little luck for the men who watched her go. Colborne felt it, preparing to resume government with a new rebellion only a day away. Charles Buller felt it, as he rode back with Colborne to the drab ceremonies in the Castle.

Once more the Provisional Administrator was to be sworn in. In spite of his own weariness and his own desire to be gone Colborne, *faute de mieux*, was held to the post. The old men were there, hopeful for the old ways. The soldiers bristled again, crisp with restored authority. "Nothing remains but military force." The murmur of oath-taking quickly came to an end, and Buller drifted off to his own quarters, "I went to the window, which commanded a fine view of the harbour. The sky was black with clouds bearing the first snowstorm of the winter, and hardly a breath of air was moving. My heart filled with many a bitter regret . . . many too true misgivings."[29]

EIGHT

"To have tranquillity..."

During the last week of September, while Durham was absorbing the disastrous news from England, there had been other unwelcome reports from around the south shore of Lake Erie. A convention at Cleveland, Ohio, between the 16th and 22nd of the month, had brought together the delegates of a recently formed society. The men came from all along the border and from both sides of it, and their numbers were estimated variously at between seventy and one hundred and twenty. They were known to the English-speaking as members of the Hunters' Lodges and to the French as Les Frères Chasseurs, but all information about them was so confused and contradictory as to be almost useless. With even the number of delegates in dispute, there was still greater uncertainty as to the membership they represented. There was no doubt that it was large, however, and no doubt of the intent. Organized in grim secrecy and bound by horrendous oaths, it was sworn "never to rest till all tyrants of Britain cease to have any dominion or footing whatever in North America."[1]

The society's convention, as a first public surfacing, had been strongly reminiscent of other occasions. There had been the usual haze of rhetoric and the usual election of committees, military, political, and financial. "The Republican Bank of Canada" had been set in train and designs for its notes displayed, picturing martyrs of the late rebellion and carrying such slogans as "The Murdered" — "Death or Victory" — and the inevitable "Liberty, Equality, Fraternity". The bank's capital of $7,500,000, not presently in hand, was to be raised by confiscation of the estates of Canadian Tories. The delegates, who had pledged themselves to raise $10,000 within a fortnight of the convention's close, had raised just $300 by November 1. Yet if the plan-making and the results seemed familiar in these aspects, they were different in many others. There was obviously work continuing under the talk, there was constant, widespread movement, and there was even a hint at last of central direction.

The new body had begun to take shape in the spring, as a coalescing of half a dozen secret and rebellious groups along the border, where the activists had full control and free rein. They had gone to work in a hot and welcoming environment, and with the blessing of hard times. The communities of patriot exiles, spraying out fiery news-sheets and revolutionary speakers, were making the cause of Canada a national preoccupation. Everywhere disgruntled men, often hungry and jobless, were looking for trouble when work was not to be found. Among the better-off there was native anti-Britishness, and the Society provided an outlet near at hand. The parish politician, who could not find jobs for his constituents, found votes easy to come by when he twisted the lion's tail. There was the sacred urge to extend republican government, and there was added charm for joiners in the oaths and secret rites. Thousands of free Americans, eager to free Canadians, were soon exchanging the handclasps, putting the fingers to nostrils, and trading the mystic jargon that made them brothers. "Laborers left their employ," wrote one recorder of the times, "mechanics abandoned their shops, merchants their counters, magistrates their official duties, husbands their families, children their parents, Christians their churches and ministers of the gospel their charges to attend meetings of the Hunters."[2]

The American government, with this groundswell heaving along the border, was doing what little it could to maintain peace. The little was done, however, with almost no regular troops and with a healthy distrust of local state militias. The citizen-soldiers raised in the frontier regions were all too likely to have taken the Hunters' oath. There was a strong probability that many of their officers had done so, and many of the state officials. The standing army of the United States consisted of barely five thousand men. It was engaged almost entirely in the south and west, keeping an eye on the new republic of Texas and fighting Indian wars. Along the whole northern border, when the troubles with Canada began, there had been a paper strength of 122 troops, garrisoned at Port Huron, Michigan. It had been increased a little by now, dubiously strengthened by a few militia units, and distributed in small detachments under General Winfield Scott. He moved about, however, with barely a corporal's guard, and with little but tact and rhetoric to discourage threats of invasion. "I stand before you," he said to noisy meetings in the restless towns, "without any troops and without arms, except for the blade at my side . . . but, except it be over my body, you shall *not* pass this line—you shall *not* embark."[3]

By late October he had evoked cheers for his nerve and impressed the stamp of authority on those with something to lose. The respectable well-to-do would wait and see. Newspapers were lecturing piously about growing public disorder and the risk of war with Great Britain, but they remained equally pious on the hope of a free Canada. The recruiting lodges of the Hunters went steadily on with their work. In General Scott's correspondence with Colborne, and in the reports of Colborne's agents, there was little to cheer the peaceful of either side. Along hundreds of miles of woods and open water the patrols of the American army were thinly spread, powerless to guard all exits. An unreliable militia might not be inclined to try. Behind them, in the United States, there were now reputed to be forty thousand Hunters. There were thought to be other thousands to welcome them in Upper Canada. And in Lower Canada, according to one of many gloomy informants, "nearly the whole population is organized into lodges."[4]

2

The reports, if not quite true, were as near the truth as Robert Nelson could make them. He had been a prime force in the movement since his release from jail in March. Active, violent, always a little mad, he had resumed as *patriote* leader in New York State and Vermont. He was soon the example and envy of the leaders farther west. With his many connections in Canada and his frequent visits to the large American cities, he exuded an aura of mystery and a sense of great affairs. He was negotiating huge loans, he was dealing with foreign governments, he had unassembled armies ready at call. From a maze of plots and plannings he had emerged with the Frères Chasseurs, and it was their rites and ceremonies, and their symbol of the rifle crossed by the long dagger, that had set the model for the Hunters. For Nelson they were now to serve as the spearhead, presaging a rising people, that would restore the one-day president, to his lost republic.

Through the late spring and summer, with Côté, Gagnon, and others of his old familiars, he had been much in the southern fringes of the Richelieu valley. It was dangerous ground for rebels, particularly a rebel president, and he had soon been recalled to the south by greater occasions. He had found emissaries, however; the emissaries had found others; and there was a steady trickle of more from across the border. As they walked the roads and drifted into the villages the waves of a second coming had lapped up through the province. Ploughmen in mid furrow, loggers busy in the woods, merchants behind their counters, and doctors, lawyers, and notaries brooding at desks had looked up to be accosted by dusty strangers, talking of familiar things. They pointed to the ravaged farms and the burnt houses, the work of the English everywhere. It called for revenge and revenge would soon be forthcoming; woe to those who opposed it. It called for a great rebuilding at the hands of oath-bound brothers; would the friends swear the oath?

They came, some of them reluctantly and pushed along by their neighbours, usually to a quiet farmhouse late at night. There would be few gathered around it and little sign of commotion inside the house. With soup in the pot at the fireplace, smoke and talk in the kitchen, and children sleeping above, the place would be wholly innocent to the eye of a chance intruder. The neophyte passed from the kitchen to another room, and was suddenly pushed to his knees. A blindfold shut off light, the door closed, and there was silence. There was a long wait, lonely and cold in the dark, and the door creaked open again. A rustle of movement came, followed by another silence, and at last by a solemn voice. The man on his knees had come to take the oath; he would now swear. He would swear to observe the signs and mysteries of the society, never revealing or speaking of them except to another member. He would live henceforth by the crossed rifle and dagger, he would be bound by all rules, he would be prompt to the aid and rescue of every brother. His means, his family, and his person he placed at the disposal of the cause. "All this I swear without restriction, consenting that, failing in any part, I shall see my property destroyed and my throat cut to the bone."[5]

With the last word of the oath the blindfold was ripped away. There was a glare of candles around the dazed postulant, and a circle of guns and daggers. They were all held by his friends, they were all aimed at his heart, and there were cold eyes behind them. He rose, bound by the oath, awed by the ring of menace, a brother of the Frères Chasseurs.

He was answerable as a new recruit to his own "Raquette", commander of a platoon of ten. "Castor" commanded a company of ten platoons. "L'Aigle" was a divisional officer responsible for an entire district, and over him, passing from region to region rarely seen, was the shadowy super-authority, the Grand Eagle. He was Edouard-Elisée Malhiot, veteran of many disasters of the first rising, and seldom at ease with his colleagues below the border. To the eloquent Doctor Côté, never at ease with anyone, he was "an ignoramus of the first class who hardly knows how to sign his name, and more than that who is nothing but vanity, presumption and the most inordinate ambition."[6] Whatever the truth, he was now the bearer of Nelson's hopes and promises. From the Grand Eagle to the lesser eagles, descending through many ranks to the scared chasseur, came the secret signs and passwords, the sleeve-pluckings and nose-pickings that linked him with unseen armies. He was warmed in his ragged impotence by the sense of gathering thousands, and newly renewed in the certainty that there would be arms for his empty hands.

154

All through the Richelieu valley that spring and summer the nightly swearings went on. Lodges sprang up in Quebec and along the whole line of the St. Lawrence between the capital and Montreal. In Two Mountains and the Grand Brûlé, northward into the Laurentians and westward to Terrebonne County at the end of the island, exiles returned as agents to build up their secret lists. They were not always welcome and not always successful, for the reminders of desolation were thickest here. They could report, however, on deep reserves of hatred, and when they crossed to the southern counties west of the Richelieu there was less diluting terror. Colborne had not marched here the year before and here, by the end of October, in Beauharnois, Chateauguay, L'Acadie, and the whole of the border region there were hundreds of sworn brothers and thousands of unsworn friends. They could neither drill nor organize, and no formations existed even on paper. But Castors and Eagles whispered from town to town, heavy with threats and plans. They were awaiting only the signal, the appointed place, and the weapons.

In Montreal the heart and centre of Frères Chasseurs planning was a comfortable little house. Ambiguously tucked away in an obscure location, it was the home of an ambiguous lawyer. It had been much haunted by Duvernay, who was now a rebel in exile, and the pleasant garden to the rear of it had been the scene of the inaugural banquet of the St-Jean-Baptiste Society. Its owner, nevertheless, seemed to belie much that was hinted at by his old associations. John Picoté de Belestre-MacDonnell was known in professional circles as a somewhat eccentric barrister but, in spite of his French antecedents, as a generally safe man. In fact, however, though he had prudently refrained from a part in the first rising, he was a virulent hater of the establishment and a born hatcher of plots. He had now come into his element as host to the Frères Chasseurs, and his house was the northern terminus for the flights of the Grand Eagle.

Behind its drawn blinds the leaders in the city were sworn. They went out to swear new brothers, and to invoke funds from sympathizers who could not quite stomach the oath. From here the tallies went south to Robert Nelson, often accompanied by sizeable sums of money. Commanders of all the regions passed through the rooms, receiving orders and disputing them, framing and re-framing plans and manifestos, and carrying the papers back to paper armies. Here came, during the late days of October, the word of the plans matured below the border, and from here MacDonnell set forth with all in train. He had battle flags in his baggage and commissions for new officers, and other papers of a still more ominous turn. There were lists of the estates to be confiscated following victory, and the names of rich merchants who were to be proscribed or held for ransom. Life would be bleak and brief for his favourite enemies in the new republic of Canada.

By November 2 MacDonnell had arrived at Berthierville, on the north shore of the St. Lawrence. He was to cross the river next morning to assume a waiting command, for the men of seventeen parishes were to rise and take Sorel. South along the line of the Richelieu and all through the border counties there were men on the move that night. They were tramping muddy roads and plodding across frozen fields, a few with old firearms and most with clubs or pikes, but each with his packet of rations slung on the end. They were knocking at farmhouse doors, bundling out timid brothers, herding them on toward meeting-points where they would find the bright new weapons. No one had seen the wagon-trains, but the rumours ran ahead of them, and in any case there was work for the fighters first. There was to be a circle of general risings, closing round Montreal. The garrison points on the Richelieu were all to be wiped out. Yet this would be only prelude to the advance of the main force. It was assembling now at Napierville, fifteen miles from the border, and it was awaiting Robert Nelson. He would cross the line with arms and supporting forces, and he would signal the march north.

3

The manor house of the seigneury of Beauharnois stood a mile or so from the village. Both looked out, however, onto Lake St. Louis, which was a widening of the St. Lawrence River to the south of Montreal. Across the lake to the northeast was Lachine, the gateway to Montreal, twenty miles away. Almost facing Lachine, on the same side as Beauharnois, was the mouth of the Chateauguay River, with Chateauguay village a mile or so inland. Fifteen miles to the east of Chateauguay Basin, still on the south side, was the more important centre of Laprairie, linking the ferry from Montreal with the province's one line of railway, which ran sixteen miles southeastward to St-Jean on the Richelieu River. The whole region, just to the west of the Richelieu and just to the north of the border, had been quiet through the first rising. But the quiet had been ominous then, and it had become steadily more so with the coursing of the Frères Chasseurs. Edward and Jane Ellice, depressed by the departure of Durham, had found a good deal more to depress them in the atmosphere of Beauharnois.

In spite of his duties as one of the Governor's secretaries, the young Ellice and his wife had spent much time at the seigneury. They were there on November 2 as work stopped on the farms and men began drifting off, and they read the signs correctly. Colborne had read them earlier, as he had for many regions, and there was now a contingent of local volunteers, equipped and supplied with arms. They were commanded by the estate manager, a man by the name of Brown, and he was keeping an eye on the village. He was more concerned with the seigneury, however, and with its one defensible point, which was the seigneury house itself. He had arranged with Ellice to store most of his arms there, and to summon his volunteers if trouble threatened.

By November 3 the weapons had been brought to the house, but that night, with rain falling in torrents and the weather bitterly cold, events overtook Brown. He found himself in the village with only a dozen men, among groups of excited tenants and some truculent-looking strangers. He dispersed a few of the noisiest and arrested a man or two, but there were others on foot and on horseback gathering from all directions. The wet roads and the fields outside the village seemed to be filling with shadowy forms. There was no time to sound a general alarm, and there was no course but retreat. Soaked, breathless, and freezing, with occasional gunshots scarring the windy blackness, the volunteers arrived at the manor gates.

Around two o'clock in the morning the household woke to a sound of yells outside. Then came bursts of firing, and bullets smashed through the windows. Ellice ordered the women and children to the basement, and went out to Brown and his men.

157

He found them clustered by the gate or sheltering along the fences, confused by the thick darkness and the welter of shouts and shots. It was obvious almost at once that defence was useless. There seemed to be hundreds closing around the house, and more coming from the distance. Ellice and Brown went out from the gate with a lantern and called for the rebel leaders.

Half a dozen appeared, some of them to figure prominently in later history. Most were debating with each other as they approached to debate with Ellice. There were two or three loud-mouthed horsemen waving swords, who seemed to be restrained with difficulty by quieter men. One of the more nervous captains, afoot, unarmed, and obviously unsure in his role, was a young country doctor, Jean-Baptiste-Henri Brien. He had been an active recruiting agent throughout the summer but had become a reluctant fighter. On this night, as the marchers passed his house, he had had to be roused from sleep and hauled along. He seemed inclined to explain himself to Ellice, and to soften some of the threats made by the others. Standing well in the background was a man who made no threats. He was Chevalier de Lorimier, a notary of Montreal and one of the inner circle in *patriote* councils. He had figured in some of the battles of the first rising, and had crossed to the United States. He had come back for a dangerous month in the northern counties as an agent of the Frères Chasseurs, returned to report to Nelson at the close of his mission, and was now returned again. Here in the rain and lantern-light, bundled up in a greatcoat and wearing green glass spectacles, with a cap pulled low on his forehead and a scarf high round his throat, he was a figure of portentous mystery, well marked by Brown. Often consulted and clearly commanding deference, he imposed a kind of silence on the quarrels round him. Little by little the shape of affairs grew clearer.

The revolution had begun. The arrest of leading *bureaucrates* was already under way. They were being taken to a camp at Chateauguay and there would be many more to follow. There was no intention to harm the people of the house. Women and children were promised every courtesy. The men, however, were now prisoners of war, and their arms and ammunition must be surrendered.

Thirty or forty of the rebels, who had grown impatient of talk, were already searching the lower floor of the house. A cheer went up as they found the stock of weapons, and the parley was soon concluded. By three o'clock the barn doors stood open and *patriotes* were circling the estate on Ellice's horses. He himself, with Brown and the volunteers, was tied up in the box of one of his wagons and jolting off for Chateauguay.

Jane Ellice, with the women and children of the household, had left the basement shelter for rooms upstairs. Here, through the rest of the night, they listened to a growing roar of new arrivals and the jubilant shouts of first-comers discovering the goods of the house. The ample larders and cellars were soon emptied, and the tumult rose as the liquid stores went down. As the lady of the house listened to the crash of breaking bottles and breaking furniture, the stamp of boots and the occasional *feu de joie*, the door of her room burst open. A huge, bearded figure stood before her, brandishing a great horse pistol and roaring drunk. He swayed forward respectfully and swept the cap from his head with his left hand. "N'ayez pas peur, Madame, nous ne voulons pas vous faire de mal, ne craignez rien."[7] Whatever the reassurance as he staggered out, it was soon dispelled as another staggered in, a little smaller and soberer and obviously much alarmed. "Listen, ladies," he advised in a shaken whisper, "save yourselves if you can. I won't answer for anything tonight—everybody's drunk and everybody's master!"[8]

With dawn on the rainy Sunday of November 4 the revels began to diminish and the women looked out the windows toward a little jetty on the lake. There was a large canoe there that might have been a means of escape, but men were already round it, and they were jabbing holes in the bottom with swords and pikes. The greater hope was the arrival of the *Henry Brougham*, the passenger steamer with mail from Upper Canada that called regularly on its way across to Lachine. They saw its smoke in the distance, but the hope dimmed even as the vessel neared. All around the sides of the wharf, behind boxes or piles of timber or whatever shelter offered, men were concealing themselves. As the steamer came to the pier they rose in a concerted rush and were aboard in a few minutes. The engines were smashed below and the feather of steam at the funnel died away. There was a long wait, and the ruffled passengers emerged, followed by the ship's officers. There were thirty men among them and they went off for the camp at Chateauguay, bound in Ellice's wagons. The half-dozen women and children were politely brought to the upper floor of the manor house and added to the group there.

Late in the afternoon there was other movement. The priest from Beauharnois village arrived at the manor, and made his way through the rebels into the presence of Jane Ellice. He had a pair of rickety carts waiting outside, and he had obtained permission for the women and children to leave. They came in the carts to the presbytery, freezing and soaked, and two hours later other wagons arrived. They were returning with the male prisoners from *Brougham*, who were in much worse state than the women. There had been no room for them at Chateauguay and they had been brought back as they went, tied up in open wagons over fifteen miles of rain-drenched country roads. They were pushed into the house with some of their guards, who distributed themselves on watch. Sitting in the midst of it all, with coughing, sneezing, and bone-chilled wretchedness everywhere, and no word of her husband, the lady of Beauharnois now counted "sixty-two people crowded in, some of them insufferably dirty — squalling children in abundance, all spoilt — and three dogs."[9]

The curé himself was as kind as his means allowed, and some food and milk were brought over from the seigneury. For all the boisterous riot of the camp outside, the guards who were near the women were kept sober. They did not steal personal possessions and they did not ask prisoners for money. Most were apologetic and regretted the necessities of war. It was time, however, for Canadians to have their rights; they had suffered long enough.

There was a curious, confident dignity about some who seemed to be leaders. The little fresh-faced farm boy, Captain Prieur, who had led the party that boarded *Henry Brougham*, was soon on a friendly footing with Jane Ellice. With the revolution begun and peace to follow he was sure that Madame would see her husband again. Delorimier came and went, a discreet, precise notary inclined to fiddle with papers. He had listed the names of prisoners on the captured ship, and been carefully intent to observe every courtesy. Official mail he had confiscated, but he would touch no private letters. He had searched the men with distaste and the ladies not at all, with the result that a consignment of money remained in an untouched bustle.

He had addressed the ship's officers in the tone of a quiet victor, regretting slight indignities and respectful to prisoners of war. He had even discussed with some of them the wider strategy of rebellion and the scope of the master plan.

It seemed to be well in train that busy Sunday. With Beauharnois manor taken, Joseph-Narcisse Cardinal, a notary of Chateauguay, had set off with an expedition to Caughnawaga. It was a village of Mohawk Indians a few miles to the north, and every brave was possessed of a well-oiled gun. Since the arms were required by *patriotes* who had already achieved a victory, it was hoped the Indians would agree to hand them over. They were to hand them over in any case, with or without agreement. Cardinal had been gone since midnight with a party of seventy-five, and though it was a hard trip through thick and rainy forest, he would certainly have arrived by dawn. He would have had to arouse the village and perhaps arrange a parley, but it could be assumed by ten o'clock that that had been done. If the braves had not been persuaded they would have been forced to donate their weapons, and Cardinal's returning foragers would be nearing Beauharnois. They were expected hourly through Sunday afternoon.

At Caughnawaga, however, events had upset plans. An Indian woman, chasing a stray cow, had seen the approach of the party and had run to inform the chief. She had found him at early mass, and there had been a prompt exodus from the church. By the time the *patriotes* entered the road to the village the woods on either side were thick with Indians. The chief appeared alone, grave and inquiring. What was the purpose of this unannounced visit? He was gravely informed by Cardinal of the *patriotes'* need of weapons. By what authority, the chief asked, was such a request made? "By this!"[10] Cardinal replied, whipping a pistol from his pocket and pointing it at the chief's head.

It was his last warlike gesture. The chief's hand shot out to knock the pistol aside. A blood-curdling war-whoop shattered the Sunday calm, and a hundred armed braves were around the *patriotes*. Of the seventy-five who came only eleven escaped, and the chief was prompt in his disposition of the others. Girod's attack on Oka a year before had been all too well remembered. By mid morning the warriors from Caughnawaga had crossed over to Lachine, to deliver sixty-four rebels to the

Lachine volunteer cavalry and be congratulated and thrust aside. For the bearskin-helmeted troopers who were now in charge of the prisoners their finest hour was at hand.

None of this, that Sunday, was known at Beauharnois. The *patriotes* waited as the afternoon wore away, impatient but still confident. They were already a force of five or six hundred men, and the number was still growing. There were hundreds more at a place that was called Camp Baker, on the Chateauguay River nine miles away. The artillery of both camps consisted of six wooden cannon strapped by iron bands and with bags of homemade slugs to serve as grape-shot. Half of the men were still awaiting firearms. But the promises came from everywhere, and the leaders grew more explicit as word of new developments reached their ears. Six thousand Americans, according to word that came to Doctor Brien, were now on the march northward and already across the border. They had only waited, according to Delorimier's version, for the first rising of the *patriotes* to clear the way. There were three great battles in progress now, or developing, and all were going well. With Montreal itself on the verge of capture, the British government was proposing to abandon Canada.

About four in the afternoon, putting the cap on all, a message arrived from Napierville, signed by Robert Nelson. The forces around Beauharnois should be prepared for an immediate march. They would be informed of their next objective within the hour.

4

In Quebec a few days previously, as Durham prepared for departure amid the rumours of new trouble, he had had a period of second thoughts. If a greater second rebellion seemed to be imminent, how could the Governor leave? He had not been freed of authority by the wreck of his failed mission; he remained the keeper of law. Sick, shaken, and furious, impotent as he now considered himself to be, he must somehow shoulder authority in the cause of public peace.

The argument had been soon dispelled by an emphatic Colborne. He was facing the possibility of armed invasion, probably directed first at Upper Canada. There would certainly be concurrent risings in the lower province, and he could form no real estimate of the actual forces involved. There were reports now on the Frères Chasseurs and the Hunters that set their strength at a quarter of a million men, distributed in the United States and the two Canadas. The reports were possibly exaggerated, or included friends and sympathizers of whom only a fraction had sworn to take up arms. Yet even this strength in fighting men was said to be forty thousand, and the secret friends and sympathizers were of as much concern to Colborne. He was watching the long border while the ground beneath him smouldered and heaved with treason. He had little trust in French-Canadian officials. He suspected that every jury had its quota of sworn chasseurs. Even the clergy, this time, were sitting in sombre silence, obviously cold to the English and obviously dreading war. It was only Colborne's troops that could make the peace and he could not command in the leading-strings of the Governor. He had no taste for the work he saw ahead; he would have much preferred to be bound for England himself. But if he remained, Durham at least should go. On November 1, as *Inconstant* swayed from harbour with the sick man safe on board, Colborne faced his task with a grim relief.

At 4.30 on the morning of November 3 he left Quebec in the steamer for Montreal. There was a slow trip upriver, for the steamer was towing barges, and it was late in the afternoon when he reached Sorel. Around the wharf there were anxious officers waiting for him, and the dusk was thick with rumours. From all down the Richelieu and from the country across the St. Lawrence there were reports of restless habitants and signs of a new rising; an attack on Sorel itself seemed quite probable. No attack had materialized by eight o'clock that evening, and Colborne continued on for Montreal. Here, however, as he stepped from the gangway early on Sunday morning, he was met by news of the capture of Beauharnois. In another hour the whole city was aware of it, and aware of the General's presence.

As the first church-bells sounded for morning mass, bugles began to compete with them and there was the thud of troops on the march. At every strategic point around the city regulars were under arms or were moving to take position. As couriers galloped everywhere, jostling crowds of civilians began to pour

163

into armouries and pour out in uniform as companies of volunteers. Some moved off in squads of half a dozen, armed, truculent and officious, shoving the whispering watchers out of their way. They were soon knocking at long-selected doors, rooting in desks for papers, and bundling pale-faced men through the crowded streets. Around the church on Notre Dame, as a trickle of silent worshippers flowed in, the clamour was rising steadily under a lowering black sky. It disturbed devotions for a while as mass progressed, but had fallen to an ominous silence as the faithful began to come out.

It seemed to one witness "as if a heavy black curtain excluding the sun's rays had extended over the city and there hung stationary in middle air."[11] Across from the church doors in the murky light, Place d'Armes glowed dull red with massed troops. In front of the troops there were cannon trained on the church, and gunners standing beside them with lighted matches. As the great bells overhead broke out in their solemn *bourdonnement* at the close of mass, military and police officers had clustered at each exit. They were now accosting many of those who emerged, and turning brusquely away with the men they spoke to. There were no warrants presented, warrants were not required; suspected rebels and sympathizers were simply marched to the jail. By noon the jail was already becoming crowded, and by tomorrow morning the act would be made legal. Colborne's restored council, in a series of new ordinances, would proclaim martial law, the right to seizure and search of suspected persons, and the right of summary arrest. Meanwhile, however, the city was being prepared for what might come.

The reports of the morning thickened with afternoon. As the search for suspected men went on in the city, many of those most wanted seemed to be missing. There was talk of a general exodus to the northern counties, and a mobilization beyond the Rivière des Milles Iles. If these regions rose, there was a threat to communications with Upper Canada as well as with Montreal. To the northeast, along the upper stretch of the Richelieu, all the familiar towns were astir again. In St-Charles, St-Denis, St-Ours, on both banks of the river, and from there west to the St. Lawrence, bands of habitants were assembling and were drifting north toward Sorel. There was another more dangerous movement to the south and west of Chambly, apparently aimed to envelop Laprairie. The railway line with St-Jean was already cut, and friends and officials of government were being herded away as prisoners. There was a report of the death of a farmer who had tried to resist the rebels and been killed in his blazing house. Against Laprairie the point of concentration seemed to be a place called La Tortue, conveniently set on a little north-bound river six miles to the west. It was rumoured, like every river and every road, to be carrying arms from the south.

With Beauharnois held by perhaps a thousand men, and the whole of Chateauguay Basin in rebel hands, the circle seemed to be closing on Montreal. Since there were at least three thousand regulars now in garrison the immediate threat was not particularly serious. But there was no measuring the real extent of the rising, and it appeared to be spreading south with each report. Toward nightfall there was word of the force at Napierville, where the strength of a dozen regions seemed to be converging. There were said to be thousands of men there from either side of the border, and with each arriving courier there was word of hundreds more.

By the same evening, however, though the murk overhanging the city had broken in icy rain, part of the gloom was dispelled. Officers came back from Terrebonne county and from all the region beyond Rivière des Milles Iles to report little but a sullen, bickering silence. There had obviously been plans and hopes for another rising, but they were withering in Terrebonne and they were dead in the Grand Brûlé and St-Eustache. Colborne was more feared there than the Frères Chasseurs; there would be peace in the northern counties. From the southern counties, moreover, through the leaden dregs of twilight, some trophies of demi-victory came plodding in.

The prisoners of Caughnawaga, brought to Lachine, had been roped together by the military for delivery to Montreal. As they moved off, bound two by two, they had gladdened the hearts of the loyal coming from church and had provided the stuff of glory for the Lachine volunteers. Ten helmeted troopers rode at their head, swords drawn, with the same number following. A file of thirty infantry with fixed bayonets paced them on either side. It was a long march on the fearful, mud-clogged roads, and the volunteers were adamant against any form of conveyance. The caught rebels must walk. As they came to the Tanneries road, entering the city proper, the word of their coming had raced far and wide. Hundreds straggled around them

165

and thousands were waiting to see them, with the proper greetings prepared. Pelted and cursed, drenched, exhausted, and
hauled along by the rope, they stumbled on with Cardinal at
their head, a man now in the last weeks of his life. Down the
length of Notre Dame Street, with the escort struggling to clear a
way ahead, they came through a narrow aisle in a massed crowd,
beaten by fists and deafened with jeering voices. Bruised from
the last blows and covered with the last spittle, they staggered on
to the prison beside the water. The gates closed, the cheers began
to grow hoarse in the pelting rain, and the swords and bayonets
clattered back to their scabbards. The pride of Lachine repaired
to the Grand Hotel. The first black day of rebellion was ending
with better omens.

5

Some twenty hours before, at around midnight on
Saturday, November 3, a small schooner moving in rainy darkness had slipped past Rouses Point on Lake Champlain and
continued northward just to the Canadian border. It carried
Robert Nelson and a dozen or so of his friends, including a
young man by the name of Charles Hindenlang and another
who was called Touvrey, both of them soldiers of fortune who
had served with the French army. Nelson had with him some
twenty thousand dollars in cash, representing the unexpended
portion of the treasury of the Frères Chasseurs. Lashed on deck
under a tarpaulin was one six-pounder cannon, and there were
crates below in the hold containing two hundred and fifty rifles
and a quantity of ammunition.

For a number of good reasons, both the force and the supplies
it carried were considerably less than planned. The plans themselves had become a trifle tentative. Around him in New York
and Vermont during the past weeks, Nelson had encountered a
cooling of first ardours. The Hunters and friends of Hunters
were as vocal as ever for the liberation of Canada. But they were
inclined to allow Canadians the first honours. The patrols of
General Scott were an increasing nuisance and the militiamen
in uniform, much more watchful of armouries and even of their

old friends, seemed infected by the cloth they wore. In the villages above the border the patrols established by Colborne were growing thicker; there seemed to be hundreds of farmers in red coats, each with a rifle and many on good horses. They were only volunteers, Nelson had urged, and would probably run with the first *patriote* success. The thousands of regulars garrisoned in Montreal were to be drawn away by an invasion of Upper Canada. The border was still open at a hundred points.

The last statement was true but the others were unconfirmed, and in any case the armies had not assembled. Nelson had had to resort to his old expedients and increase the ration of promises that reinforced persuasion. For his agents moving in Canada there had been reports of growing strength in the United States. To hesitant Hunters still south of the border he had enlarged on the mighty rising that awaited their movement north. By November 2, as Côté, Gagnon, and a dozen or so of his vanguard left for Napierville, he did not seem to have convinced many Americans. But he had convinced himself, within bounds of proper prudence, as the schooner carried him north on November 3. About one o'clock on the morning of Sunday the 4th, with American patrols eluded and no alarm in Canada, he stepped ashore at a place called Vitman's Quay. It was three miles north of the border and twenty miles from Napierville, but it seemed at the moment almost near enough. There were no welcoming voices and there was no mass of men gathered in the darkness; there was only wind and rain.

For half an hour the party shivered on the quay. As nothing happened one or two ventured off, scouting the black silence. They returned from a nervous tramp along the near roads and wood trails with half a dozen equally nervous farmers. There was no *patriote* army hereabouts, but there were all-too-plentiful loyalist volunteers. There was a strong company at Hemmingford, fifteen miles to the west, there was another company at Lacolle, six miles north, and there might be more at Odelltown, which was three miles nearer than Lacolle. Farther above these towns, Ile-aux-Noix, the ancient gate of the Richelieu, was garrisoned by regular troops. The schooner would certainly be taken if it tried to proceed upriver, and there were neither wagons nor an escort to convey the arms by land. In the bleak small hours, with the help of the conscripted farmers, the cannon and the crates of rifles were off-loaded from the schooner and hidden around the wharf. Horses were found for Nelson and his two French officers, and with the rest of the party left to guard the arms, they set off northwest for Napierville.

Here, about nine o'clock on the morning of Sunday the 4th, they rode in on better weather and a much more heartening scene. The town glowed with the red, green, and white of *patriote* flags, the streets and the fields around it were alive with men, and more could be seen on the way from all directions. As Nelson and his aides were recognized there was a pandemonium of cheers only slightly dampened by the empty-handed arrival. The arms, it was soon explained, were almost here, only a few miles south. The President climbed to a rostrum, inevitably introduced by Doctor Côté, and in a succession of confident speeches the republic was re-proclaimed. Nelson, after a deflating first arrival and an edgy ride in the dark through hostile country, looked out on a force of nearly three thousand men, still growing. If he thought of the fact that one in ten had arms, and that he only had arms for another one in ten, it was not allowed to mar the inauguration.

With the President confirmed, the election of officers followed. Under Doctor Côté as Commander-in-Chief of the forces, Charles Hindenlang the professional was to organize companies and battalions. A Quartermaster General was to see to the provisioning of the army, and leading Eagles turned to the other work. By the morning of Monday the 5th all was under way. Patrols were scouring the country for recruits and food. Selected local *bureaucrates* had been consigned to the town jail, and their houses had been taken over for the army's use. The curé had been ejected from his presbytery to make room for *patriotes*, and Côté, a zealous priest-hater, had seized the parish funds to pay for supplies. The money was soon gone and was soon being hastily supplemented by notes of the new republic, but with or without payment supplies were coming in. In late afternoon, as Hindenlang completed his work of organization, the army marched past Nelson in grand review. The sight was at least remindful of the first, most urgent mission, and a part of the force moved off the same night.

It was an élite body of five hundred, and it was expected to return next day with Nelson's weapons. Moving in early darkness under the command of Côté, Gagnon, and Touvrey, it angled across to the bank of the Richelieu River and began the tramp south. As it approached Lacolle it swung a little to the west, giving the town a wide berth, and continued south apparently quite unseen. Between Lacolle, however, and the arms at Vitman's Quay there was one more little river to be crossed by a single bridge. There were also volunteers on watch at the bridge. The *patriotes* stumbled onto them, the volunteers made off, and the way was cleared with hardly a dozen shots. The noise, however, had been enough to arouse Lacolle, and by the time the *patriotes* arrived at Vitman's Quay there was a general alarm northward.

The silence around the quay was again oppressive. The guards and the crates and the cannon were all there, but there had been no increase in the interval. No more arms or armies had arrived by Lake Champlain, though Nelson had thought they would, or had said he thought they would. For all the impressive assembly around Napierville, the fighters below the border remained prudent. The fighters around Vitman's spent the rest of the night in hiding and looked north at daylight to be faced by patches of red, growing on every road and frosty field.

There was a company of volunteers coming from Hemmingford and closing in on the west. The volunteers of Lacolle were moving south. There were others coming from the east across the Richelieu, and they were all nearing steadily. Fire spattered and the *patriotes* drove between the approaching groups, trying to break the ring. The charge faltered as the fire grew, and within a quarter of an hour it came to a wavering standstill. Then suddenly it broke, and the last flurries of fighting dissolved into wild pursuit. With eleven of its dead behind it and its new arms and its old strewn on the fields, the *patriote* army scattered. Commander-in-Chief Côté, with unerring instinct, made straight south for the border. Most of the men followed him while a few broke east and west, with volunteers on horseback hard at their heels. By the morning of November 7 a handful of stragglers somehow reaching Napierville had spread the news through the camp. By that night, of the three thousand who had gathered there about twelve hundred remained.

On the morning of Thursday the 8th, in the light of changed circumstances, the President of the republic came to a new decision. By nine o'clock, at the head of his twelve hundred, he was moving south for Lacolle. The lost arms were presumably still there, and might be recovered in battle. In any case, Lacolle was nearer the border. By dusk, with the force diminished at every crossroads, he paused in the fields and brush outside the town. There were no lights in the distant houses and no one seemed to be stirring, but he did not resume the advance. There were certainly volunteers somewhere about; his force by now was reduced to eight hundred men, and it would be wise to reconnoitre. He ordered a night encampment, the *patriotes* settled down, and he rode off in the darkness intent on his own mission. It proved unfortunate, later in the small hours, that Hindenlang the soldier had sent out mounted patrols. Three of the horsemen cantered in at daylight with the President riding among them, tied hand and foot.

He had not been heading for the border, Nelson protested; he had been making his own reconnaissance for the march south. It had not seemed so to the patrol; the officers were hard to convince, and the camp awoke to discover itself in uproar. Dawn broadened and a rainy day came on as the acrid arguments mounted and the semi-trial was held. Clubs and pikes were brandished over the President, musket muzzles glared at him, and there were loud, unpleasant suggestions for his prompt disposal. He should be delivered over to the enemy bound and gagged; he should be killed here on the spot. He was not yet gagged, however; his gift of talk was functioning, and he was still alive at the end of the first hour. Revolted by the thought of treachery, grieved by doubts and suspicions, he had only one wish — to lead his friends to battle. By the end of another hour, under the stern eyes of his friends, he had had the wish granted.

The *patriote* force resumed its southward march, with the centre commanded by Hindenlang, the left surrounding the President, and the right spread out through the fields along the road. There was no sign of an enemy as it swept on by Lacolle, and for a mile or so to the south the road was open. Then there was a little crossroads opening out in the woods above Odell-town, and here the picture changed. The *patriotes* were faced by the bulk of a square stone church, with a stone fence beside it and a cluster of barns and buildings near the fence. Standing ominously just in front of the church was the lost cannon that had been brought north by Nelson. There were volunteers around it, some of them training the gun, and many muzzles poked from the church windows. The advance came near and smoke clouded the muzzles; there was a blistering hail of shot. The cannon barked with authority and the *patriotes* took cover, sheltering behind barns and fences. From here, for those who had firearms, the volunteers in the open were easy targets. Most of these were soon retiring on the church, and the cannon itself fell silent as its gunners ran or were dropped. For the next two hours, with *patriote* marksmen inching forward from shelter and the windows spouting fire as they showed their heads, the battle became a desultory stalemate.

The volunteers had been trapped, Nelson claimed. He exuded confidence from his post on the left wing, but it was less shared by the men in the *patriote* centre who were taking most of the fire. There was obviously a strong force inside the church, and it did not seem to consider itself trapped. Instead, the tempo of battle abruptly rose. The doors of the church burst open and three hundred volunteers came surging through, making a rush for the barns held by the French. They were beaten back but they left the buildings ablaze, and the first determined sortie was followed by five more. At the end of a savage hour, with a low stone fence their only remaining shelter, the *patriotes* were huddling grimly under plunging fire from the church.

It was worst for the men in the centre who had borne the brunt of the attacks, and most of their ammunition was now gone. Hindenlang moved to the left to consult Nelson, but the President was not to be seen. He had not, in fact, been seen for the past two hours. The news raced back to the men along the fence, and they had hardly time to absorb it before another rush came on. This time, moreover, it came with redoubled force, for the roads were crowded with arriving volunteers. Two hundred men from Hemmingford and a hundred from across the Richelieu came on with the men who poured through the church doorway. All of them were well-armed, many were well-horsed, and hardly an exhausted *patriote* had powder or bullets left. With fifty dead and as many more wounded, the last of the three thousand broke up in a *sauve-qui-peut*. By dusk, with Nelson safely across the border, Hindenlang was tramping north in a file of prison-

171

ers. Patrols of volunteers were scouring the country, the homes of rebels blazed in the windy darkness, and over abandoned Napierville the flags drooped in the rain.

6

On that same day, Friday November 9, Colborne marched for the south from Montreal. For several days he had been moving troops from the city across the St. Lawrence and assembling them in two camps, the one just west of the Richelieu and the other on the east bank. He had now in hand most of his available forces, including the Grenadier Guards, the First Dragoon Guards, the 7th Hussars, four regiments of infantry, two batteries of artillery, some five hundred volunteers, and about four hundred Indians. As the force got into motion that Friday morning it was about eight thousand strong, marching in two columns with the Richelieu River between them.

Montreal was left behind thinly defended, for the mood of siege had passed. Two days earlier John Picoté de Belestre-MacDonnell, hands bound and roped in a file of prisoners, had been dragged along through the streets. His papers, flags, and commissions had been captured with him, and none of them had seen use. There had been no attack on Sorel, and he had not even seen the men he had gone to command. Malhiot the Grand Eagle, who had mobilized the seventeen parishes, had melted off with the dissolution of his forces.

He was believed to have taken to the hills around Boucherville with the last of the arms and perhaps two hundred men. Belestre-MacDonnell himself, in the friendless gloom of the morning of November 4, had set off down the St. Lawrence paddling a canoe. He had been taken at Trois-Rivières and brought to Montreal with a column of troops. As he staggered along half-fainting, pelted with stones and filth, he was a sign of changed conditions.

Colborne was quite at ease now on the state of the northern counties. In Quebec city, in spite of some spacious plans to blockade troops in the citadel, there was only the usual mutter and the usual calm. East of the Richelieu River, and along the upper Richelieu itself, there was every sign of *patriote* disintegration. The gatherings were breaking up, men were returning home, or they were clustered in hilltop hiding-places locked against the St. Lawrence.

Some thirteen thousand habitants appeared to have risen, or at least to have left their homes prepared to rise. With a half or more of them now well dispersed, the remaining centres of trouble could be marked off. They were all in the southern counties west of the Richelieu, and two were west of the present line of march. Chateauguay was unsubdued and Beauharnois manor and village were in rebel hands, but the plans for dealing with them were under way. They involved once more the volunteers from Glengarry, who were coming from farther west across the St. Lawrence. For the two columns of the army, as it moved down from the north, the rebel force at Napierville remained the first objective. It was dwindling and moving south by all reports, and there was word late in the day that it had been stopped and scattered. But if there were to be no rebels to fight there would still be rebels to punish, and the files of infantry and cavalry ground on.

The column on the right came down well to the south, crossed the river a little above Lacolle, and swung north to throw a loop round Napierville. The other column moved direct for the town. Both entered it in the evening within an hour of each other, and found little to do. The battle was over at Odelltown, and in Napierville itself the last friends of the *patriotes* had abandoned the last houses. There were only wrathful *bureaucrates* to be freed from the village jail, and the work of burning and manacling that must follow all rebellion.

The last was to be well done. The two columns of the army, dividing again to sweep the whole of the region, were reinforced with enthusiasm by local volunteers. The first column, commanded by General Clitherow, turned northeast for the Richelieu and crossed the river. From there it turned for the border and cut a southward swath, searching for any sign of rebel movement. There was no sign to be seen. The troops tramped and clanked over empty roads, platoons and companies scoured the lesser trails, and horsemen rode through the fields on either flank, threading their way through copses, galloping into farmyards, and hammering at house doors. Village windows were shuttered, there was no one working on the land, those seen were usually women tending the lank brown cattle. Most of the men were in cellars, or they were hiding in patches of wood, or they were plodding off in irons. Everywhere along the march there were the known rebels to be searched for and the official arrests and burnings, but the country smoked with other trails where the volunteers had passed. Not even Colborne's placarded dispensation could save some of the houses, and rebel-hunting was to continue as the sport of a long winter.

Colborne himself had gone south to Odelltown to survey conditions on the border. As the second column of the army left Napierville it was under command of General Macdonell. He moved north and west, with patrols sent out to the southward, under another haze of smoke. Chateauguay and Beauharnois were his new objectives, but on the night of November 11 he came to a halt. He had burned four houses in the course of a ten-mile march, and had taken several rebels whose houses would be burned next day. He was a little in doubt, however, as to where he was most required. Word had just reached him that the Chateauguay camp was abandoned and that Ellice and all the prisoners had been released. He could find no rebel forces along his route, and he requested orders from Colborne. Should he continue on to the west for Beauharnois, or should he comb south for the border?

In the event he moved west, but by then it hardly mattered. The border was sealed by volunteer patrols, riding everywhere, searching everywhere, herding bewildered fugitives away from safety. La Tortue was no longer a threat to Laprairie; the last of its men had trickled down to Napierville. Some had gone on to Odelltown, and been part of the rout there. Others had tried for the border and a few were coming back, but by the night of November 11 there was nowhere left to turn.

For the *patriotes* waiting at Beauharnois on November 4 there had been no second order from Robert Nelson. Instead there had been a letter from Doctor Côté, arriving on November 8, at about the time he was resuming residence in the United States. It had been written days earlier in the flush of the assembly at Napierville, and before he left for the arms at Vitman's Quay. The *patriote* legions, he said, were gathering strength in the south; the Beauharnois men were to march at once to join them.

Three times, after the letter arrived, Delorimier had read it out to his moody force. Each time there had been only deeper silence. Rumours outpacing the letter had told of the lost arms, of Côté's defeat and departure, and of the dismay in Nelson's camp as it absorbed the shock. There had been even grimmer word, arriving on November 8, from Coteau-du-Lac to the west across the St. Lawrence. Troops had been seen there, and men more feared than the troops. The Glengarry Highlanders were arriving, fifteen hundred strong, and they were preparing to cross the river. They could be on the near shore by morning, and they would be not much more than twenty miles away. On the night of the 8th, with a handful left to guard the manor and the village, the three hundred men who still remained in Beauharnois moved out to make their stand.

They marched southwest toward the little village of St-Timothée, just across the river from Coteau-du-Lac. By the morning of the 9th, as men came down to join them from the region around Chateauguay, they were a force of five hundred. While they were still north of the village they came to a halt, disposed themselves in the scrubby fields by the road, and waited the day out. Toward dusk there was word from the river that troops were crossing. There was no sign of the Glengarries but a hundred and fifty regulars appeared on the road, apparently the force's vanguard. The *patriotes* waited till the body drew abreast of them, and then broke from cover and came surging across the fields. The confused troops, suddenly taken in flank, retired in much disorder along the road. As they struggled to re-form their ranks there were loud shouts from the attackers calling for a second charge, but there were more shouts against it. The *patriotes* drew off to debate and assess their chances, and the chance flickered away. By last light, with a level gleam of bayonets along their front, the regulars were in position and waiting. As dark came and no more fighting developed they retired a little farther, but their campfires glowed in the distance throughout the night.

In the morning the British did not attempt to advance, and there were still no bugles by early afternoon. The *patriotes* had drawn back northward along the road and were sheltering in clumps of wood. A stone fence commanded part of the road, and their six wooden cannon were in place behind it. They did not trust the guns, they had only their homemade slugs to use as shrapnel, and there was hardly powder enough for their own weapons. They were bickering now and they were dwindling, harried by mounting rumour. Wives came into the camp from nearby farms, pleading for some to leave. Hurrying men went past them, talking only of disaster, looking only for hiding-places, taking other men with them. There was terror over the country and all around them, and there was smoke, now, blowing across the St. Lawrence. It rose from burning buildings, a sign of the marching Scots, and as the afternoon wore on there were fires on the near shore.

In the woods and behind the fence the force of five hundred was diminished by almost half. Ahead of them down the road the soldiers of yesterday's fighting had not moved; they too were awaiting the Scots. There could be no thought now of another charge by the *patriotes*; too many men were gone. The remainder gathered in groups reciting litanies, some with guns in one hand and rosaries in the other. There was more smoke at dusk, always a little nearer. It was patched with flame as the night closed in around them, and courage drifted away with the last hopes. The wild yells of the Highlanders began to rise on the wind and the groups in ambush simply melted away, scattering back on Beauharnois or trudging off to the east.

Around nine o'clock that evening Jane Ellice and the others sheltering in the priest's house heard distant shots and yells. They had been left lightly guarded throughout the day, and the town around them had seemed almost empty. For days past they had sensed a change in their captors, as the mood of confidence shifted to nervous bluster and shifted again to fear. Some had approached the captives, anxiously explaining: they had been forced to do what they did. Others had been brusque and sharp and a little threatening; the prisoners would move with the rebels if they changed camps, and they would not like what awaited them. There had been less food and fewer privileges, and there had been more debating groups in the streets outside. Two nights before, as endless comings and goings appeared to harden to a purpose, they had watched most of the fighters march away. Now, nearing from the distance and growing everywhere about, there was a wild tumult of returning. Suddenly the door of the presbytery burst open and men, women, and children came flooding in, some of them trampling each other in a rush for safety. A British officer followed them, pistol in hand, but he was only a protector now. The wild wave of the Glengarry men, uncontrollable by anyone, had pushed the troops of the vanguard on ahead of it and was sweeping over the town.

Until four the next morning Jane Ellice watched from a window of the presbytery as fires rose in the village, glowed over the manor house, and dwindled east with pursuit to the Chateauguay River. By dawn the Highlanders had abandoned the chase of rebels and were back in town to resume the work of pillage. It was more or less completed by eleven o'clock in the morning. At about the same time the presbytery door opened and Edward Ellice walked in, waking his wife from a brief and restless sleep.

A shaggy and grimy spectre after nine days in captivity, he was not improved by the mud of a long ride. Three days before, as most of the rebels decided to abandon Chateauguay, he had been brought south in a cart with the other prisoners. The men in charge of the cart intended to join the *patriote* force at Napierville, and they had left on the night of the 9th. By the 10th they had been nearing the town, a dwindling party, always keeping to wood trails, beaten by sleety rain, and troubled by meetings with fugitives who reported the force dissolved. At the last camp, in woods three miles from Napierville, the final word had come: a British army had occupied the town, there were British armies everywhere.

As rain changed to snow and the fireless, lightless party huddled under stripped branches, the prisoners had watched their captors in a last bitter debate. Some had spoken for killing them, some for letting them go, while others had begged Ellice to use his influence to save them. He had been well cursed when he protested that he had no influence, but the rebels had cut his bonds and disappeared. He and the other prisoners had made for Napierville, and Ellice had found a horse. He had ridden to Laprairie, crossed to Montreal, and set off for Beauharnois within the hour.

Shortly after noon that day, as the regular troops restored a measure of order, the seigneur and his lady walked through the streets of the town. The church was still standing, for the Glengarry men were Catholic or Presbyterian and there were no Orangemen here. A few terrified worshippers were creeping home from mass. There were bloody pools in the streets and the doors of smouldering houses stood wide open, with the interiors stripped and smashed. The manor and the seigneury buildings had been half-burned and wrecked, and there were acrid clouds of smoke for miles beyond them. They would not be soon forgotten, the Glengarries boasted. They had left a trail through the country six miles wide, and whatever they they had missed in coming they would burn on the way back.

By Monday morning the Scots had been gathered together for the homeward march. They moved off, to the great relief of the regulars, with their newly acquired horses and their packs and wagonloads of plunder. Returning civilian loyalists began the work of search and inquiry into the acts of suspect rebels. It would be long, diligent, and productive, and it was well begun that evening as the Ellices left for Chateauguay to be rowed across to Lachine.

Chateauguay itself was still in an earlier stage. Drunken, marauding Indians filled the village, as loyal and thirsty as the Scots, and now aping them. As the Ellices reached the wharf and their boat moved out on the river "the water was lighted up by the reflection of the villages, burning in all directions."[12] From Montreal "the country back of Laprairie presented the frightful spectacle of a vast expanse of livid flames, and it is reported that not a single rebel house had been left standing."[13] The report was not quite true, but it was near enough, and the *Herald* commented in philosophical mood. Humane men might grieve but hard necessities remained, even if the French Canadians were to be swept from the face of earth. "To have tranquility we must make a solitude."[14]

7

On November 13 Colborne returned from the south to Montreal. His operations were now almost concluded. On the 15th a column swept down from Sorel, clearing the wedge of territory between the Richelieu and the St. Lawrence. A patrol sent into the hills around Boucherville discovered the Grand Eagle flown. His camp and the breastworks round it were all empty, and there had been no attempt to carry away its stores.

The troops found powder and shot, a few more wooden cannon, and even some thirty firearms that had been left behind in the flight. Arms were no longer sought by eager *patriotes;* they were flung away by desperate, broken men. The only men with firearms in the whole desolate countryside were the patrols of regulars marching and counter-marching, the volunteers at their work of hunting rebels, and the guards who were bundling away their gaunt prisoners.

In Upper Canada the expected invasion of thousands had dwindled to an attack on Prescott by about eight hundred men. It had been a bungled crossing of the river in two schooners, one of which was driven off. The other had landed less than half of the force at a place called Windmill Point, a mile or so below Prescott. Here, around the stone windmill that gave the place its name, there had been a sharp and bloody engagement, but the position of the invaders was hopeless. For three days they had held on in the mill, but on November 17, surrounded by two regiments of British regulars and thousands of volunteers, the trapped men had surrendered. There would be more raids, each a little more desperate, each more stupid and hopeless, and tavern heroes on the safe side of the St. Lawrence would be bellowing for another year. But here, as in Lower Canada, rebellion's back was broken and the transport ship and the scaffold would complete what work remained.

A cloud of warrants hung over Montreal, and there was no more space to fill in the new prison. On Jacques Cartier Square by the waterfront, close to the column raised for Horatio Nelson, the "old" prison had been reopened, squeaking with rats and stinking of ancient wretchedness. It was becoming crowded too and there was soon to be a third prison, converted from a vacant warehouse near the second. Patrols and bailiffs were still tramping the streets, making their new arrests. Commissions and courts of inquiry sat each day, ridding the cells of small fry, clearing the way for new. Important prisoners remained, with or without evidence, so long as a breath of old suspicion touched them. LaFontaine had been in jail since November 4, and Edouard Fabre and Louis-Michel Viger had soon joined him. Delorimier and Prieur had arrived, taken close to the border. By November 18 Doctor Brien was sitting in a cell apart, writing for his life. There would be friends helped to the scaffold by that confession. Roped strings of prisoners, coming by country roads, arrived each day at Longueil and Laprairie. They were ferried across by steamer and met by English crowds as they reached the wharf, with snowballs and rotten apples and eggs and filth and spittle. In the grey city under its grey skies the hate, suspicion, and rancour of half a century had come to its flowering time.

Over it all Colborne presided grimly, not liking the work. Lady Colborne spoke of "the horrible Herald"[15] and Colborne shared her opinion both of the newspaper and of its friends. Yet rebellion had threatened the Empire a second time. Justice would have to be done and seen to be done. By the 19th of November the *Herald* was approving unctuously of "the new gallows made by Mr. Brondson. We believe that it is to be set up facing the prison so that the incarcerated rebels may enjoy a sight that doubtless will not fail to assure them sound sleep and agreeable dreams. Six or seven of them can be strung up at once without difficulty on the new gibbet, but a yet greater number at a pinch would it accommodate."[16]

Mr. Brondson's work was soon in its proper place. Other arrangements were made with due celerity. On the 28th of November, with the gallows overlooking the prison wall, the trials by court martial commenced.

NINE

"Dans l'abaissement"

For a little over five months, from the 28th of November to the 1st of May, the quiet, orderly drone of the trials continued. At the centre of the long table, flanked by a dozen officers, sat Major-General Clitherow, President of the court. The deputy judge advocate, another military officer, was in charge of the prosecution. He was assisted by two barristers and there were two appointed for the defence, but they were the only vestiges left of civil procedure. The thirteen hard-faced soldiers were judge and jury alike, for there was now no hope in another Court, or in any twelve men, for a true verdict rendered according to the evidence. Outside in the streets were the English mobs and newspapers, bellowing for rebel blood. Everywhere, silent around them, was the smouldering hate of the French. In the last depths of division, with the Conquest reasserted and never again to be accepted, the uniforms and the bayonets kept the law. The court martial was, in Colborne's opinion, "the only tribunal which, in the deplorable state of this province, can be relied on to dispense impartial justice between the Crown and the subject."[1]

Joseph-Narcisse Cardinal and eleven of the others taken at Caughnawaga were the first men to be arraigned. The proceedings went on, cool, fair, and inexorable, within the framework set by the victors. On December 8 two of the accused were acquitted and ten were found guilty, though with varying degrees of guilt. By December 14 the court's recommendation for mercy had been applied to six of the ten. On December 21, with the sentence of death in abeyance on two more, Cardinal and Joseph Duquette went to the scaffold.

They came out onto the snowy courtyard of the new prison, a man of thirty and a lad of twenty-three. For Cardinal, the older of the two, there had been no hope. He had been a leading notary in Chateauguay, a member of the provincial Assembly, and an unrelenting enemy of the bureaucratic régime. Determined and hard-headed, he had seen the hopeless folly of the first rising and had played no open part. Yet he had found himself at its close a lost man, surrounded by triumphant enemies, watched with grim suspicion, and driven by desperation toward the plans of the new leaders. He was soon with Robert Nelson below the border, and he had returned from there to recruit for the Frères Chasseurs. A known commander of rebels, he had blundered at Caughnawaga and been taken, arms in hand, accepting his fate from the first hour of capture. "Save that I leave you", he had written to his wife and five children, "nothing could make me desire life, and I should receive mercy with more repugnance than satisfaction."[2]

It was different with Joseph Duquette, the younger notary. Frail, sickly, and intense, a one-time student of Cardinal's, he had no wife or children and had had little time for his profession. Caught up in the first rising and driven south of the border with other rebels, he had returned to Canada under Durham's amnesty. But it was the same Canada for the *patriote*, the worse for its blackened fields, and he had soon been active with Cardinal in the work of the Frères Chasseurs. He was as guilty as but no guiltier than most of the men tried with him, and might well have hoped to be spared along with others. He still hoped, unmindful of the high policy that demanded stern examples. He walked stiffly, his face beaded with sweat, his eyes glazed and incredulous, behind the chief he had followed

182

to Caughnawaga. He was still following as they came to the wooden steps; there was to be no mercy for either.

The high platform, raised above the prison gate, was in full view of the crowds. They surrounded the walls and packed the near streets, in separate, murmurous seas of English and French. Cavalry held them back and troops were lined in the courtyard, forming an aisle to the scaffold. Beyond them, kneeling in snow with his pectoral cross raised, was the young assistant to the Bishop of Montreal, destined himself to be long remembered and remembering as Bishop Ignace Bourget. A priest walked with the prisoners, paced by the conducting officers, and there was a low murmur from behind them of men kneeling in the cells, reciting the *De Profundis*. The noose swung down from its beam, framed against a black sky, and under it Humphrey, the hangman, was a folk-image of his trade. He moved out, as the party came to the platform, huge-handed, bent almost double, with no mask hiding his scarred, grotesque face. The rigid officers in scarlet stepped away. Cardinal walked to the square beneath the rope and stood, nerveless and cold, as the loop settled and was drawn. There was to be no speech from the gallows; he did not desire the privilege. He looked out in silence over the thousands of upraised faces, the grey city and the grey river, the land in which he no longer wished to live. The trap fell, the rope ran out to stop with a sudden jerk, and he was a corpse twitching below.

There was to be no such cleanly end for the young Duquette. His legs gave as he was signalled over to the square, and he had to be held erect, shivering and sobbing. The rope was got into place and the trap was sprung, but the hurried hangman had set the noose badly. It slipped up to tighten across the mouth instead of the throat, and the writhing form plunged sideways. It crashed face first into one of the beams below and swung away unstrangled, with the bloody mask emitting its screams for mercy. They were to be heard for twenty minutes as Humphrey hauled the body back to the platform and began his work again. Then the trap opened, the rope fell straight and true, and the crack of snapping vertebrae brought release.

The courts droned on, the list of the guilty lengthened, and there remained the sorting out of the prime examples. By January 18 the choice had fallen on five. Joseph-Marie Robert was fifty-eight years old, François-Xavier Hamelin was twenty-one, and the two Sanguinet brothers, Ambroise and Charles, were men in their late twenties. The Sanguinets were members of an old seigneurial family that had been dispossessed by officialdom a quarter of a century earlier. Robert was a prosperous, influential farmer who had resigned his militia commission under Gosford and become a marked man since then. He had played no part in the first rising and had been hesitant to join the second, but he had been forced on like the Sanguinets as one of the natural leaders. Hamelin had simply followed the older men. They had all been prominent, however, at a little roadside skirmish on November 3, in which a house had been burnt down and a loyalist farmer killed. They were to go to the gallows now, convicted murderers. Pierre-Théophile Decoigne, a thirty-year-old notary, had been one of the force at Napierville and had fired on the Queen's soldiers. Distinguished for courage then, and selected now to exemplify the cost of treason, he walked along with the others.

By ten o'clock on the morning of the 18th the five bodies in their convict uniforms lay stretched out in the snow by the courtyard gate, awaiting their rough coffins. Passing them on the way inward came one of the Black Marias from the old jail, with prisoners for a trial that had been delayed an hour by the hangings. It was then in its eighth day, and when it was concluded on the 21st Jean-Baptiste-Henri Brien, François-Xavier Prieur, and Chevalier Delorimier were among those sentenced to death.

Eight others had been tried with the three, and of all the eleven men Delorimier had been declared most guilty. He had been known in Montreal, since the election of Tracy in 1832, as one of the brilliant youth in the Papineau party. He was charming, eloquent, dangerous, and the only one of the principals now in the toils. He had been Secretary of the Permanent Central Committee in Montreal, and he had fought at St-Denis in the first rising. He had been present at St-Eustache, though he had left before the battle, and he had returned to the county later to recruit for the Frères Chasseurs. To all this was added the guilt of Beauharnois, which had been found, by itself, enough to condemn Prieur. Delorimier fought his case like a skilful advocate but he had been a doomed man from the first.

For Brien, as was well suspected, the sentence was a mere formality. He had pleaded guilty on the opening day of his trial, and had accompanied his plea with a document that was not read in court. It was the confession that would help to convict some he had worked with, and it would turn him out of prison a few months later, free, banished, and execrated, to hide from other *patriotes* for the rest of his life. Yet if it was all guessed at now it was still only half-believed, and he shared a cell with Delorimier among the men waiting for death.

Prieur found himself with Hindenlang, who proved a difficult companion. The French soldier of fortune, denying the right of a British court to try him, had remained defiant to the end. He had seemed principally concerned that his name be spelt correctly in the indictment that would become history. Shut off now from his hated English judges, he alternated constantly between fits of high heroics and moods of black depression, and he varied some of his rantings with attacks on priests and the Church. For the stolid little farmer, who had fought and lost and accepted his fate and was now inclined to pray, he made the days long and many of the nights sleepless.

By February 12 there were almost fifty condemned in the cells on the main floor of the new prison. On the two floors above them the lesser prisoners were herded in great common rooms. Around the élite below, confined two by two, the long, dark corridors were restless with coming and going. New men under sentence were marched in, guards stamped back and forth, and visitors arrived with their gifts and tears and rumours. The final rumour for some hardened on the night of the 12th; there had been seven coffins delivered to the prison courtyard.

Two were not to be used. On the night of the 14th there were five places of honour at a macabre banquet held by permission of the authorities in the corridor outside the cells. One was reserved for Delorimier and one for Charles Hindenlang, but Prieur had been passed by. Another place was for Pierre-Rémi Narbonne, one of the last and bravest of the force destroyed at Odelltown. A sometime painter and sometime county bailiff, he had lost an arm in childhood and been given little as recompense in thirty-three years of life. Taken in the first rising, he had been freed under Durham's amnesty, but had come out of prison to find his wife dead. Destitute, with three children, and his old employment closed to a former rebel, he had placed his hope of revenge in the Frères Chasseurs. It was gone now, along with all other hopes, and only the defiant anger still remained.

185

The other two who were to walk with him in the morning had
both been taken at Odelltown, but were wanted for other
reasons. François Nicolas, a teacher of forty-one, and Amable
Daunais, a twenty-year-old farm boy, had been accused with
others of helping to kill an informer amid the tumult of the first
rising. Expressly excluded from amnesty, they had been tried
by a civil court, and their acquittal in spite of the evidence had
been a sharp rebuff for authority. Authority had not forgotten
when the men were taken again, and they were dying for the
old murder as well as the newer treason.

From the opened cells in the corridor other prisoners
gathered about the table. Candles were lighted and wine began
to flow, while the guards watched stolidly and curious officials
found cause for looking in. Brien was not at the table, nor could
he bear to spend the last night with Delorimier; he had begged
for Prieur to replace him and was now in Hindenlang's cell.
Delorimier himself was long in joining the others; he was walking with his young wife in another section of the corridor. She
fainted, still clinging to him, as the order came to leave, and he
carried her over to friends waiting by the doorway. The door
closed behind her and his face set in a clear and final calm. "The
worst blow has been struck." He moved over to stand in his
place at the table and, still standing, raised a glass to his friends.
Then he turned for his cell, where there were pens and paper
waiting. Through most of the night, as the sombre revel
dwindled away in the corridor and Hindenlang's oratory flared
and smouldered down, he wrote while Prieur watched.

There was a generous note to Brien, treating him as a fellow
sufferer, though he knew what the man was. There was a last
letter to his wife, and there were words for his small daughters.
They would be cared for, he hoped, in his name, for "I have not
been insensible to the woes of my kind." It would be forty-five
years later, when the wife and daughters were discovered in
obscurity and indigence, that that wish would be granted.
There was a note to Prieur with the lock of hair he had asked
for, and at last as dawn neared and it was time for the visit of
the priest, he wrote of the hope he died with: "My friends and
my children shall see better days; they shall be free . . . that is
what fills me with joy when all about me is desolation and
grief . . . The Canadian in peace shall see happiness and liberty
reborn on the St. Lawrence . . . the blood and tears flowing

today on the altar of Liberty water the roots of the tree which shall fly the flag marked with the stars of the two Canadas."[3]

In the assembly room in the morning there were the guards and silent officers and the five cups of coffee. The arms were bound to the sides and the jacket collars opened to leave the space clear at the throat. The door swung, giving on sudden daylight, and the crowd was a murmurous roar beyond the walls. The way led straight to the scaffold through a double file of troops. Hindenlang gasped and swayed as the sight struck him, but Delorimier touched his arm. "Courage, my friend." It was enough to recall the pride and restore the mask, and the soldier's head snapped up. "Death is nothing to a Frenchman."[4] He walked out to shout another defiance from the wind-blown platform and go the way he had wished. Nicolas and Daunais went quietly, without speech, but the fumbling work of Humphrey had reserved a last horror for Narbonne. The cord encircling his body had been too loosely tied. As the trap fell his single arm wrenched free and his hand shot out to tighten on the rope above him, holding its length slack. Twice he was knocked away and started to fall, and twice that desperate grip fastened again. It was only with a third blow, and with a last strangling scream, that the body dropped to stretch the rope to its limit and the final plunge brought silence.

Delorimier followed, the last man of the day, and with his going Humphrey's employment ceased. The courts martial went on, naming the men for death. Twelve additional sentences were given in February, twenty in March, twenty more in April and one on May 1. By May 6, the day the court dissolved, one hundred and eight had been tried, ninety-eight condemned, and twelve of the condemned hanged. Of some twelve hundred other prisoners who had passed through the various jails, most were now freed. Thom and his like were yelling for more hangings, but there were other English answering them now, weary and sick of blood. It would not cement peace, and it would not drown the fires that had troubled the peace. They would have to be dealt with otherwise when the wreckage was cleared away.

There was still more than enough of it as martial law was suspended and civil law returned. In the cells of the new prison eighty-six men remained under sentence of death. There were several others apart from them who haunted the official mind, and two at least were *causes célèbres* with the public. John Picoté de Belestre-MacDonnell, the half-way English traitor, was still awaiting his trial. Old Captain Jalbert, the only one who had been captured of the accused murderers of Weir, had lain in prison for nearly eighteen months. With habeas corpus restored, the bodies would have to be brought forth, and authority pondered the problem throughout the summer. By the end of August Colborne had reluctantly parted with Belestre-MacDonnell. Flagrantly guilty as he was, there had been no "overt act";[5] he had run instead of fighting. He had best be released, the Attorney General advised, for lack of sufficient evidence. In the case of Jalbert, however, the opinion given was gingerly optimistic. If the required witnesses could be gathered, and could be made to tell the truth, there was good hope of a conviction.

On September 3 the trial of Jalbert opened in the Court of Queen's Bench before three judges and a jury and a crowd of English spectators who were sure of a quick decision. The authorities by then had come to share the confidence, for the time allotted to the session was very short, with the court's mandate expiring on September 15. Yet day by day, in the midst of mounting fury and incredulity, proceedings all went wrong. The Attorney General produced his required witnesses, and was soon regretting most of them. The wildly conflicting testimony, confused as the savage morning two years earlier, brought back all the rancours but could prove little or nothing. Weir had been hacked to death by many men, but there was only one in the dock. Where had Jalbert been? What had Jalbert done? Old men had forgotten and younger men lied; farm boys and farm girls collapsed in tears on the stand. They could be bullied, threatened, and stormed at but they could not be pinned down, and the case went to the jury with the senior judge himself conceding its weakness.

Of the twelve jurors seven were French Canadians, and they were all firm for acquittal. They were joined by three Englishmen who remained stubborn to the end. For five days the twelve were kept in their room, locked ten to two, part of the time with bailiffs who were instructed to hold them "without meat, drink, fire or candle, and to suffer none to speak to them nor speak to them themselves except to ask if they are agreed."[6] They were called back for the last time at a quarter before midnight on the night of the 15th. The courtroom was packed to the doors, the mood of the crowd was obvious, and it had dined well. According to the Attorney General, it was suffocating him with its "Bacchic vapours".[7] The presiding judge put the usual question to the foreman and received the usual answer; there had been no verdict reached. He rose, dismissing the court, and as midnight struck Jalbert was a free man. Instantly the mob was swarming over the benches, wrestling with bailiffs trying to protect the prisoner, and pummelling the offending jurors with fists and canes and clubs. Once more, and an hour later, it was only the tramp of soldiers that restored peace. Whatever the form of law in the distracted country, it was the bayonet that still ruled.

2

Ten days later, on September 25, 1839, the last phase of the clearing away began. François-Xavier Prieur, with fifty-seven of the others in the condemned cells, was ordered to prepare for departure the next morning. For these men the sentence of death had been commuted to transportation, and the old three-decker *Buffalo* was now waiting at Quebec. Behind them, as they left for the convict colonies of south Australia, there would be twenty-eight remaining who would linger for a while yet. Authority, pondering their dossiers, had set them to one side; they were either the less important or the less guilty. In a few months they would simply be turned out, free to return to what was left of their homes.

For the fifty-eight, the morning of the 26th began early, with a flooding in of agonized friends and families. Many had travelled through the night on an hour's notice, many distracted wives had brought their children, and the partings in those gloomy corridors would be a long and living memory. For little Prieur, who had no wife or children, it would be his mother's face and her words, "You will come home — you will come back to us again."[8]

At ten the order came for visitors to leave, and the weeping crowd was jostled out to the courtyard. There was a great clang, heard along the line of cells, as a pile of fetters was dumped in the assembly room. Then the cell doors opened, the fifty-eight came out as their names were called, and the fettering up began.

Shackled two by two in the familiar fashion, the prisoners were marched to the courtyard. There was one great breath of crisp September air, a glimpse of reddening maples over the walls, and then they were through the gateway. Around them, beyond the lines of cavalry and infantry, were the faces of wives and children and the known voices, merging now in the low, long murmur of the crowd, building its memories too. It was a swift and passing blur, almost too brief to sense, for there was none of the ceremony this time of the sending off to Bermuda. Below at the quay, waiting to take them to Quebec, was the steamer *British American*, and they were herded down to her side at a half-trot. In fifteen minutes they were lined up on the foredeck and the ship was under way.

At Quebec *Buffalo* was waiting, an old man-o'-war, with ports in her heavy sides for thirty guns. By eleven o'clock on the morning of the 27th the prisoners had been marched on board. Following them, manacled in the same way, came eighty-four men condemned in Upper Canada and two ungrateful felons who had been allowed to share the dignity of political prisoners. In the reek of the third deck, well below the waterline, handcuffs were knocked off, mattresses handed round, and one hundred and forty-four men shoved to their places.

They moved bent double, and half the group would be shut away from the other. A double corridor ran the length of the ship, divided down its middle by a rough partition of packing-boxes and crates. At either end was an iron grille and a sentry, and the lanterns there provided the only light. The partition rose to the full height of the 'tween-deck, which was about four and a half feet, and on either side was the living-space for the prisoners. A long common shelf, built out from the inner hull, would serve both as a bench and as a locker for their few possessions. Below that, with about ten feet to stretch out in, and rubbing shoulder to shoulder, each man spread his mattress.

Dinner came down and they munched on their first meal, of corned beef and biscuit. Five hours passed, and buckets of oatmeal soup were handed round. Blankets came, thin and rough as the mattresses, one for each two men. They were allowed a trip to the water-closet on the next deck above, always under guard of a burly sentry. Then, forbidden to talk, in blackness and foul air, they waited out the night alone with their thoughts. As dawn came, though there was no change in the darkness, they could guess at the sounds above. Chains scraped; the anchor was coming up. A tug hooted, there was a groan and swaying of timbers, and the hard deck beneath them began to heave. There was a shudder and boom of cannon overhead, and then the guns from Cape Diamond acknowledging the ship's salute. The echoes died, the tug hooted in departure, and they were under way for Australia.

They saw the last of the St. Lawrence during their daily hour in the air, when they were allowed to march on the deck in two groups. Then came the plague of seasickness and most lay huddled below, with the vomiters prodded by sentries to the tub on the next deck and other prisoners swabbing the mess behind them. The salt beef and the oatmeal, the suet pudding and biscuit and maggoty bacon came on unrelentingly at the appointed times. The food was not much worse than that of the sailors, but it was always bad and strange. Thirst was an incessant torture, for even the foul green water was strictly rationed. Lice came, and the bodies crammed in the darkness became masses of red-scratched sores.

Yet the iron routine had one impersonal purpose, to deliver the bodies whole. The lice were scrubbed away at the laundry tubs, and the clothes pipe-clayed stiff. The weekly shave with the one communal razor left faces gashed and raw from the cold salt water, yet they remained the faces of men and not animals. The guards were always quick with the fist and boot, but they were seamen and not jailors. In spite of all orders there was sometimes rum for a sick man or a stolen ration of water, and in one case there was a flogging for the guard who brought it. Lime came down as a fumigant when the ship nosed into the zone of tropic fevers, and the sharp, clean stink of whitewash grew over the other smells. During the first long leg of the voyage around the hump of South America one of the Upper Canadian prisoners died. There were to be no more deaths, however, and on November 30, when the ship put in to Rio de Janeiro after sixty-three days at sea, there were no sick to be removed.

For five days, during the allotted hour each day, there was at least the sight of land from a still deck. There were fresh vegeta-

191

bles and meat, replacing the rotting remnants of the first provisions, and lime juice came aboard to prevent scurvy. On December 5 the ship sailed again, and there were sixty-five days more of open sea. On February 8, 1840, Cape van Diemen lifted out of the haze, and on the 13th *Buffalo* came into Hobart Town, Tasmania. It was the destination for the prisoners from Upper Canada, and they clanked up from the 'tween-deck, shackled once again. There were six days in Hobart Town and six more days at sea, with a new emptiness in the hold and a new tension building among the men remaining below. Then there was another stillness and the scrape of the anchor chains. They were in the approaches to Sydney harbour.

The wide-flung arms of the Church embraced them here. Within an hour of the ship's anchoring the Catholic Bishop of Sydney was down in the hold, accompanied by an Irish priest who spoke French. For three hours they listened, comforted and advised, and heard the men's confessions. They returned two days later carrying the Host, and in the cramped gloom of the 'tween-deck, with candles glowing around a homemade altar, high mass was sung. Afterward there was anxious talk. The destination of the prisoners was Norfolk Island, hundreds of miles from Sydney and a hell-on-earth reserved for the worst convicts. Sydney itself was wary of French rebels and wanted them far away. It would be hard, as it was everywhere, to change the minds of authority, but the Bishop would do his best.

Five days passed and there was only the agony of waiting, interspersed with the chill of officialdom when the men were brought on deck. They were marched up in groups, to fill out forms and be questioned, and marched back below. With that done, there were more long days of silence, but the good news finally came on March 11. The Bishop had been successful to the extent of his bleak hopes; he had saved the French Canadians from Norfolk Island. They were to go to a place called Longbottom, a few miles up the coast.

At two that afternoon they were brought to the deck of *Buffalo* for the last time, manacled and in pouring rain. A schooner was lying under the side of the warship, and the handcuffed men went clambering down to board her. Their scraps of baggage followed, the schooner rounded away, and they were bearing north for the Paramatta River. About four they saw its mouth, a narrow gap in the flat, desolate shoreline, and the ship put in to a quay. There were soldiers lounging about it, and bullock carts were waiting for the prisoners' gear. It was only a mile to Longbottom and the men were expected to walk, but they had not set foot on land for a hundred and sixty-five days. As they plodded after the carts many stumbled and fell, and even those who completed the journey were racked with cramps for a week.

The camp was a gaunt quadrangle of sheds, barracks, and storerooms, enclosing a muddy square. A prisoner who crossed the square without permission would be subject to fifty lashes. For today there would be no work, it was late and it was too wet, but tomorrow the men would be digging and cutting stone. They were marched to stores to draw their convict uniforms and then to their sheds to be fed and locked up. They listened through the night to the drip of leaking roofs and tossed on their straw mattresses, seven thousand miles from home.

In the morning they were routed out in their rough brown shirts and trousers and formed in a wavering line in front of their huts. Guards went down the line with stamps and paint pots, marking jackets and trouser legs with the black LB for Longbottom. One of the prisoners grinned wanly at his neighbour; in the far-off days at Chateauguay they had both been promised medals. "Be content, my boy. This is the decoration — your Cross of Honour."[9]

TEN

"Let me take this instrument . . ."

It was almost a year and a half now since Durham
had left for England, and Durham himself was in the last
months of his life. He was to die on July 28, 1840. He had
arrived in Plymouth on December 1, 1838, to receive no welcome from any of Melbourne's cabinet. By December 7 he had
reached London, by December 10 the resignation of his commission had been accepted, and by February of 1839 his report
had been completed. It had appeared first in *The Times*, forcing
the hand of a government that had been half inclined to
suppress it, and by March of 1839 its contents were known in
Canada.

The magnificent, magniloquent essay was already the sign
and portent of a new era. The sick man had done what he had
come to do; there was no hope and no vista that would ever be
the same again. He had cleared away the past and its feudal
rubble. He had struck down, with searing and eloquent scorn,
the ancient pretensions of councils and the hopes of colonial
aristocrats. He had searched through every evil that plagued the

colony, untangled the long skein of misgovernment and indifference at home, judged the conditions of life, and appointed remedies. He had looked out over the vast extent of the continent and the years that lay ahead and had painted a thrilling picture of the nation that would one day rise, made of itself, governing itself. He had told the imperial mother in plain terms what that government must be, rooted in and responsible to the people. Yet he had seen it all through the eyes he had first come with, as the work and hope of a people wholly British.

The two nations who were now warring in the bosom of a single state must be made one nation. The last hope of *la nation canadienne* must be brushed away. "I entertain no doubt of the national character which must be given to Lower Canada; it must be that of the British Empire; that of the majority of British America; that of the great race which must, in the lapse of no long period of time, be predominant over the whole North American continent." He saw, respected, and patronized the many virtues of the French, but "the remnants of an ancient colonization...are and ever must be isolated in the midst of an Anglo-Saxon world ... It is but a question of time and mode; it is but to determine whether the small number of French who now inhabit Lower Canada shall be made English under a government which can protect them, or whether the process shall be delayed until a much larger number shall have to undergo, at the rude hands of its uncontrolled rivals, the extinction of a nationality strengthened and embittered by continuance."[1]

He was for no rudeness, and there was to be no revengeful triumph for predestined masters. With the coming of responsible government the *bureaucrates* and the councils would all go down. Rising in their place, yet not usurping their powers, the confraternity of the merchants would unite the Canadas, in cool and reasoned fulfilment of the long-delayed dream. The upper province was bankrupt, because its thriving, striving Englishmen had mortgaged themselves to the future. The lower province was solvent because the French had clung to the past. That stubborn apathy must go now in a new and common striving. With all debt pooled, and the reluctant partner saddled with his due share, there was hardly a hope or promise that could not be speedily redeemed. The fruits of trade would be shared by east and west, progress and education would be one and indivisible. The half-built canals and waterways would be driven on to

195

completion, and the long-unbuilt begun. The St. Lawrence, linking them all, opened up by them all, would be the imperial road of commerce from the mid continent to the sea. It would be lined at last with a people wholly British, and the work would be done at leisure by the forces of time and growth. "If the population of Upper Canada is rightly estimated at 400,000, the English inhabitants of Lower Canada at 150,000 and the French at 450,000, the union of the two provinces would not only give the English a clear majority, but one which would be increased every year by the influence of English emigration. And I have no doubt that the French, when once placed by the legitimate course of events and the working of natural causes in a minority, would abandon their vain hopes of nationality."[2]

2

Louis-Hippolyte LaFontaine had been released from prison in December of 1838. By the spring of 1839, as the one man capable of leadership among desperate French Canadians, he was facing the prospect offered by Durham's Report. He saw it darken steadily as the gallows was torn down, the exiles sailed for Australia, and the prisoners remaining behind them emerged as free men, bitter, destitute, and silent. By October Colborne was gone, already replaced by Charles Poulett Thomson, the brisk Manchester businessman who was soon to become Lord Sydenham and governor of the United Canadas. By July of 1840 the Act of Union had passed in the British Parliament, and on February 10, 1841, it was formally proclaimed in Canada. To a people "dans l'abaissement" the future was now revealed.

For Melbourne's government in England one dominant idea had emerged from the report. "It is laid down by us all as a fundamental principle that the French must not be reinstated in power in Lower Canada."[3] That had been well assured by the new creation. The United Canadas were to be governed by a single Parliament, elected not on the basis of but in defiance of population. The four hundred thousand of the upper province and the six hundred thousand of the lower were each to be represented by forty-two members in a House of eighty-four. A governor would remain supreme, to be advised but not controlled by an appointed council. Councillors themselves would be answerable only to the governor, and as blithely free as they had ever been from control by the elected House. They were to sit now only at the governor's pleasure and not for life, and they were vaguely enjoined that the exercise of authority must be "in accordance with the well-understood wishes of the people". Yet it was still the Governor-in-Council who would interpret every wish. The promise of Durham's statistics had been considered insufficient, and the best of his hopes ignored. There was to be no truck nor traffic with his theories of colonial rule. The vision of responsible government had been deformed by a grudging Torydom with its face turned to the past.

Yet the past was gone, somehow blown away with the wars and ruin. There were young men now who sensed it, and they were not all of them French. There was to be no return, even in the name of progress, to the cliques and the Family Compacts that had forced rebellion on. It was the conviction of Robert Baldwin, the reformer of Upper Canada, who had turned away from Mackenzie but not from Mackenzie's goal. The same conviction made young Francis Hincks, the ambiguous juggler and twister of later years, into a clear-eyed man of the people for these times. The two of them plunged together into the fight for responsible government, and they saw that their ally loomed from among the French. He was sought in a new mood, presaging a new time. "There is and must be no question of races," wrote Baldwin to LaFontaine. "It were madness on one side and guilt, deep guilt, on both to make such a question."[4] Over and over Hincks wrote in assurance "that your brother-reformers in Upper Canada will meet you and your compatriots as Canadians, that no national animosities will be entertained, that we desire your friendship, esteem and co-operation."[5]

On July 14, 1841, the first Parliament of the united Canadas met in Kingston, seemingly a docile tool for Sydenham's use. English was the only language of official proceedings. The Council bristled with Tories, and was wholly dominated by the English. The electoral methods of the businessman anxious to get on with progress had made every other assurance doubly sure. There were forty-two English members from Upper Canada, and nineteen members from the lower province whom

197

the Governor could safely refer to as "my candidates". He had bribed, intimidated, and gerrymandered to help them on to election, and his agents' imported bully-boys had defeated LaFontaine. Etienne Parent, among the leaderless twenty-three from Lower Canada, elected as French reformers and tainted as French rebels, spoke for the mood of all. "God in His mercy has left hope to the oppressed, and it is all that remains to us."[6]

Yet before the session was over there were portents broad in the sky. Robert Baldwin, elected for two ridings and obviously a coming leader in Upper Canada, had been appointed to a seat in Council as a move to appease reform. He resigned on the first day, disputing the Council's status. It had too few French, and most were the Governor's creatures; no such council could enjoy the confidence of the House. That it enjoyed the Governor's confidence was not enough; only the elected members spoke for "the well-understood wishes of the people". Within another three months Louis-Hippolyte LaFontaine, the twice-imprisoned Frenchman and friend of rebels, sat as the member for York in Upper Canada. He had, at the urging of Robert Baldwin, been elected by acclamation to Baldwin's second seat. A year later Baldwin, defeated by outraged Tories in his own riding, was the elected member for Rimouski in Lower Canada. He spoke no French and LaFontaine halting English, but the message was clear in both tongues on either side of the Ottawa. A majority of the two peoples had been joined for a common work; they intended to rule their rulers by the parliamentary process.

The other fact was not long in emerging, as election after election spelt it out. It was the rebellious, beaten French, wholly united and grimly set on survival, who must become the senior partner. The leaders returned to seats in their own provinces, but the weight of the alliance swung inexorably east. The leader in Upper Canada, bent on responsible government, contended with other English aims and factions. The leader in Lower Canada, for as long as the one great issue hung in the balance, had the single goal of a people clear before him. It would remain clear; it had always been clear for this man; the ten great years had begun for LaFontaine.

He was thirty-four in 1841, three years younger than Baldwin and a man of the same grey cast: stolid, pragmatic, banking his fires deep. He had held apart from rebellion and been called a traitor by his friends. He had been the man the friends turned to when they were helpless amid the ruins, and he had been called a rebel by the English. He had seen a ray of hope in the coming of Durham, and had been rebuffed and disappointed. He had been locked away by Colborne at the start of the second rising, though he thought it madder than the first. He had come for a second time from a British jail, to be faced by Durham's Report and then the result of the Report, distorted in the Act of Union. He had faced Sydenham as he had faced Colborne, a man adamant for justice but seeking it through the law, and he had not yielded to the despair and bitterness round him. He had searched out amid Durham's arid eloquence the one hope for the French, and he had taken the extended hand of Robert Baldwin. "I am in favour of this English principle of responsible government...the reformers in the two provinces form an immense majority...our cause is common." He had turned then, holding the detested Act, to the people of his own province: "Let me make use of this very instrument to save those whom it was designed to ruin, to place my fellow-countrymen in a better place than they have ever occupied."[7]

It was bruising, bitter politics through the reigns of three governors and part of the reign of a fourth. The great cross-currents ripped their way through the country, forcing up other issues, creating new divisions. Yet the central issue remained, and the two unchanging men; the alliance held. There was always Baldwin standing with LaFontaine. For the first time in these Canadas that title of fellow countryman bridged the Ottawa, and sounded an echo even across the Atlantic. Sydenham died and Bagot came to replace him, speaking French, liking the French, a shrewd, well-willed diplomat, alert to the new day. There were no more rigged elections, the wind was allowed to blow the way it set, and it shredded away the authority of Tory councils. The majorities grew in the House, always a little more dominant, always a little more French. "It is impossible to conceal from oneself the fact that the French members of the Assembly possess the power of the country."[8]

Bagot died and the dying Metcalfe came, eaten away by cancer yet a man of the old stamp, a governor who meant to govern. The half-won grip of the people was to be pried loose from the sceptre. "It is now, perhaps, too late to remedy the evil,"[9] but he tried to his last day. There were more times like the old times of Papineau, with tottering ministries shored up by officialdom and rebellious Houses standing prorogued and empty. Yet over it all and always a little louder was the well-understood wish, irresistible now. It had found itself in the voices of two men, it spoke in two tongues; it demanded the reins of government for men answerable to Parliament and through Parliament to the people. Elgin came, the last of the four governors and the son-in-law of Durham, sensing the Report's greatness, anxious to redeem its faults. The inevitable was clear before him and he welcomed it as a fact. He opened Parliament in 1849 with LaFontaine and Baldwin as his principal ministers, and he read the Speech from the Throne in English and French.

Durham's memory was vindicated, responsible government had come; and every other hope was stood on its head. Of Elgin's two First Ministers the first was a French Canadian, and the Governor's own voice, speaking in its own tongue, had lifted the pall of conquest from *la nation canadienne*.

3

The Speech from the Throne was delivered in Montreal, the new capital of the province, and among those who listened were Louis-Joseph Papineau and Wolfred Nelson, honourable members of the House. Nelson had returned in 1842, Papineau three years later, and they had both discovered constituents who were eager to have them back. They were no longer friends, for the quarrel over St-Denis lay thick between them, and Nelson's charges of cowardice bespattered the returned leader. Yet they were linked by a bond that united many others; they were free men under pardons that had been won by LaFontaine.

It had been his steady, dogged purpose from the day he began his work in the united province: to erase the stains of disloyalty, to restore the banished men, and finally to repay the innocent whose homes had been plundered and burnt. He was to close the books of rebellion with the Rebellion Losses Bill, and the cloud of that coming battle loomed ahead. There were no innocent *patriotes* to an English Tory, and there were too many to the French. The innocent Wolfred Nelson was demanding twelve thousand pounds. He would not get it, but many would get their due, and in the meantime the other work was complete. The Queen's onetime enemies were again forgiven subjects, and if there was flint in the smile of amnesty there was gold for at least one.

In 1845, as the result of three years' effort by LaFontaine, Papineau's sentence of exile came to an end. He returned at his surly leisure, indifferent to all forgiveness, and unforgiving. Six years before, as the flames of the second rising smouldered down, he had wearied of the friends in Albany and the friends had wearied of him. He had sailed for France in February of 1839, and it had been a relieved parting on both sides. Life had been dull in France, lightened by a few friendships with some of the great of Paris, warmed by the presence of the family as they came to join him. Yet there were no means for the entertainment of the great; the straitened Canadian exile had been compelled always to be a guest, and invitations had dwindled. Listeners had grown fewer, and writings had remained unread. One by one the family had drifted home, drawn by their own affairs. He had moved from house to house, each one a little smaller, frequently pressed for money, always with the old thoughts and the old angers. These were not relieved by the warmth of the welcome home, or by the acclamation to Parliament, or by the presence of LaFontaine. The cheers came from the few, and they were surrounded by a chill silence. The little receptions and triumphs were a minuscule of the past, the crabbed writing on the wall; Papineau might be remembered but it was LaFontaine who ruled.

Yet if there was to be no rule there were old rights, and Papineau remained unchanged in changing times. He had not forgotten the salary of Mr. Speaker, so long unpaid in the stormy days of Gosford. Neither had LaFontaine, and the Parliament of the United Canadas was acquiescent. In 1846, with due authorization by a unanimous vote and "as a right and not as a favour",[10] came a government cheque to Louis-Joseph Papineau for forty-five hundred pounds. On the drab old seigneury of La Petite Nation the beautiful Montebello began to rise.

There was to be less than that for lesser men, but there were no forgotten exiles. As the hope of amnesty broadened into fact it promised to embrace the men sent to Australia. It did not embrace their return, for if the Queen's ship had taken them they must find their own way home, and it was a long way for the penniless. Yet they had long-remembering friends and there were even a few enemies who were now inclined to forgive. In 1843, with the assistance of Ludger Duvernay and supported by LaFontaine, Edouard Fabre organized L'Association de la Délivrance to provide the men with passage money as soon as they were pronounced free. Some twenty-five hundred pounds were soon raised, and the long list of donors included Governor Metcalfe. Yet even with the funds in hand the men were scattered in Australia, some of them still not pardoned and seven thousand miles away. It remained to contend with the creeping progress of the amnesties, the red tape of officialdom, and the endless snags and difficulties of communication by sea.

4

François-Xavier Prieur and his fifty-seven companions had spent about six months in Longbottom, digging stone, breaking it, and hauling it off by bullock cart over the raw, half-built roads of New South Wales. They had suffered a great deal from the fierce Australian mosquitoes and almost as much, for a while, from a brutal camp commander and guards who were usually drunk. When the guards turned to attack the commander, however, and the commander called on his prisoners to lock them up, the human pests had become almost neutralized. The Canadians had had better food and better treatment. Guards had winked when they stole corn from the bullocks and ground it into meal for "coffee". The commander had allowed some after-work commerce, and the prisoners had roamed the shore along the bay, collecting shells that they sold for making lime. Two men had gone off, grey-faced, lying on straw in a cart, to die in a Sydney hospital eight miles away. The remaining men, however, when the time came for the next phase of their punishment, were in reasonable health and spirits.

Prieur became one of a group commuting to Sydney, still in the brown uniforms bearing the LB stamp but less heavily guarded. They left their huts in bullock carts each morning and were brought back each night, but their long day was spent on the city streets with only a foreman watching. They were hauling stone and cutting wood for paving-blocks, and they were now a species of trusty. There was many an ex-convict among the citizens passing round them, and the booming town seemed friendlier as it grew accustomed to the French rebels. When the next phase came on, some fourteen months later, they found themselves for a while in much demand.

They were now bondsmen, still under supervision but permitted to hire out. Acquired en bloc by farmers in need of labourers, they were part of an official transaction which earned them 7s. 6d. per week. Of this, half went to the farmer to pay for provisions and half to the prisoner's credit in a government bank, for his use when he became a free man. In the meantime, living in huts apart from the main house, supplied with rations and cooking their own food, the prisoners were strictly confined to the limits of the master's property. It was rather more comfortable for some than the next stage of the process, when they were dumped out as ticket-of-leave men onto a country sunk in one of its sudden depressions.

Prieur, in this state, was free to work where he pleased and for whom he pleased, so long as the police approved. The difficulty now, however, was to find any employment. He whipped eggs and scoured pans in a confectionery shop till the shop went out of business. There was a brief stint as a factory hand till the factory also failed. Then, with his pockets empty and evicted from his last lodgings, he strayed into the shop of a prosperous merchant who proved to be a former convict. For Prieur everything changed from that day. Abruptly he was a respected clerk, one of a genial family, with pleasant work at a counter and an airy room of his own in the merchant's house. Yet it was too much and it was not enough. The old friends came by, he wanted to be with them, and the master was sympathetic when he left.

By 1843, with nine others of the exiles, he was established in an abandoned sawmill, nine miles from Sydney along the Paramatta River. There was some rusting old equipment, their pooled resources supplied a little more, and through the next year they fought the bush for a living. Well back from the river there were great trees, five or six feet in diameter and a hundred feet tall. They hacked them down, hauled them back to the mill, sawed them into four-foot billets, and split the billets for laths. At night, when darkness put an end to the work, they sat at supper around their own table, talking of home and singing the old songs.

The cargoes of laths were freighted down to Sydney, and little ever came back but provisions for the next stint. The fees of carters and bargemen took the rest, but there was better than money here; they were almost free men. Then as a bush fire swept over the property they were once more jobless wanderers.

It was not so bad, tramping round Sydney now, swag on back, stick in hand, for everyone seemed to know and like the Canadians. Times were still hard, but Prieur discovered some businessmen from France who were establishing themselves in the city and required the services of an interpreter. He had a spell of that till his employers discovered the real quality of his English, and then he was back on a farm.

By 1845, when the first word came that some of the men had been pardoned, he was in the baking, blacksmith, and grocery business with three others of the Canadians. They had established themselves at a crossroads boasting two taverns and three huts and bearing the name of Irishtown. By the time their work was finished they had added a long, bark-covered stall to serve as a smith and a forge, a mud hut that was both a dwelling and a shop, and a Canadian outdoor oven that they had built of potter's clay. The great news from Canada, however, disrupted all plans, and it was followed by word of still other pardons, including one for Prieur. He and his partners were soon back in Sydney, and a first group of the exiles was arranging passage home.

He was not yet to be one of them. There was delay in confirming pardons and there was confusion in forwarding money. For Prieur none came, and he had no money of his own. There were farewells to luckier friends, another job as a clerk in a drygoods shop, and more months of waiting, the worse now that it could be so near its end. "Every Sunday I spent the afternoon on a rock in a solitary little bay overlooking Sydney harbour. There I dreamed of my homeland and my family."

Mailboats came, but they brought no news or money. The

Governor sent for Prieur to inform him that the sum for his passage had been raised in Canada, but it did not come to hand. Finally there was one more job. Philip Mesnier, another French merchant established in Sydney, had become disgusted with his prospects and intended to return to Europe. He required help in the winding up of his affairs, and the fee would be a passage home. It was the last work in Australia for the thirty-year-old convict who was to die forty-six years later as Superintendent of Prisons for the Dominion of Canada. By January of 1846 he was preparing to leave with Mesnier. In February, installed as a cabin passenger in a comfortable first-class ship, and with thirteen fellow exiles still waving from the dock, Prieur sailed for London.

He arrived in June and was soon in touch with friends. The long arm of L'Association de la Délivrance was groping out for him here. An agent found him in lodgings to deliver greetings and money, and by July 13 he was outward bound for Canada. On September 2 he saw the Gaspé shore, and his delight evoked a party. An English major, one of his fellow passengers, arranged the affair with the captain and several others, and there were many drinks to Canada and to Prieur and the safe return. On September 10 the ship dropped anchor at Quebec, and the calèche of the debarking passenger climbed to the Canada Hotel. As the driver whipped away with a brisk "Marche donc!", the creak of Longbottom's bullock carts and tired "Hi-djii" that had urged the beasts on became a remote and dying echo.

Friends crowded in on him during his few hours at Quebec, and there were more to be seen next day in Montreal. Duvernay called and Prieur was taken to Fabre, and from him to LaFontaine. He discussed the work of deliverance and examined some of the snags. They were many but it was going well; within another fifteen months, except for the two who had died and one who married and stayed, all the men would be back. But that was for the future then, and home was near.

On the morning of September 12 he took the steamer for Beauharnois and went on from there by land. The farm was outside St-Timothée and the carriage seemed to crawl; it was two o'clock in the morning when he reached his door. There had been rumours for weeks that he was on the way home but there had been no certain word, and he came on a sleeping house.

205

Suddenly, with the knock, there was a great stirring and rising, and he was enveloped in reaching arms. His mother's tears were wet on his cheeks again. "It's Xavier—yes—yes—it's Xavier, our dear boy!"

All the lamps in the house were soon blazing, and there began to be answering gleams from the night outside. In other farmhouses round them "the old men who often get up at night to light their pipes at the stove door" looked out of their windows and roused their families. "Look! It must be Xavier Prieur come back from exile. They will be very happy there."

The mothers and sons and daughters and the hired hands and girls began to tumble out in their night-clothes. "We must go welcome him"—"*should* we go?—maybe we will disturb them." But the final answer was always much the same: "What! —does one disturb his neighbors when he goes to celebrate with them for the return of a son? Get dressed, the lot of you!"

The wagons began their clatter over the roads, stopping at any houses that were still dark. "Get up—get dressed! Xavier Prieur's home—aren't you coming to see him?" More gleams began to speckle the countryside, the Prieur house was filled, and François-Xavier was enveloped by heavy-coated, big-booted men and women with woollen shawls over their heads and clothes hastily flung on, talking, embracing, laughing, and shedding tears. It went on till five in the morning, when his mother put an end to it. "This is only the beginning of what you have to tell us. The rest will keep—you are tired."

His room had been ready for weeks, dusted each day, fresh-smelling and immaculate, with the thorn-crowned Christ on the wall and the gay coverlet on the bed. He was alone in it at last, looking around him wonderingly as distant lights on the countryside began to pale with dawn. "Yes. Yes, I am really home."[11]

5

On April 25, 1849, Lord Elgin, the Governor General, sanctioned the Rebellion Losses Bill, passed by the government of LaFontaine and Baldwin. It was to compensate Lower Canadians, as Upper Canadians had already been compensated, for the various injuries they had suffered through no fault of their own. It had been fought to the last ditch; it was suspect in many of its items; but it had seemed to a majority in Parliament to be a reasonable price for peace.

That afternoon, as Elgin left the Parliament Building, his carriage was chased and pelted by an English mob. That evening on Place d'Armes George Moffatt was present, as he had been at the May Day Riot of 1832, seventeen years older but still of the same mind. He was chairman of a great meeting that had been summoned by crier and broadsheet through the course of a riotous day. The theme of every speaker was a demand for the recall of Elgin and the disallowance of the Rebellion Losses Bill, and the evening did not end with the last speech. Possibly it was not meant to, for the crowd that broke away and flooded up through the darkness onto a Parliament still in session had strange constituents for a mob. As the doors were battered in, the members driven from their chamber, and as flames rose from the gutted and smashed interior to envelop the whole building, it was the well-dressed and respectable of commercial Montreal who stood and watched from the sidewalk. They watched for five days more, still approving, as hordes of their friends and disciples roamed the streets, burning, savaging, wrecking LaFontaine's home, destroying the "Sodom and Gomorrah"[12] that had given domination to the French. But it was of no use. Elgin was not recalled, the motherland remained unmoved; the sceptre had crossed the Atlantic and had changed hands. The power wrenched from the oligarchy was held by the two peoples and the future lay with them now, to make of it what they could.

In 1851 LaFontaine resigned and retired from political life. The effects of his work were clear, and though he was a man who was rarely eloquent he had proud words in farewell. "The Union," he said, "was designed to annihilate French Canadians. But the result has been very different. The very race that had been trodden into the depths now finds itself, in some sort by this Union, in a position of command today. Such is the position in which I leave the people of my race."[13]

Yet he was leaving Papineau behind him, and he was leaving because of Papineau. A man as unchanged as Moffatt, Papineau was to remain in Parliament for three more years, bitter, obstructive, repudiated, but tearing at LaFontaine's name, tearing at all he had done. "On his return from exile," LaFontaine confided to a friend years later, "Papineau claimed incessantly that I had sold out to the English. I scorned these accusations at first, but I saw that they took hold among the young Liberals, who believed them. I could not hold on and I resigned."

In the same year Baldwin also retired. The work of the two was done; and it was a work already threatened. They had ended the long nightmare and opened a new day, but time and growth worked on, building the inexorable pressures. The empty land called out, the new millions were coming, and they would not be long denied. There were still the inevitabilities foreseen by Durham, and there was still the need that had found its voice in Papineau. The "remnants of an ancient colonization" were still and always would be "isolated in the midst of an Anglo-Saxon world". They must die or grow to build a place in that world; there was no other choice. The choice had been made and determined now by LaFontaine and Baldwin. It would be confirmed by the young Macdonald and the young Cartier, and the work that would fall to them. Yet over the work of all, challenging the work of all, would be the hovering, restless spirit of the older man.

By 1854 Papineau had had enough of Parliament, and Parliament enough of him. It was, said the politicians combing the constituencies, as hard to find support for Papineau as to find ears of corn after the harvest. They did not search very carefully, or they were unable to feel the stirring of renewed growth. The cause of the flawed man had been greater than the man himself, and it would make no truce with progress on any terms but its own. Already those young Liberals whom he had detached from LaFontaine were asserting themselves in the face of an English continent, in the face of all growth "which imposes upon us a double nationality . . . an invasion of ideas and institutions foreign to our own . . . so as to render the one necessary, the other useless . . . to make us lose ours and adopt the other."[14] Papineau had failed in much and betrayed many, but he had quickened instincts never to rest again. Narrowed by his horizons but fed from its own roots, the French fact was alive in North America. It would not die, and it could not live in impotent isolation. It must reach out, broadening beyond Papineau, to the ground of the other fact, the other people.

It would be assaulted there, with ever-increasing force, by "ideas and institutions foreign to our own". Foreign but not hostile; it was the only key to the future. There was no refuge for the French in Papineau's arid dream; but the other hope of a nation wholly British was as dead as the eighteenth century. There would somehow have to be melding, a weaving of strands in common; yet there could be no breaking of either thread, whatever the resulting pattern. Out of the brutal lunacies of rebellion the stark imperatives of nationhood began dimly to emerge. They were a challenge to the nineteenth century, and they remain a challenge still.

6

Many of the surviving *patriotes* died early, broken and burnt-out men. Girouard was dead by 1855, though he had had some peaceful years. He had resumed his practice as a notary in St-Benoit, and had helped to rebuild the town. He was much respected by the French, regained the trust of the English, and was a friend of LaFontaine. But he would not re-enter politics. With his sketch-pad and his books, and a growing family round him, he waited out the end in a changing province.

For W. H. Scott, though he died four years earlier, there had been a more eventful aftermath. By 1844 he was restored to his business and prospering in St-Eustache. He was soon sitting for the riding of Two Mountains in the new provincial Parliament. A lifelong Presbyterian, for all his Catholic constituency, he remained true to his convictions at some considerable cost. On the day before he died, in December of 1851, he was married at last to the Catholic Marie-Marguerite Paquet, who had lived with him as his wife for twenty years and was the mother of his five children. Through all those years Scott had firmly refused to change his faith, or to enjoin change on the children. With equal firmness Marie-Marguerite had gone to mass each Sunday, though she could not receive communion. The death-bed union, whatever it did to solve the problems of eternity, did not lessen the earthly problems of inheritance. Scott's estate was sizeable, and he had been sixteen years in his grave when the last litigation was disposed of by the Privy Council in London.

Lucien Gagnon did not live to see amnesty. He died of consumption in 1842, an exile in New York State. He was brought back to his home parish of St-Valentin and buried according to his wishes in the *tuque bleu* and *étoffe du pays* of the *patriote*. Doctor Côté outlived him by eight years, and was also buried at last on his own soil. He had contrived to live, however, with storm and stress around him to his last day. While he took advantage of amnesty, he made no peace with the Church, and came home to a hostile parish to preach as a Baptist minister. Death found him in Vermont, the orator still, attending a Baptist convention.

Captain Jalbert died peacefully in St-Denis, some five years after his trial. Bonaventure Viger, the lively fighter, survived both risings, as well as exile in Bermuda, to become a prosperous farmer. As he grew older, it was said, his pride in the old battles gave way to pride in his cheese, which was noted throughout his county. François-Xavier Prieur, equally adaptable, became a prosperous merchant, a pillar of the Conservative party, and finally a Superintendent of Canadian prisons. George Etienne Cartier had become his friend, somewhere along the road of his own transition, as he rose from the status of rebel to become Prime Minister of his province and a maker of Confederation.

Wolfred Nelson lived on until 1863, never wholly at peace with former friends. But he remained the public servant, as member of Parliament and Mayor of Montreal. Finally, like Prieur, and with the same appropriate irony, he became one of the high officials in charge of prisons. Robert Nelson, as he departed Canada in 1838, had continued his southward journey to California. There, amid the hectic years that preceded and followed the Gold Rush, he somehow acquired a fortune and was somehow swindled out of it. He returned to New York and medicine, and was once again successful. By the early 1860s he was a prominent consulting surgeon and a writer on medical subjects. Occasionally he was in Montreal, though only to assist his colleagues on important operations. He had made the vow, he said, that he would never live in Canada while it was under British rule. It is not known that he was ever asked to recant, and he died in New York in 1873.

Edmund Bailey O'Callaghan, like his enemy Adam Thom, made no return to the storm he had helped to rouse. With his last farewell to Papineau in 1839 he seemed to have bade farewell to Canadian affairs. New York State was safe, peaceful, and inviting, and its public service required a man of letters. It accepted the Canadian rebel and soon tamed him. He died in 1880 as Archivist and State Historian and compiler of works of record.

Thom, high in the councils of Durham by 1838, returned with the Governor to England. He is said to have influenced Durham in some parts of the Report. In 1839 he was chosen by the Hudson's Bay Company to act as a councillor and magistrate in the courts of the Red River. He proceeded without delay to become as much detested by the Métis as he had been by the French Canadians, and he was removed from the bench in 1849. For five years longer, and in various other capacities, the country retained the blessing of his presence. It saw the last of him in 1854, when he returned to his native Scotland.

The Abbé Etienne Chartier, after his flight from St-Eustache, had arrived in Vermont and soon gone on to Albany. For months he had haunted Papineau, but had not been much in favour. As rebuffs came, he had inclined toward other leaders and had used his time in private to produce a malignant pamphlet. As an open letter to Papineau, unctuously and acidly dwelling on faults and failures, it would not have been much welcomed and he could not find courage to show it. But he had carried it on to Paris when he followed Papineau there, and had at last succumbed to temptation and let it appear in print. It broke the last link with Papineau and forged no link with any of the other leaders; the Abbé was too well known. He went on to Rome and then recrossed the Atlantic, in the hope now of regaining favour with the Church. Forgiveness was long in coming, and for a while restricted when it came. For several years, confined to the United States, he served at clerical duties in Indiana, and then in New Orleans. By 1845, however, with amnesty in effect, he had returned to his home province and resumed his usual course. Between 1845 and 1851 he held four curacies in Lower Canada and one in Arichat, Cape Breton. He died in a Quebec hospital in 1853.

Thomas Storrow Brown, who had gone as far as Florida in his southward flight from St-Charles, returned by easy stages to Montreal. By the early 1860s he was well established there, prospering modestly in business and with much explained away. He was slowly going blind as the result of his damaged eye, but he was to live long as a patriarch and a friend of the temperance cause. In 1864 he would certainly have been a spectator, and probably a lively commentator, at an imposing state funeral. LaFontaine came to his end in that year, dying a judge and baronet, and a disappointed man.

Papineau still remained, half a legend now. He lived on in retirement in his beautiful Montebello, while much was forgiven and forgotten by all but him. "I remain always unchanged . . . the political state of the country is more a stench in my nostrils than it has ever been . . . birthplace, old relatives, family interests chain me here like an oyster on the rock where I was born." Yet friends came to him still, and there were always the mellowing acres of the beloved seigneury, with respectful tenants doffing their bright caps. There were always the young men, scattering his seed in furrows far beyond him. He watched some of them in battle with George Etienne Cartier, that rebel of St-Denis, and he watched Cartier beat them and Confederation come. For the last time, on September 23, 1871, a lovely autumn landscape brightened round him. He sat at his study window and the white head drooped. "I shall see no more my garden and my flowers."

Notes

Chapter 1

1. Chester Martin, *Foundations of Canadian Nationhood* (Toronto: University of Toronto Press, 1955), p. 11.
2. Governor Murray to Lords of Trade, October 29, 1764, in W.P.M. Kennedy, *Documents of the Canadian Constitution* (Toronto: Oxford, 1918).
3. General Murray, "Report on State of Government", June 5, 1762, in Arthur G. Doughty, *Documents Relating to the Constitutional History of Canada* (Ottawa: King's Printer, 1907).
4. Instructions to Governor Murray, December 7, 1763, in Kennedy, *Documents of the Canadian Constitution.*
5. Aberdeen to Amherst, April 2, 1835. Enclosure no. 1, PAC.
6. T. Fred Elliott, quoted in Gérard Filteau, *Histoire des Patriotes* (Montreal: Editions L'A.C.F., 1938-42), vol. 1, p. 145.
7. Papineau to Neilson, June 27, 1823, Neilson Papers, PAC.
8. Helen Taft Manning, *The Revolt of French Canada* (Toronto: Macmillan, 1962), pp. 344-5. Also *The Vindicator*, Montreal, January 3, 1832.
9. Journals of Legislative Council of Lower Canada, January 17, 1832.
10. *The Vindicator*, May 15, 1832.

Chapter 2

1. Papineau to Neilson, June 1832, in Helen Taft Manning, *The Revolt of French*

Canada (Toronto: Macmillan, 1962), Appendix p. 383 (Ref. Neilson Papers, vol. 7, pp. 443-51).
2. *Report of the Permanent Committee of the Faculty of Medicine*, Quebec City, November 19, 1832.
3. John J. Bigsby, *The Shoe and Canoe* (London: Chapman & Hall, 1850), vol. 1.
4. *Report of Commission Appointed by the Sanitary Board of Thirty Councils to Visit Canada*, Philadelphia, 1832.
5. Robert Rumilly, *Papineau* (Paris: Ernest Flammarion, 1934), pp. 83ff.
6. John J. Heagerty, *Four Centuries of Medical History in Canada* (Toronto: Macmillan, 1928).
7. *Report of Commission Appointed by the Sanitary Board of Thirty Councils to Visit Canada*, Philadelphia, 1832.
8. Donald Creighton, *The Empire of the St. Lawrence* (Toronto: Macmillan, 1956), p. 276 (Ref. Montreal *Gazette*, September 11, 1832).
9. Rumilly, *Papineau*, pp. 83ff.

Chapter 3

1. Fernand Ouellet, *Histoire Economique et Sociale du Québec, 1760-1850* (Montreal: Editions Fides, 1966).
2. Ibid.
3. Helen Taft Manning, *The Revolt of French Canada* (Toronto: Macmillan, 1962), p. 319.
4. Thomas Storrow Brown, *Brief Sketch of the Life and Times of L. J. Papineau*, pamphlet, Redpath Library, McGill University, Montreal.
5. Aberdeen to Aylmer, April 2, 1835, Enclosure no. 4, PAC.
6. Mason Wade, *The French Canadians* (Toronto: Macmillan, 1955), p. 145.
7. Ibid.
8. Gérard Filteau, *Histoire des Patriotes* (Montreal: Editions L'A.C.F., 1938-42).
9. Papineau in speech at St. Laurent, May 15, 1837, in *Read and pass to your Neighbour*, pamphlet, Redpath Library, McGill University, Montreal.
10. T. Fred Elliott, *The Canadian Controversy*, pamphlet, PAC.
11. Glenelg to Gosford, July 17, 1835, in W.P.M. Kennedy, *Documents of the Canadian Constitution* (Toronto: Oxford, 1918).
12. Sydney R. Bellingham, Memoir, PAC, MG 24, Series B25, vol. 2.
13. Filteau, *Histoire des Patriotes*, quoting T. Fred Elliott, secretary of Gosford Commission.
14. Glenelg to Gosford, July 17, 1835, in Kennedy, *Documents of the Canadian Constitution.*
15. Ibid.
16. Ibid.
17. Ibid.
18. "Lord John Russell's Ten Resolutions", March 6, 1837, in Kennedy, *Documents of the Canadian Constitution.*
19. Donald Creighton, *The Empire of the St. Lawrence* (Toronto: Macmillan, 1956), p. 314.
20. Adam Thom in *Montreal Herald*, quoted from pamphlet, Redpath Library, McGill University, Montreal, 170 T36-20.
21. Colborne to Fitzroy Somerset, February 10, 1836, Colborne Papers, PAC, MG 24, Series A40.
22. Address of Assembly of Lower Canada, August 26, 1837, in Kennedy, *Documents of the Canadian Constitution.*
23. Journals of the Assembly of Lower Canada, August 26, 1837.

Chapter 4

1. Gosford to Glenelg, September 8, 1837, C.C. Correspondence, PAC.
2. Mason Wade, *The French Canadians* (Toronto: Macmillan, 1955), vol. 2, pp. 172-6, quoting Gérard Filteau.
3. Colborne to Gosford, October 6, 1837, *Imperial Blue Book*, 1838, PAC.
4. *Morning Herald*, Quebec, November 10, 1837.
5. L.-O. David, *Les Patriotes de 1837-1838* (Montreal: Eusèbe Sénécal & Fils, 1894), p. 23.
6. Ibid.
7. F.-X. Garneau, *Histoire du Canada*, 4th ed. (Montreal: Beauchemin & Fils, 1882), vol. 3, p. 341.
8. Amury Girod, Journal, PAC.
9. Quoted in *Imperial Blue Book*, 1838, PAC.
10. *Montreal Herald*, November 20, 1837, quoted in *Imperial Blue Book*, 1838, PAC.
11. Girod, Journal, p. 373.
12. Gérard Filteau, *Histoire des Patriotes* (Montreal: Editions L'A.C.F., 1938-42), p. 27.
13. Trial of Jalbert, C.O. 42/296 ff., 85-93 v., PAC.
14. Ibid.

Chapter 5

1. Gore to Colborne, November 25, 1837, C.O. 42, PAC.
2. Gérard Filteau, *Histoire des Patriotes* (Montreal: Editions L'A.C.F., 1938-42).
3. L.-O. David, *Les Patriotes de 1837-1838* (Montreal: Eusèbe Sénécal & Fils, 1884), p. 138.
4. Sir George Bell, *Rough Notes by an Old Soldier* (London: Day & Son, 1867).
5. Wetherall to Colborne, November 27, 1837, C.O. 42, PAC.
6. D. B. Read, *The Canadian Rebellion of 1837* (Toronto: C. B. Robinson, 1896), p. 254 ff., quoting Captain Beauclerk.
7. Trial of Jalbert, C.O. 42/296 ff., 85-93 v., PAC.
8. Ibid.

Chapter 6

1. Colborne to Fitzroy Somerset, December 7, 1837, C.O. Correspondence, *Imperial Blue Book*, 1838, PAC.
2. C.O. 42/276, p. 63.
3. Ibid.
4. Gosford to Glenelg, October 5, 1837, Correspondence Relative to Affairs of Lower Canada, Accounts and Papers, 1838, vol. 39, Enclosure no. 36.
5. Amury Girod, Journal, PAC, vols. 1-14, Geo. V, V.A. 1924.
6. Ibid.
7. Notes of Alfred Dumouchel, *Bulletin des Recherches Historiques*, vol. 35, 1929, pp. 31-51.
8. Girod, Journal.
9. Ibid.
10. Abbé Emile Dubois, *Le Feu de la Rivière du Chêne* (Montreal, 1937), p. 140.
11. Ibid., pp. 123-4.
12. Notes of Alfred Dumouchel.
13. *Journal Historique des Evénements arrivés à Saint-Eustache*, par un Témoin oculaire, Mtl. (Montreal: John Jones, 1838).

14. L.-O. David, *Les Patriotes de 1837* (Montreal: Eusèbe Sénécal & Fils, 1894), p. 49.
15. Dubois, *Le Feu de la Rivière du Chêne*, p. 122.
16. Ibid., p. 159.
17. Sir George Bell, *Rough Notes by an Old Soldier* (London: Day & Son, 1867).
18. Colborne to Fitzroy Somerset, December 22, 1837, C.O. 42/274, PAC.
19. Maitland to Colborne, December 20, 1837, C.O. 42/274, PAC.
20. Dubois, *Le Feu de la Rivière du Chêne*, p. 332.
21. Ibid., p. 179.
22. Ibid., p. 180.
23. Ibid., p. 180.

Chapter 7

1. Philip Whitwell Wilson, ed., *The Greville Diary* (London: Wm. Heinemann, 1927), vol. 1, p. 30.
2. Jean Bruchési, *Histoire du Canada* (Montreal: Editions Beauchemin, 1959), p. 463.
3. Chester W. New, *Lord Durham* (Toronto: Oxford, 1929).
4. Gosford to Glenelg, December 23, 1837, Accounts and Papers, 1838, vol. 39.
5. Gérard Filteau, *Histoires des Patriotes* (Montreal: Editions L'A.C.F., 1938-42), vol. 3.
6. Ibid.
7. Ibid.
8. Colborne to Glenelg, March 9, 1838. Accounts and Papers, 1838, vol. 39.
9. Ibid.
10. Albert B. Corey, *The Crisis of 1830-42 in Canadian-American Relations* (Toronto: Ryerson, 1941), p. 35.
11. C. P. Lucas, ed., *Lord Durham's Report on the Affairs of British North America* (Toronto: Oxford, 1941), vol. 1, p. 106.
12. A. & Bertrand Desrosiers, *L'Accalmie* (Montreal, 1937).
13. Lady Durham, Journal, Literary and Historical Society of Quebec, Historical Documents, Series 9, Part 1.
14. Mrs. Edward Ellice, Diary, 1838, PAC, MG 24, Series A2, vol. 50.
15. Charles Buller, "Sketch of Lord Durham's Mission to Canada in 1838", in C. P. Lucas, ed., *Lord Durham's Report on the Affairs of British North America*, vol. 3.
16. Ibid.
17. Filteau, *Histoire des Patriotes*, vol. 3.
18. Wolfred Nelson Papers, PAC.
19. C.C. 42/282, p. 190, PAC.
20. Major John Richardson, *Eight Years in Canada* (Montreal: B. Dawson, 1847).
21. Buller, "Sketch of Lord Durham's Mission to Canada in 1838", p. 357.
22. Durham to Glenelg, August 9, 1838, C.O. 42/283, PAC.
23. Ibid.
24. Ibid.
25. Lafontaine Papers, PAC.
26. Lady Durham, Journal.
27. Ibid.
28. Richardson, *Eight Years in Canada*.
29. Buller, "Sketch of Lord Durham's Mission to Canada in 1838", p. 371.

Chapter 8

1. Albert B. Corey, *The Crisis of 1830-42 in Canadian-American Relations*

(Toronto: Ryerson, 1941), p. 76.

2. Ibid.

3. Ibid., p. 64.

4. Ibid., p. 192.

5. J.-B.-H. Brien, Account reprinted in *Canadian Antiquarian and Numismatic Journal,* PAC.

6. Wolfred Nelson Papers, PAC.

7. Mrs. Edward Ellice, Diary, 1838, PAC, MG 24, Series A2, vol. 50.

8. Ibid.

9. Ibid.

10. Major John Richardson, *Eight Years in Canada* (Montreal: B. Dawson, 1847).

11. Ibid.

12. Mrs. Edward Ellice, Diary.

13. Jean Bruchési, *Histoire du Canada* (Montreal: Editions Beauchemin, 1959), p. 467.

14. Ibid.

15. J. D. Borthwick, *History of the Montreal Prison* (Montreal: A. Periard, 1886).

Chapter 9

1. Colborne to Glenelg, December 19, 1838, Dispatch 93, C.O. 242/296.

2. L.-O. David, *Les Patriotes de 1837-1838* (Montreal: Eusèbe Sénécal & Fils, 1884), p. 201.

3. Ibid., pp. 252-3.

4. Ibid.

5. Ogden to Colborne, July 23, 1839, C.O. 242/296, PAC.

6. J. D. Borthwick, *History of the Montreal Prison* (Montreal: A. Periard, 1886).

7. Ibid.

8. François-Xavier Prieur, *Notes of a Convict of 1838* (Sydney, Australia: D. S. Ford, 1949).

9. Ibid.

Chapter 10

1. C. P. Lucas, ed., *Lord Durham's Report on the Affairs of British North America* (Toronto: Oxford, 1941), vol. 2.

2. Ibid.

3. Donald Creighton, *The Empire of the St. Lawrence* (Toronto: Macmillan, 1956), p. 330. Also Chester W. New, *Lord Durham* (Toronto: Oxford, 1929), p. 490.

4. Mason Wade, *The French Canadians* (Toronto: Macmillan, 1955), p. 229.

5. Ibid.

6. Ibid., p. 232.

7. Stephen Leacock, *Lafontaine*, The Makers of Canada Series, vol. 5 (Toronto: Oxford, 1926), p. 89.

8. Wade, *The French Canadians*, p. 238.

9. W. P. M. Kennedy, *Documents of the Canadian Constitution* (Toronto: Oxford, 1918), p. 569 (Metcalfe to Stanley).

10. Robert Rumilly, *Papineau* (Paris: Ernest Flammarion, 1934), p. 244.

11. François-Xavier Prieur, *Notes of a Convict of 1838* (Sydney, Australia: D. S. Ford, 1949).

12. Creighton, *The Empire of the St. Lawrence*, p. 379.

13. Leacock, *Lafontaine*, p. 380.

14. Quoted in Wade, *The French Canadians*, p. 262.

15. Ibid., pp. 256-7.

16. Rumilly, *Papineau*, p. 305.

Select Bibliography

In the preparation of this book, while Colonial Office correspondence, private and state papers, and manuscripts available in public archives have been consulted, I have depended very largely on work already published by scholars and writers. If anything has been accomplished here, it is a work of collection and synthesis rather than of original scholarship. It has been done with the hope, not of adding anything to the story of political evolution during the 1830s and 1840s, but of giving depth to the background against which the changes came. That background, in my opinion, is relevant and important today.

BELL, Sir George. *Rough Notes by an Old Soldier*. London: Day & Son, 1867.

BELLINGHAM, Sydney R. Memoir. Public Archives of Canada, MG 24, Series B25, vol. 2.

BENDER, P. *Old and New Canada*. Montreal: Dawson Bros., 1882.

BIGSBY, John J. *The Shoe and Canoe*. London: Chapman & Hall, 1850.

BORTHWICK, J. D. *History of the Montreal Prison*. Montreal: A. Periard, 1886.

BOSWORTH, Newton. *Hochelaga Depicta*. Montreal: Wm. Greig, 1839.

Select Bibliography

BOYD, John. *Sir George Etienne Cartier, Bart.* Toronto: Macmillan, 1917.

BRIEN, J.-B.-H. Account reprinted in *Canadian Antiquarian and Numismatic Journal*, PAC.

BROWN, Thomas Storrow. *Brief Sketch of the Life and Times of L. J. Papineau.* Pamphlet, Redpath Library, McGill University, Montreal.

BRUCHESI, Jean. *Histoire du Canada.* Montreal: Editions Beauchemin, 1959.

BRUNET, Michel. *French Canada and the Early Decades of British Rule.* Pamphlet translated from the French by Canadian Historical Association, 1963.

BULLER, Charles. "Sketch of Lord Durham's Mission to Canada in 1838". In *Lord Durham's Report on the Affairs of British North America,* edited by C. P. Lucas, vol. 3. Toronto: Oxford, 1941.

CARRIER, L. N. *Les Evénements de 1837-38.* Quebec, 1877.

CHRISTIE, Robert. *A History of the Late Province of Lower Canada.* Quebec: T. Cary & Sons, 1848-55.

COREY, Albert B. *The Crisis of 1830-42 in Canadian-American Relations,* Toronto: Ryerson, 1941.

CREIGHTON, Donald. "The Economic Background of the Rebellions of 1837". *Canadian Journal of Economics and Political Science,* August 1937.

_____. *The Empire of the St. Lawrence.* Toronto: Macmillan, 1956.

DAVID, Laurent-Olivier. *Les Patriotes de 1837-1838.* Montreal: Eusèbe Sénécal & Fils, 1894.

DECELLES, Alfred D. *...Papineau, Cartier.* The Makers of Canada Series. Toronto: Oxford, 1926.

DOUGHTY, Arthur G. *Documents Relating to the Constitutional History of Canada.* Ottawa: King's Printer, 1907.

DUBOIS, Abbé Emile. *Le Feu de la Rivière du Chêne.* Montreal, 1937.

DURHAM, Lady. Journal. Literary and Historical Society of Quebec, Historical Documents, Series 9.

DURHAM, Lord. *Lord Durham's Report on the Affairs of British North America.* Edited by C. P. Lucas. Vol. 3. Toronto: Oxford, 1941.

ELLICE, Mrs. Edward. Diary, 1838. PAC, MG 24, Series A2, vol. 50.

ELLIOTT, T. Fred. *The Canadian Controversy.* Pamphlet, PAC.

FAUTEUX, Aegidius. *Patriotes de 1837-1838.* Montreal: Editions des Dix, 1950.

FIDES, Montreal. *Les Troubles de 1837.* Dossier d'histoire du Canada.

FILTEAU, Gérard. *Histoire des Patriotes.* 3 vols. Montreal: Editions L'A.C.F., 1938-42.

FRASER, John. *Canadian Pen and Ink Sketches.* Montreal: Gazette, 1890.

GARNEAUX, F.-X. *Histoire du Canada.* 4th ed. Montreal: Beauchemin & Fils, 1882.

GIROD, Amury. Journal. PAC.

GOUIN, Jacques. "William Henry Scott". *Asticou,* Cahier 6. Societé historique de l'ouest de Québec.

GREVILLE, Charles. *The Greville Diary.* Edition edited by Philip Whitwell Wilson. London: Wm. Heinemann, 1927.

GUILLET, Edwin C. *The Lives and Times of the Patriots.* Toronto: University of Toronto Press, 1955.

HEAGERTY, John J. *Four Centuries of Medical History in Canada*. Toronto: Macmillan, 1928.

KENNEDY, W. P. M. *Documents of the Canadian Constitution*. Toronto: Oxford, 1918.

KILBOURN, William. *The Firebrand*. Toronto: Clarke Irwin, 1956.

LEACOCK, Stephen. *Lafontaine*. The Makers of Canada Series. Toronto: Oxford, 1926.

LYSONS, Sir Daniel. *Early Reminiscences*. London: John Murray, 1896.

MANNING, Helen Taft. *The Revolt of French Canada*. Toronto: Macmillan, 1962.

MARTIN, Chester. *Foundations of Canadian Nationhood*. Toronto: University of Toronto Press, 1955.

MASSICOTTE, E. Z. *Faits Curieux de l'histoire de Montréal*. Montreal: Librairie Beauchemin, 1924.

NEW, Chester W. *Lord Durham*. Toronto: Oxford, 1929.

OUELLET, Fernand. *Histoire Economique et Sociale du Québec, 1760-1850*. Montreal: Editions Fides, 1966.

————. *Louis-Joseph Papineau: un être divisé*. Pamphlet, La Société Historique du Canada, 1960.

————. *Papineau, Textes Choisis*. Quebec: Les Presses de l'Université Laval, 1959.

————, with Jean Hamelin. *La Crise Agricole dans le Bas-Canada, 1802-37*. Paris: Etudes Rurales, Sorbonne, October-December 1962.

ORMSBY, William, ed. *Crisis in the Canadas 1838-1839: the Grey Journals and Letters*. Toronto: Macmillan, 1964.

PRIEUR, François-Xavier. *Notes of a Convict of 1838*. Translated by George Mackaness. Sydney, Australia: D. S. Ford, 1949. (*Notes d'un Condamné Politique de 1838*, Montreal, 1884.)

READ, D. B. *The Canadian Rebellion of 1837*. Toronto: C. B. Robinson, 1896.

RICHARDSON, Major John. *Eight Years in Canada*. Montreal: B. Dawson, 1847.

RUMILLY, Robert. *Papineau*. Paris: Ernest Flammarion, 1934.

SEGUIN, Robert-Lionel. *Le Mouvement Insurrectionnel dans la Presqu'île de Vaudreuil, 1837-1838*. Montreal: Librairie Ducharme, 1955.

WADE, Mason. *The French Canadians*. Toronto: Macmillan, 1955.

Index

Act of Union, 1840, 196-7
Addison's Tavern, 122
Albany, New York, 133
Alburgh Springs, Vermont, 134
American Revolution, 3-4, 33, 40
Amnesty, 141
Assembly of Lower Canada, 5, 6; its
    membership, 6-8; in operation, 8-12,
    33-4; and Papineau, 35, 37-8; 42, 46-7
Assembly of the Six Counties,
    St-Charles, 55-9
Association de la Délivrance, L',
    202, 205
Australia, exiles to, 189-93, 202-6
Aylmer, Matthew, Baron, 18-19, 40
Ayotte, Madame, 86

Bagg, George, 16
Bagot, Sir Charles, 199
Baldwin, Robert, 197-200 passim,
    206, 208
Banque du Peuple, La, 39, 54, 62, 68
Beauce, the, 32
Beauharnois, seigneury of, 137, 155;
    taking of, 156-62, 163, 165, 173; 174-8

Beauport, 29
Belestre-MacDonnell, John Picoté de,
    155-6, 172, 188
Beloeil Mountain, 79
Bermuda, exile of prisoners to, 140-4, 148
Berthierville, 156
Billet, Pierre, 17
Blanchard, Captain, 72
Board of Magistrates, Montreal, 14, 38
Boards of Health, Quebec and Montreal,
    21, 23-30 passim
Bonacina's Tavern, Montreal, 59
Boucherville, 172, 178
Bourdages, David, 73
Bourdages, Louis, 73
Bourdages, Raymond, 73
Bourget, Bishop Ignace, 183
Bourguignon, Louis, 96
Break-Neck Stairs, Quebec, 20
Brien, Dr. Jean-Baptiste-Henri, 158,
    162, 179, 184-6 passim
British American, steamer, 190
British American Land Company, 43
"British Party", 10, 130, 139
Brockville, 29

Brown, Mr., 157-8
Brown, Thomas Storrow, 52, 56, 59, 60; at battle of St-Charles, 80-3, 89; 90, 211-12
Bruneau, Julie, 35
Buffalo, H.M.S., 189-93 *passim*
Buffalo, New York, 131
Buller, Arthur, 137
Buller, Charles, 137, 138-9, 141, 143, 145, 147, 149
Bureaucrates and bureaucracy, 5, 8, 9-11, 30, 34, 35, 41, 94, 146, 158, 168

Calvaire, Mount, 92
Camp Baker, 162
Canada, 1, 3, 162, 166; under Union Act of 1840, 196-200
Canada, steamer, 142
Cape Diamond, 41, 191
Cape Van Diemen, 192
Cardinal, Joseph-Narcisse, 161, 166, 182-3
Carillon, 97, 113
Caroline, steamer, 132
Cartier, George Etienne, 73, 76, 90, 208, 210, 212
Cartier, Henri, 73, 90
"Castor", 154, 155
Caughnawaga, 29, 112, 161; delivery of prisoners from, 165-6
Chambly, 29, 61, 62, 63, 78, 79, 81, 84, 164
Chambly County, 55
Champ de Mars, Montreal, 28, 46
Champlain, Lake, 134, 166, 169
Champlain Canal, 11
Champlain Street, Quebec, 20, 23
Chartier, Abbé Etienne, 103-4, 109, 110, 111, 211
Château Clique, 13
Chateauguay County and village, 155-78 *passim*
Chateauguay River, 157, 162, 165
Chatham, 97, 123
Chaudière River, 32
Chauvin, Casimir, 17
Chénier, Dr. Jean-Olivier, 56, 96, 99, 100, 102, 103, 105-12 *passim*; in attack on St-Eustache, 119-22 *passim*
Cholera Cemetery, Quebec, 26
Cholera epidemic, 19-30
Chouayens, 94
Church, Roman Catholic, 2, 3, 4, 6, 36
Church of England, 3
Civil List, 9, 10, 13, 37, 41, 42, 43

Clergy Reserves, 8
Cleveland, Ohio, 150
Clitherow, Major-General John, 140, 142, 181
Colborne, Sir John, 45, 52, 53, 60, 63, 64, 79, 84, 89, 92, 97; in attack on St-Eustache and St-Benoit, 112-24; 129, 131, 132, 135, 136, 139, 140, 149, 152, 155, 157, 162-5 *passim*, 167, 172, 174, 178-80 *passim*, 181, 188, 196, 199
Colborne, Lady, 137, 180
Colleges, ecclesiastical, 6-8
Colonial government, as established 1791, 4-5
Colonial Office, 1, 4, 40
Committees of Liberty, 52
Committees of Public Safety, 52
Congreve Rocket, 115
Constitution of 1791, 8, 9, 35
Constitutionalists, 38, 44
Côté, Dr. Cyrille-Hector Octave, 56, 58, 59, 88, 133, 134, 135, 153, 154, 167, 168-9, 174, 175, 210
Coteau-du-Lac, 175
Courier, Montreal, 62
Court martial, trials by, 180, 181-7
Coves, The, Quebec, 20
Craig, Governor Sir James, 10, 13
Craig Street, Montreal, 28
Crown lands, 9, 10
Crown Reserves, 8, 11

Daunais, Amable, 186-7
Davignon, Dr. Joseph-François, 61-2
Decoigne, Pierre-Théophile, 184
De Lorimier, Chevalier, 158, 160, 162, 175, 179, 184-7
Demaray, Pierre-Paul, 61-2
Desève, Father, 106, 107, 109, 122
Deux Montagnes, county of, 92
Doric Club, 52, 60
Duquette, Joseph, 182-3
Durham, John George Lambton, First Earl of, 128-9, 136, 138-9, 140, 141, 144-9, 150, 157, 162, 163; Report, 194-6, 197, 199, 208, 211
Durham, Lady, 137, 148
Duvernay, Ludger, 15-16, 22, 38, 155, 202, 205

Eastern Townships, 14
83rd Regiment, 113
Elgin, James Bruce, Earl of, 200, 206-7
Elizabethtown, New York, 134

Ellice, "Bear", 137, 146
Ellice, Edward, 137, 157-60 *passim*, 174, 177-8
Ellice, Jane, 137, 138, 157-60 *passim*, 176-8 *passim*
Emigrant Fund, 21
Erie, Lake, 150
Erie Canal, 11
Executive Council, 5, 43

Fabre, Edouard, 39, 68, 179, 202, 205
Family Compact, 145, 197
"Fence-post brigade", 76
Fils de la Liberté, Les, 52. *See also* Sons of Liberty
First Dragoon Guards, 172
Franklin, Benjamin, 1, 4
French Canadians, 2-4
"French Party", 10, 14
Frères Chasseurs, Les, 150-2; oath-taking, 153-4; organization, 155-6; 157, 158, 163, 165, 166, 167, 182, 184, 185

Gagnon, Lucien, 56, 88, 133, 134, 135, 153, 167, 169, 210
Gaspé, 2
George III, 4, 35
Girod, Amury, 56-7, 61, 96, 97-112 *passim*, 124, 125-6, 161
Girouard, Jean-Joseph, 94-5, 96, 99, 100, 101, 103, 104, 122, 124-5, 140, 141, 144, 147, 209
Glenelg, Lord, 127-8, 144, 145, 148
Glengarry County volunteers, 94, 97, 123, 173, 175-8 *passim*
Globenski, Maxime, 112, 114
Gore, Colonel Charles, 63, 64; attack on St-Denis, 73-7, 79; return to St-Denis, 84-8
Gore, the, 97, 123
Gosford, Earl of, 40-3, 45, 46-7, 48, 49, 53, 59, 60, 62, 91, 105, 129, 130, 132, 135, 138, 201
Gosford Commission, 40, 41, 43
Grand Brûlé, 61, 92, 93, 96, 98, 112, 123, 165
"Grand Eagle", 154, 155, 172, 178
Grande Côte Road, 98, 110, 114, 119
Grenadier Guards, 172
Grenville, 97, 123
Greville, Charles, 127
Grey, Earl, 127, 137
Griffin, Lieutenant, 86-7
Grosse Ile, 21-4 *passim*, 29

Habitants, 5, 6, 31-2, 40
Hamelin, François-Xavier, 183-4
Hastings, frigate, 136
Head tax on immigrants, 21-2
Hemmingford, 167, 169, 171
Henry Brougham, steamer, 159, 160
Herald, Montreal, 178, 180
Hickory Island, 135
Hincks, Francis, 197
Hindenlang, Charles, 166, 168, 170, 171, 185-7 *passim*
Hobart Town, Tasmania, 192
Hôpital des Emigrés, L', 24
House of Commons, British, 12, 36, 46
Humphrey, Montreal hangman, 183-7 *passim*
Hunters' Lodges, 150-1, 153, 163, 166, 167. *See also* Frères Chasseurs, Les

Immigration, 6, 8, 11, 19-30 *passim*
Inconstant, frigate, 148, 163
Ile-aux-Noix, 167
Irish, 14, 19
Irishtown, New South Wales, 204

Jacques Cartier Square, Montreal, 179
Jalbert, Captain François, 57, 59, 69-70, 78, 90, 210; trial of, 188-9
John Bull, steamer, 84

King's Prerogative, 9, 11, 37, 41, 42
Kingston, 29, 135
"Knights of the Cross", 12

L'Acadie County, 55, 155
Lachine, 29, 112, 156, 161, 165
Lachine volunteer cavalry, 112, 162, 165
Lachute, 93, 97
Lacolle, 167, 169, 170, 173
Laflamme's Tavern, 112
LaFontaine, Louis-Hippolyte, 32, 62, 91, 130, 146, 179, 196-202 *passim*, 205, 206, 207-8, 212
Lagorce, Abbé Charles-Irénée, 78
"L'Aigle", 154, 155
Lake of the Two Mountains, 92, 124
Lake St. Louis, 156
La Minerve, Montreal, 15, 38
Languedoc, François, 17
La Petite Nation, 12, 33, 35, 53, 201
La Petite Ste-Rose, 113
Laprairie, 157, 164, 165, 174, 178, 180
Lartigue, Bishop Jean Jacques, 59
La Tortue, 165, 174

Le Canadien, Quebec, 130
Legislative Council, 5, 9, 10, 14, 41-3 *passim*, 49
Lévis, 29
Liberty Pole of St-Charles, 55, 57, 58, 84
Little River, 29
Longbottom, prison camp, 192-3, 202
Longueil, 61, 63, 180
Lower Canada, 4, 5-12 *passim;* agricultural distress, 31-2; 42; commercial depression, 44-5; 133, 152, 163, 196
Loyalists, 4, 5
Lysons, Lieut. Daniel, 86, 89

M'Coll, Duncan, 96
Macdonald, Sir John A., 208
Macdonell, General J., 174
McGill, Peter, 45
McGregor, Doctor, 86-8
Mackenzie, William Lyon, 54, 131, 132, 134, 135
MacNab, Sir Allan Napier, 132
Maillet, Jean-Baptiste, 66, 69
Maitland, Colonel John, 113, 115, 118, 119, 123
Malhiot, Edouard-Elisée, 154, 172, 178
Markham, Captain G., 75
Melbourne, Lord, 127, 128, 129, 144, 148, 196
Merchants, British, 4, 5, 9, 11-12, 35-6, 38, 39, 144, 146
Mesnier, Philip, 205
Metcalfe, Charles, Baron, 199, 202
Migneault, François, 66, 69
Mississquoi Bay, 88-9, 90, 135
Moffatt, George, 14-17 *passim*, 22, 207
Montebello, 201, 212
Montreal, 2, 12; election and riot of 1832, 16-17; cholera epidemic, 27-9, 33, 44; troops in, 46, 52-3, 59; 77, 108, 109, 112-13, 126, 129, 155, 156, 162, 163-6, 172, 179, 207
Montreal volunteer cavalry, 61
Moore's Corners, 89
Mountain, George Jehoshaphat, 26
Mountain Street, Quebec, 20, 26, 137

Napierville, 156, 162, 165, 167-72, 173, 174, 177
Napoleon, 9
Narbonne, Pierre-Rémi, 185-7
Nation canadienne, la, 40, 200
National convention, 54

Navy Island, 132
Neilson, John, 36, 37
Nelson, Robert, 56, 101, 133-5, 153, 155, 156, 158, 162; Napierville expedition, 166-72; 174, 175, 182, 210
Nelson, Wolfred, 50, 54, 55-6, 57, 58, 61, 65-6; at battle of St-Denis, 66-78, 81, 82; flight and capture, 90; 140, 141, 142, 143, 147, 200, 201, 210
New England, 33
New France, 2, 13, 33, 34, 35
New York State, 129, 131, 134, 153, 166
Niagara Falls, Durham's review of troops at, 145
Niagara River, 132
Nicolas, François, 186-7
Ninety-Two Resolutions, 37-40
Norfolk Island, 192
Notre Dame, church of, 17
Notre Dame Street, Montreal, 28

O'Callaghan, Edmund Bailey, 38, 54, 55, 61; flight from St-Denis, 68-9; 89, 97, 210-11
Odelltown, 167, 170, 174, 186
Oka, Indian mission, 102, 161
Ordinance of exile, 141, 144, 147, 148
Ottawa River, 2, 4, 12, 92

Pagé, Louis, 72
Papineau, Joseph, 33-4
Papineau, Louis-Joseph, 12-17 *passim*, 18-19, 32-40, 45-7 *passim*, 49, 52; and agitation leading to rebellion, 53-62; 63; flight from St-Denis, 68-9, 89-90; 94, 95, 97, 99, 100, 101, 106, 130, 133-4, 140, 200, 201, 207-9, 212
Paquet, Marie-Marguerite, 209
Paquin, Abbé Jacques, 98-9, 100, 103-11 *passim*, 122, 123
Paramatta River, 192-3, 203
Parent, Etienne, 130, 198
Parliament, first, of the united Canadas, 197-8
Peel, Sir Robert, 127
Permanent Central Committee, 39, 54
Perrault, Ovide, 73, 77
Philipsburg, 89
Place d'Armes, Montreal, 16, 112, 164, 207
Plains of Abraham, 1, 24, 26
Point Lévis, 45
Pointe-aux-Trembles, 125
Port Huron, Michigan, 152

Pot-au-Beurre Road, 65, 67
Prescott, 29, 179
Prieur, François-Xavier, 160, 179, 184-6 *passim;* exile with other prisoners to Australia, 189-93, 202-6; 210

Quebec, city, 2, 15, 16, 18; during cholera epidemic, 20-6; 44; troop reinforcements and entertainment 45-6; 50, 136, 155, 163, 172

"Raquette", 154
Rebellion Losses Bill, 200, 206-7
Reformers, English, 11, 34-5
"Republican Bank of Canada", 151
Richelieu County, 55
Richelieu River and valley, 32, 50-2, 53; during first rebellion, 62-90 *passim;* 153, 155, 156, 164, 169, 172, 173, 178
Rimouski County, 32, 198
Rivière des Milles Iles, 92, 93, 97, 98, 112, 113, 118, 164, 169
Rivière des Prairies, 50, 52, 97, 113, 125
Rivière du Chêne, 93, 115, 118
Robert, Joseph-Marie, 183-4
Rouses Point, 166
Rouville, Hertel de, 79
Rouville County, 55
Royal Artillery, 63
Royal Regiment, 63, 113
Russell, Lord John, 43, 94, 127
Ryland family, 49

St. Andrews, 97, 123
St-Armand, 89
St-Benoit, 50, 93, 94, 99, 103, 107, 108, 110, 115; occupation and burning, 122-3
St-Césaire, 88-9
St-Charles, 50; meeting of the Six Counties at, 54-9; 63, 66; attack on, 78-84; 85, 89, 101, 102, 164
St-Denis, 50, 63; attack on, 64-78, 81, 82; 84, 101, 102, 164
St-Eustache, 50, 53, 93, 94, 98, 99; preparations for resistance, 101-12; attack on, 112-22, 124, 165
St-Germain, Madame, 67, 70, 85
St. Helen's Island, Montreal, 17, 28
St-Hilaire, 79
St-Hyacinthe, 53, 85, 89
St-Hyacinthe County, 55
St-Jean-Baptiste Society, 39, 155

St-Jean d'Iberville, 61, 135, 157, 164
St. Johns, 29
St-Joseph, Mount, 92
St. Lawrence River, 2, 4, 6, 11, 30, 32, 45, 92, 155, 156, 172, 173, 178
St. Louis, Castle of, 41, 137
St-Marc, 54, 61, 89
St-Martin, 97, 108, 109, 113
St-Ours, 65, 77, 81, 84, 164
St. Paul Street, Montreal, 27, 28
St-Polycarpe, 125
St-Timothée, 175, 205
St-Valentin, 210
Ste-Rose, 98, 101, 102, 110, 113
Ste-Scholastique, 50, 93, 94, 95, 119, 123
Ste-Thérèse-de-Blainville, 93, 123, 125
Sanguinet, Ambroise, 184
Sanguinet, Charles, 184
Scott, William Henry, 94-5, 96, 99, 100, 102, 105-6, 123, 209
Scott, General Winfield, 152, 166
Seigneuries, 2, 5, 8, 93
7th Hussars, 172
Sewell, Judge Jonathan, 48
Simpson, John, 140, 143
Sons of Liberty, 52; riot in Montreal, 59-60, 81
Sorel, 63, 64, 66, 77, 84, 88, 156, 163, 164, 172, 178
Speaker of the Assembly, 8, 12, 37
Swanton, Vermont, 88
Sydenham, Lord, 196, 197, 199
Sydney, Australia, 192, 202-5 *passim*

Tanneries road, 165
Ten Resolutions, 43, 44, 46, 94
Terrebonne County, 155, 165
Thirteen Colonies, 1, 3, 5, 14, 36, 40, 46
32nd Regiment, 64, 113
Thom, Adam, 45, 53, 59, 62, 68, 146, 187, 210-11
Thomson, Charles Poulett, later Lord Sydenham, 196
Three Rivers, 29, 134
Touvrey, C., 166, 169
Townshend, Major, 97, 113, 123
Townships, 6, 8, 12
Tracey, Daniel, 15-16, 22, 27, 38
Treaty of Paris, 1, 3
Turcotte, Father, 98, 99, 105-6, 122
Turton, Thomas, 137, 141, 147
24th Regiment, 64
Two Mountains, county of, 92

Union Bill, 1822, 11-12, 35-6
United States, 4, 14, 37; commercial depression, 44; 52, 100, 106, 145; standing army, 152
Upper Canada, 4, 11, 19, 29, 45, 54, 60, 68, 93, 97, 131, 132, 135, 144-5, 152, 163, 164, 179; political prisoners, 190-1; 196

Van Buren, President, 129
Van Rensselaer, General Rensselaer, 135
Varennes, 61, 125
Vaudreuil, 125
Vendus, 94
Verchères, county of, 55
Vermont, 88, 129, 131, 134, 153, 166
Vestal, frigate, 143
Victoria, Queen, 44, 127, 128
Vindicator, The, Montreal, 15, 38, 54, 68
Viger, Bonaventure, 80, 90, 210

Viger, Louis-Michel, 39, 53-4, 62, 68, 179
Vitman's Quay, 167, 169, 174
Voyager, immigrant ship, 23

Wakefield, Edward Gibbon, 137
War of 1812, 35
Warrants, issuance of, 61
Weir, Lieut. George "Jock", 64-6; killing of, 69-70, 121; finding of body, 86-8
Wetherall, Lieutenant, 120
Wetherall, Lieut.-Col. G. A., 63, 64; in attack on St-Charles, 78-84; in attack on St-Eustache, 113-23 *passim*
William IV, 37, 41, 44
Windmill Point, 179
Wolfe, General James, 1, 47
Wool, General John E., 134, 135

Yamaska River, 88-9
York, Upper Canada, 30, 198